MINNESOTA

WISCONSIN

MICHIGAN

Lake Superior

Georgian Bay

Lake Huron

Lake Michigan

IOWA

Lake Ontario

NEW YORK

MAINE

VT.

N.H.

MASS. BOSTON

HARTFORD PROVIDENCE

CONN. R.I.

NEW YORK CITY
MAY 8, 1984

FLINT

DETROIT

Lake Erie

CLEVELAND

YOUNGSTOWN

PENN.

WEST POINT

CHICAGO

INDIANA

OHIO

PITTSBURGH

PHILADELPHIA

TRENTON

N.J.

MD.

DEL.

ILLINOIS

INDIANAPOLIS

MORGANTOWN

WASHINGTON, D.C.

WEST
VIRGINIA

OCEAN

KANSAS CITY

ST. LOUIS

LOUISVILLE

VIRGINIA

MISSOURI

KENTUCKY

KNOXVILLE

NORTH CAROLINA

TULSA

OKLAHOMA
CITY

WEST MEMPHIS

TENNESSEE

CHEROKEE

SOUTH
CAROLINA

ATLANTIC

ARKANSAS

TUPELO

BIRMINGHAM

ATLANTA

DALLAS

MISSISSIPPI

ALABAMA

GEORGIA

TEXAS

FLORIDA

LOUISIANA

GULF OF MEXICO

MONIQUE DE MONET · PHILIP DE MONET · RICARDO DE MONET · JOAN CARLOS DE OLIVERA · JOSE SEBASTIAO DE SOUZA · ANITA DEFRANTZ · STEPHEN L. DEMENNA · RICK DERENZIS · ANTHONY DEWITT · CARY MARTIN DEAN · CYNTHIA DEE THOMAS · WAYNE A. DEEGAN, JR. · RONALD DEFOSSE · MOIRA DELANEY · NORMA DELANEY · VIRGIL DELANEY · MARY DELISTRATY · JOE DELLINGER · KAREN C. DEMARS · KATHRYN D. DENNING · RUTH A. DENSTAEDT · GARY L. DEPOLO · WARNER K. DEPUY · DOUG DERRICK · BRYN ELIZABETH DESSENT · THOMAS M. DETELICH · ANN SCHULTZ DETERS · JUDITH A. DETWILER · CARLOS LOPEZ DEUSTO · JOE DEVORE · CHIP DEWEY · KAY DEWHITT · RAYMOND DEYNE · SCOTT B. DIAL · ART DIAZ · JOHN DICKEY · MICHELLE K. DICKINSON · BRUCE DICKSON · DERON DICKSON · RANDY A. CROYTS · GLORIA E. CRUM · JAMES P. CRUTCHER · JIM CRUZ · KATHRYN CULLIGAN · RUSSELL A. CULLY, JR. · JIM CUMMINGS · JIM CUMMINGS, III · STEVE CUMMINGS · GLEN CUNNINGHAM · TIM CUNNINGHAM · WILLIAM J. CUNNINGHAM, JR. · RONALDO CUNYA · JOSEPH CUPARI · JOHN C. CUSHMAN · JOSEPH W. CUSICK · JEANNE D'AMICO · DANILA DA RODDA · NEIL D. DABNEY · JIM DAGGS · WILLIAM DAGGS · GRANT DAHLKE · WILLIAM DAHLMAN · ERIC DAHLQUIST · RICHARD G. DAILEY · ROBERT L. DALESSIO · JOHN S. DALEY · EDDIE DALTON · ANTHONY F. DALY, M.D. · ELIZABETH DALY · GAIL DALY · PATRICK S. DALY · MICHELLE DAME · KIMBERLY DANIEL · JOSEPH DANIELS · WILLIAM DANNEMEYER · JOHN M. DARGA · DENISE DARLING · DOMINIQUE DAVALOS · SALVADOR DAVALOS · ROLAND DAVIDE · MICHAEL DAVIDSON · CAROLYN L. DAVIES · GREGORY DAVIES · ALEXANDRA DAVIS · ANDY DAVIS · CHRISTOPHER DAVIS · JIM DAVIS · PATRICIA DAVIS · RICHARD DAVIS · ROBERT N. DAVIS · ANDREW COOK · BENJAMIN H. COOK · LAURA COOK · MARK COOLIDGE · KAYLE COONS · CAMERON COOPER · CRAIG R. COOPER · KEN COOPER · STACEY R. COOPER · RONALD CORDEAU · HARRY CORDELLOS · ANN CORNELL · FELIX ALBERTO COSCIO · JOHN COSGROVE · CINDY COSMI · CINDY COSTELLO · RICHARD COSTELLO · CLINTON B. COTTER · TERRY COTTER · TERRI COTTLE · BARBARA J. COTTON · WILLIAM A. COULTER · DENNIS COUNCIL · ROLAND COUVILLON · JOHN COVENDAL · JERRY COWART · LANCE COWART · JOHN COWLIN · SHIRLEY CRADDIC · JENNIFER CRAIN · ALEXIS V. CRAMPTON · RONALD CRASKA · ARTHUR CRAWFORD · BRIDGET CRAWFORD · JAMES W. CRAWFORD, II · MATT CRAWFORD · ROGER CRAWFORD, II · TONY CRAWFORD · BRIAN CRETS · JEAN CREWS · DON CRIST · JIM CROCKETT · KIMBERLEY CROMMELIN · WILLIAM CRONIN · ROBERT F. CROSBY · ROBERT G. CROSS · STEVE CROSS · MICHAEL CROSSLEY · ARLEN B. CROUCH · GARY CROWE · TERESA CROWELL · DICK COCHRAN · BOB COFFEE · NANCY ANN COFFEY · ALEX COFFIN · ELIZABETH A. COGSWELL · DOUGLAS COHEN · JOAN F. COHEN · LOUIS COHEN · STEVEN COHEN · SHAWN M. COHNHEIM · RUSSELL C. COILE, JR. · JACK COKLEY · AUGUST R. COLACHIS · JAMES W. COLACHIS · CARTER L. COLE · DALLAS COLE · GERI ANN COLE · BRUCE COLEMAN · DEIRDRE COLEMAN · ZEDELL COLEMAN · GARY COLES · WAYNE COLLETTE · CHRIS COLLIER · EVAN COLLIER · KENNETH COLLING · DALE COLLINS · JOSEPH L. COLLINS, JR. · LEE COLLINS · MIKE COLLISHAW · MARY ANN

★ ★ *One with the Flame*

COLSON · JUNE MARIE COLTON · TIMOTHY D. COLVIN · ANDREA L. COMAI · MARILYN COMBELLICK · SEAN CRAIG COMBS · WILLIAM H. COMBS · JAMES A. COMYNS · S. THOMAS CONLAN · WILLIAM CONLON · JOHANNA CONNELL · JUSTIN CONNELL · THOMAS K. CONNELLAN, PH.D. · JIM CONNELLY · JOHN CONNELLY · KAY CONNELLY · JACK W. CONNER · GEORGE CONOPEOTIS · ROGER F. CONOVER · GEORGE E. CONSTANTINO, JR. · SAL CONTRERAS · MARION MCKNIGHT CONWAY · BENNY CHAN · DAVID CHANEY · KIRA CHANEY · R. CHAPIN · JEFF CHAPMAN · BOYCE CHASE · L. ASHTON CHASE · CARI CHENEY · MICHAEL CHENEY · JASON H. CHENG · GARY CHERER · MANJYOH CHIEMI · CAROL CHILCOAT · DEANN CHILCOTE · TIFFANY CHIN · ALLAN D. CHLOWITZ · SUSAN CHOI · SPENCER CHRISTIAN · GEORGE CHRISTIE · ROBERT J. CHRISTOFF · LYDIA CHRISTOPHER · TERESA LYNN CHRISTOPHER · KATE CHRISTOPHERSON · MICHAEL L. CHUMA · MARGARET EVELYN CHUMO · MARLENA LYN CHUMO · MICHAEL LEE CHUMO · N. FREDERICK CHURCHMAN · RON CIANCI · ROBERTA CICCARELLI · CARL R. CICCHETTI · D. L. CLABORN · KENNETH CLAPPS · DEBBIE CLARK · DENIKA CLARK · DOUGLAS CLARK · ELLERY H. CLARK, JR. · JOHN CLARK · MARY CLARK · RHONDA CLARK · TODD CLARK · BRIAN CLARKE · JAMES T. CLARKE · ANDREW I. CLAUSEN · ANN CLAYCOMB · MICHAEL PATRICK CLEARY · PENSE WELSH CLEARY · SCOTT A. CLEGG · DAVID E. CLEMENTS · RON CLEMONS · JACK CLIPPER · FRANK COBARRUBIAS · BARBARA CARLSBERG · LORI CARLSON · RICHARD CARLSON · WILLIAM CARMEN · FAUSTINO CARMONA, JR. · CHESLEY CLAUDE CARNEY, II · F. CARON · DANE M. CARPE · ROSEMARY CARPENTER · CINDY S. CARR · RUTH CARR · JOSEPH R. CARRAH · LEV

"Your courage is strong
As the world cheers you on
Let pride be your name
And your spirit is one with the flame."

From "Carry the Fire,"
© 1984 by AT&T.
Music and lyrics by James Singer;
vocals by Richie Havens

One

FRONTISPIECE: *Lou Ribbins, 87, carries the Olympic flame for one kilometer of the 1984 Olympic Torch Relay, into the "Little Italy" section of Cleveland, Ohio.*

with the Flame

CARRYING THE OLYMPIC TORCH ACROSS AMERICA

BY MICKEY HERSKOWITZ

NAL BOOKS

NEW AMERICAN LIBRARY

NEW YORK AND SCARBOROUGH, ONTARIO

PHOTOGRAPHIC ACKNOWLEDGMENTS

Courtesy of Anheuser Busch, Bud Light division, 14 (3); Associated Press/Wide World Photo, 26, 27 left, 29, 33, 39 bottom, 53 bottom right, 63 (2), 66 (2), 67 right, 179 left, 180 left, 184, 185 left, 188 right; The Bettmann Archive, 30; Courtesy of David W. Brown, New Jersey Olympic Committee, 24, 27 right, 28, 31, 32; Garry Bryant/*Standard-Examiner*, Ogden, Utah, 158 (2); Courtesy of Classic Coachworks, Little Rock, Arkansas, 18 left; Bob Collister, 8, 12, 15 (2), 16, 42, 45, 76, 78 (2), 85 bottom, 86 left, 87 top right, 91, 101, 102, 122, 124, 148 left, 149, 177 left, 177 bottom right, 199, 201, 203, 215, 217; Ralph Crane/*People Weekly* © 1984 Time Inc., 38 (2); Steve Cross, 150; Larry Davis/© 1984 *Los Angeles Times*, 181 top; Tim Farrell/*Gannett-Westchester Newspapers*, 51 left; Jo Fielder © 1984, 53 left; Gary Friedman/© 1984 *Los Angeles Times*, 188 left; Mike Gaffney, 40 far right, 48, 61 right, 72 (2), 125, 207; Mary Ann Gotheridge/*Orange County Register*, California, 182; James F. Green, 75; Courtesy of Robert Haas, 40 far left, 40 center; Don Host/*The Register Star*, Rockford, Illinois, 86 right; Don Ipock/*The Kansas City Times*, 127 right, 213; E. Ray James/*Mountain Mail*, Salida, Colorado, 156 left; Brad Justad, 193; Shelly Katz/*Black Star*, 136; Rex Larsen, 100 (2), 103 left; Courtesy of Bill Mattman, 53 top right, 54 left; Photo Researchers, 64, 172, 185 right, back cover; Steve Purcell/*The Denver Post*, 50; Jake Rajs, 192; Howard E. Ruffner/*Black Star*, back cover; Courtesy of Richard Sargent, 39 top; Jim Sczepanski, 17; Denny Silverstein, 190 right; *The South Reporter*, Holly Springs, Mississippi, 54 right; Chris Springman, 23 right, 90 (2); Courtesy of Bill Thorpe, 61 left; Courtesy of U.S. Olympic Committee, 62, 67 left; *Wenatchee World*, Wenatchee, Washington, 160.

All other photographs courtesy of AT&T.

Cartoon on 37 by Edward Stein, Courtesy of *Rocky Mountain News*, Denver, Colorado

NAL BOOKS TRADEMARK REG. U.S. PAT. OFF. AND FOREIGN COUNTRIES
REGISTERED TRADEMARK—MARCA REGISTRADA
HECHO EN HARRISONBURG, VA., U.S.A.

SIGNET, SIGNET CLASSIC, MENTOR, PLUME, MERIDIAN and NAL BOOKS are published *in the United States* by New American Library, 1633 Broadway, New York, New York 10019, *in Canada* by The New American Library of Canada Limited, 81 Mack Avenue, Scarborough, Ontario M1L 1M8

Library of Congress Cataloging-in-Publication Data
Herskowitz, Mickey.
One with the flame.

1. Olympic torch relay—United States.
2. Olympic Games (23rd: 1984: Los Angeles, Calif.)
i. Title. GV 721.92.H47 1985   796.4'8   85-21800   ISBN 0-453-00504-7

End paper map designed by Pat Tobin
Designed by Barbara Huntley
First Printing, November, 1985
1   2   3   4   5   6   7   8   9
PRINTED IN THE UNITED STATES OF AMERICA

To that volunteer army called the Telephone Pioneers,
the men and women who helped form a bridge across America.
In spirit, as well as action, they were true guardians of the flame.
And to the millions who stood at the crossroads
who waited and cheered. They also served.

*"Thus the sum of things is ever being reviewed,
and mortals dependent one upon another.
Some nations increase, others diminish,
and in a short space the generations of living creatures
are changed and like runners pass on the torch of life."*
—Lucretius (99–55 B.C.)

Two torchbearers pass the fire in New York's Orange County. And at that brief moment, as they grip each other's hands, the hope of world harmony seems a more reachable dream.

ACKNOWLEDGMENTS

The list of people who contributed to the making of this book is long, although not as long as the roster of those who helped carry the torch across the continent. In special cases, they were the same people.

For the massive research that went into these pages, the offices, files, and sources of AT&T were made available. For these courtesies we are indebted to Walt Cannon, Charlie Mitchell, and Rick Wilbins. No one, it should be noted, felt more strongly than Wilbins that the relay was worthy of a book nor did more to make it happen.

Ben Arthur Passantino, who is as resourceful as he is tenacious, served many roles: researcher, writer, photograph selector, and utility editor.

Doris Jelicks worked endless hours collecting interviews and verifying names and facts.

Material and insights were provided by Jim Messenger and other members of the AT&T media center group; Nick Kilsby and Bill Morrison of the public relations firm of Burson-Marsteller; and Ruth Berry. Ginny DiBernardo and Donna-Lynn Farino were generous with their time and secretarial skills.

Howard Ruffner helped assemble literally thousands of photographs, from which the final selections were made, and Bob Totten assisted in critiquing the final selections. Dave Brown was responsible for the historical photos in the chapter "Of Flags and Flames." Paul Owens was a valued contributor from the West Coast. Other support came from Thomas Shepherd as well as from Lonna Barrett, Ann Newland, Irma Stowbridge, Patricia Tokash, and Shorna Walden. At a time when the Los Angeles Olympic Organizing Committee was trying to close shop, Carol Daniels, an attorney, made available information from their archives. At New American Library, Joe Esposito was truly an editor tested by fire.

A final "thank-you" is essential: to Dick Boehner and to all the AT&T cadre runners, who shared with us their thoughts and their emotions as they shared their torches with the entire country.

CONTENTS

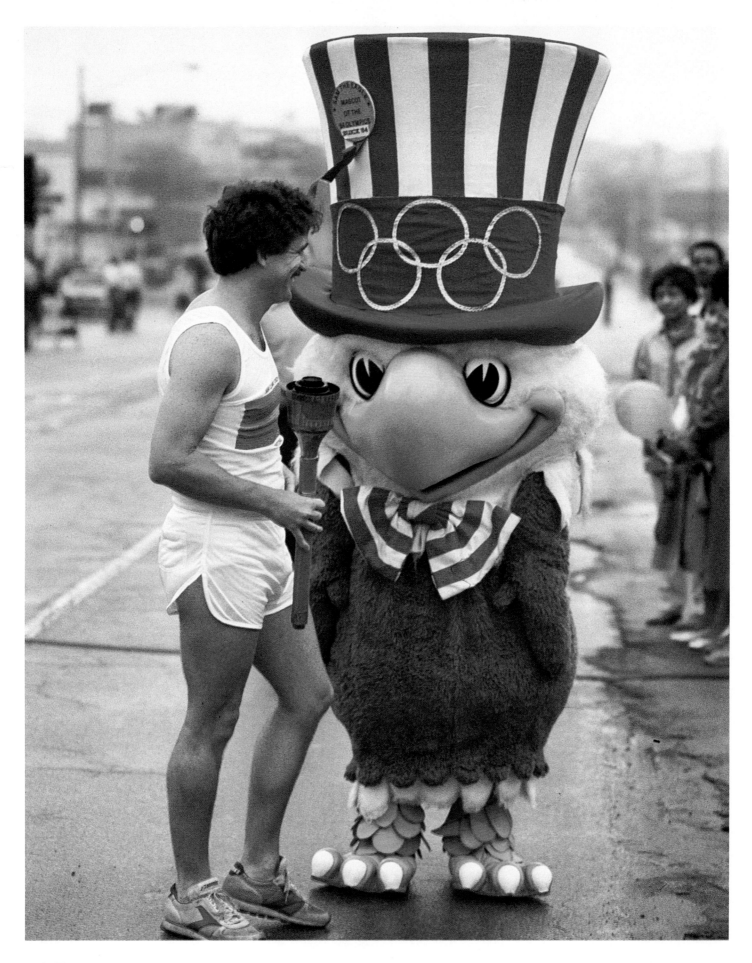

SOMETHING HAPPENED

Sam the Eagle, mascot of the 1984 Olympics, appears to stare with admiration at the Olympic Torch, which took on the symbol of American achievement as the relay wound through the country.

We were moths drawn to the flame, the Olympic flame, every blessed one of us. Or so it seemed. In 1984, a torch moved, and an entire nation moved with it. Why? What forces were joined to make this event a part of our permanent record?

The point of this American journey, this Torch Relay, was to carry the fire to the opening ceremony for the 1984 Summer Olympics. No country had ever designed a more extravagant plan to get it there: a chain of 4,200 runners would follow the sun to Los Angeles, across 33 states and 9,000 miles. So many people, using so much time (82 days) at such an expense ($10 million). The sponsor was AT&T, a company experienced at long-distance connections.

The image of the Olympic Torch be-

came a kind of Rorschach test for those who held it and those who merely watched. For some it was a child of the Lady in the Harbor. For others it was the Loneliness of the Long-distance Runner. In Oklahoma it reminded some of hard times overcome: the Dust Bowl, when children slept with wet rags over their faces and listened to the trucks and cars, mattresses and a few pieces of furniture tied to the top, rattling toward California. It was the taming of the frontier, the promise of the West, the linking of America.

Remember this television commercial? It became one of the most familiar and popular in all of 1984: two farmers waiting near a fence line, squinting against a late-afternoon sun, looking toward an open road. One adjusts his cap and, in a voice as dry as wheat,

allows: "They should be coming now."

And moving at a steady clip along the dark surface of the road, in twilight's last gleaming, past the two men standing in the field, was a runner bathed in the flashing blue headlights of a trailing car, carrying the Olympic Torch.

The picture on the screen was only a TV commercial for beer, the one product that may now be regarded as more American than apple pie. But the viewers saw something else, deeper and wider and beyond the obvious: The torch as sixty-second theater. In the spring and summer of 1984, those who carried the fire saw scenes like that one repeated everywhere along the route: through Pennsylvania and West Virginia; past the

■ 13 ■

The message was the media. A year before the relay left New York, ad executives for Bud Light met to discuss plans for three Olympic-related television commercials. The strategy was to tie their message into a "least common denominator" of American society. They chose to highlight "a torch relay which would nearly evoke tears from two American farmers." It worked and won a Clio award, to boot. Then something magical happened: The commercial came true.

cotton fields of Georgia and the wheat fields of Kansas; across the oil and cactus belt that binds Oklahoma and Texas; into the highlands of New Mexico, Idaho, and Oregon.

In one of those states a little girl approached a torch relay runner waiting by the roadside. She pointed to a farmer who had been plowing in the field and said he was her father. She wanted the runner to know that her father never stopped plowing when his kids came home from school but that he had stopped to wave to the torch. She was impressed.

Months after the Olympics had ended, the stories continued. The runners who passed the torch, and the millions who lined the streets and roads and fields to watch and wave and cheer, still felt warm all over when they talked or thought about it. They had seen the light, but what exactly was it, this Olympic Torch that drew together Americans so powerfully, so mysteriously, so wonderfully? What deeper chords had it touched?

There were no losers, so it could not have been a sports event. It did not stand still long enough to be a pageant. Perhaps the relay was, as one runner said, "a nine-thousand-mile parade."

Did the Torch Relay in fact give America hope that a long national losing streak had ended? Vietnam, Watergate, the Iranian hostages, the pain of the economic recession in 1981 and '82. We had been the first to put a man on the moon, and the people were enthralled, but then, we didn't stay because we found out there was nothing to do there. When was the last time we celebrated a triumph so clear and pure that everyone could share it?

The reaction to the Torch Relay startled us. Something kept attracting the people—hundreds, and then thousands, until the total was in the millions. There were fireworks and sirens. Bands played. People sang. Some just started to run alongside the torchbearer. No one seemed to mind.

The sight of the torch rekindled a sense of American patriotism. The Stars and Stripes suddenly came in vogue.

The mood of the nation rose as the relay carried on its journey; bands struck up tunes for its passage in big cities, small towns, and tiny villages. Horns honked and stereos blared. A symphony followed them across the land.

It took a while for the national media to discover that the American people were having one gigantic flag-waving, hand-clapping parade. An extended transcontinental block party. *The New York Times* called it a phenomenon. But ordinary folks knew what it was all along. As the relay crossed the Central Colorado Rockies, at 11,000 feet, a man named Irwin Krueger, standing on the side of the road, said, "I could have told you. People really care about their country. People care."

It was a simple statement by an old Marine who had fought in the South Pacific forty years ago. One of his wife's relatives was Scott Carpenter, the astronaut. "But that moon stuff was so far away," he said, "so technological. Well, it was just hard. But this, this torch, you understand."

The commentators kept saying, and the writers kept writing, and even the runners repeated at stop after stop the same thought: "Something is happening here. But what? Is it the torch? The conquest of time and distance and hardship? Or a reaction to the Russians trying to rain on our parade?" In Purcell, Oklahoma, a mechanic said no, it wasn't the Russkies, "It's people trying to achieve something. I like that. It gives meaning to life." Another said: "We're all hungry for heroes but not big ones. Not anymore. Little heroes."

Maybe that was the point, after all. These were not pampered and high-priced athletes running and jumping for glory and six-figure contracts. These were ordinary people doing an extraordinary thing, and that has always been America's strength.

"Nobody can really explain what happened here," said Dick Boehner, one of the architects of the relay, near the end. "There was just something magic about it. The torch is a symbol that goes far beyond the flame. Some see it as the international peace symbol. Some, as a sign of national patriotism. Others, for things I can't even imagine. But everyone sees it in a positive way. It has been a giant national celebration."

Throughout the relay, only the flame really moved. Each runner kept his or her torch but lighted the next one. And so it went, hand to hand, person to person, across the country. More than 30 million people saw the torch move—live. The $12 million collected for charities as part of the relay made the relay among the largest fund-raisers in the country's history. The torch, slowly zigzagging its way across the country, was one of the unforgettable images of the year. And, some would argue, the real legacy of the 1984 Games, and of 1984.

□ □ □

The Torch Relay was a story with many beginnings. If you wanted to get historical, one could go back to ancient Greece, or to Amsterdam in 1928. If you wanted to be technical, you might plug into 1982, when the first codes were fed into a computer to produce

■ 15 ■

Outside Landon International House, a dormitory at Michigan State University, elementary-school children waited for a memory to be born. For most it was their first time to witness history outside of a textbook.

an operating plan. And if you wanted to get up close and personal, the place to begin was New Jersey, in March of 1984, during the second of two trial runs to prepare for the relay.

Flights from around the country had delivered some two dozen men and women to the Newark International Airport. They had come together for a test run of the Olympic Torch. Most were volunteers—some runners, some members of the Telephone Pioneers of America, a distinguished service organization of telephone company employees and retirees. While the runners ran with the torch, the Pioneers drove the vehicles and operated the ham radios. Runners and Pioneers all were dressed for travel and the late spring chill in zippered jackets and baseball caps, a few in sweatsuits, as if a marathon might break out at any moment.

There was something almost mili-

tary about the project from the beginning. Not in its precision—at least not then—but in the movement of people and vehicles and, yes, in the time spent waiting and searching and scouting. Some sat on their suitcases, read a newspaper, waited for a pay phone to become available, checked their watches.

A series of public address announcements indicated that they were joined in a common cause. Ears cocked whenever the disembodied voice repeated: "Will the drivers for the Olympic Torch Relay please come to the baggage area?"

They sparked only an occasional curious glance from their fellow travelers. Who knew what a "torch relay" was? The word *Olympics* may have sounded familiar. It is a very tall and evocative word, a dominant word. It has flags in it and even a little circus. At the same time it's a very sober

word, a clean and dynamic word, one that anybody would be proud to take home to meet their mother.

For the people milling around the baggage room, this trip represented their ticket to the Olympics. They had come together to conduct a test run of 800 miles, across parts of eight states, in eight days. It was a rehearsal for the real thing, delivering the torch from New York to Los Angeles for the opening of the 23rd Olympic Games.

Three vans had been assigned to collect them. One was needed elsewhere. A second broke down. The third got lost. You could not have asked for a better start.

Everyone received his or her written orders at the same time, usually between five and six each morning. Until

Bob Etzel passes the flame to Gordon McKinnie while hundreds from the suburbs near Shawnee, Kansas, either watch or, with their cameras aimed and focused, attempt to capture the exchange on film. The 1984 Torch Relay may well be the greatest spectator event ever—and the most photographed, too.

then no one knew for sure the route the runners would take or where the night would end. It was like a giant scavenger hunt. The Olympic Committee in Los Angeles kept saying that the last-minute orders were necessary for security reasons. It was also a convenient way to test people for stress.

What made the simulation run a grand and crazy time was this: It was okay for things to go wrong. You actually hoped they would. What better way for the managers to learn what or how much to fix before the actual run in May?

For those who wanted glitches, conditions were ideal. Through New Jersey, Pennsylvania, Delaware, Maryland, Virginia, West Virginia, Ohio, and Michigan, they traveled,

past woods and rivers and over mountains. Cross-country running taken to its extreme. Although the trial run involved only one shift of sixteen runners, and a fraction of the support crews and vehicles that would be needed later, the mix was representative of the longer task that was to come.

One of the motor homes got stuck in the mud in a field at the Aberdeen Proving Grounds in Maryland, and the U.S. Army sent a truck to pull it out. Then the truck sank up to its axle and the army had to send a tank to haul out both of them. For a while it was like watching *The Creature from the Black Lagoon.*

Half the caravan got lost trying to find the battlefield at Bull Run, and the entire relay was brought to a stop by a blizzard between Maryland and West Virginia. They broke for lunch at

a bowling alley and a shopping center and an Amish farmhouse, where you could shop in a log cabin scented with herbs and buy bags of noodles made from organic wheat. Once a woman charged them fifty dollars to park in front of her motel.

The thing is, you did not have to be a runner or a Pioneer to be swept up in the spirit that was already taking shape. You could be a writer, along for the ride, or a fly on the wall.

I was there, riding most of the week in a GMC van with a Pioneer named Harold Littell, from Akron, Ohio. A cherubic fellow, Harold wore glasses and had a voice like a tambourine.

One day we were lost, as we frequently were. At an intersection I finally spotted directly in front of us a motor home with the striped markings that identified it as an official torch vehicle. With great relief I assured Har-

A shell of one of the GMC motor homes used in the relay awaits the mastermind of Classic Coachworks' Al Taylor. Because the relay was of a magnitude never before attempted, nearly every aspect of it required "custom" attention.

Almost a dead ringer for Larry (Bud) Melman, the funny character who appears on Late Night with David Letterman, *Harold Littell became a fixture on the relay. A Telephone Pioneer, on the 82-day relay he was sentry to the torch supply truck.*

old that we were saved. He was not so confident. He made a sweeping gesture with his hand.

Two buses, a van, and a Buick had pulled up to the intersection from all four directions. As people do when they are agitated, there was a great deal of running in circles and a flapping of maps. "One of us isn't lost," said Harold. "Now all we have to do is figure out which one."

Although I never ran, no one questioned the fact that I seemed to have nothing to do. If asked, I identified myself as an observer. One of the things I observed were the two press buses, which were equipped with typewriters and telecopiers and photocopying machines. Quietly I tried to work in one, but a problem developed. Whenever the bus turned, the typewriter I was using skidded to the other corner. If the typewriter re-

mained stationary, my chair slid to the other wall. You would be amazed at how little I got done.

You knew everything would work out when two of the public relations people began to complain of boredom. There were simply great deserts of time when all you could do was sit in a car or truck and watch the runner plod ahead at six or seven miles an hour. Out of that monotony, Linda MacDougall, then with AT&T in Kansas City, and John Pashdag, a publicist for General Motors, had shared long conversations and occasional moonlit walks.

Their boredom reassured the relay managers. If people didn't get bored, they reasoned, it meant that the pace and intensity would remain so high on the official run that most of the travelers would be wrecks by the third week. For those with a little romance

in their souls, it should be noted that a few months after the Olympics, Linda MacDougall and John Pashdag were married.

The simulation run more or less matched an actual week on the New York to Los Angeles safari. There were two types of runners: those from AT&T, and those running for charity, "average" folks, many non-runners. The charity legs were called YLKs— for Youth Legacy Kilometers. In relay shorthand, these also became known as "Wild Ks." YLK runners, or their sponsors, each contributed $3,000 to a designated charity for the privilege of running six-tenths of a mile with the torch.

The other group of runners, from AT&T, were swift, strong, experienced. Their role: to escort the YLK entrants, help them light the torches, prop up those who struggle to finish,

The "core caravan" formed a protective pod for the runner, the torch, and the flame. Shown in this photo is the lead car, followed by the torchbearer, the security vehicle, and the Emergency Medical System truck.

and run with the flame during stretches when there were no YLKs scheduled. The AT&T runners were divided into four teams of four—three groups of men, one of women—each assigned to a specially constructed and fitted motor home, manned by a volunteer driver and radio operator. These four people learned the true meaning of communal living. They shared a tiny bathroom with a tinier shower; a refrigerator stuffed with sodas, fruit, candy bars, fruit juice, and half-eaten sandwiches. Each bus was equipped with a color television set that was never in range of a station when you actually had time to watch.

You felt a surge of admiration for any runner who fit inside his sleeping berth. One runner slept by pressing

his head against a bulkhead, his feet against the other, and slightly flexing his knees. He nicknamed his motor home *Das Boot*—the name of a classic German film about U-boats in World War II. He said he would always feel a special kinship with other claustrophobics who went down to the sea in submarines.

It must be true—the theme runs through many of their remarks—that the runners came to regard the relay as a mission. But in the beginning it was the idea of having fun (a track 9,000 miles long to run on) that outweighed the appeal of doing good (advancing the torch). They certainly did

not see themselves as heroes; nor for that week as project managers or computer analysts. They were runners, and the price they were willing to pay was high.

When the time came to make a distinction between the AT&T torchbearers and those who ran the charity kilometers, the relay managers decided to stick with the name they were already using—the AT&T *cadre*. Meaning an elite, or honor, guard. Several, in fact, had competed on AT&T's national championship running teams.

You have to understand runners. In a sense, the road is the temple where

they come to worship. After eight hours on a job they are back on the streets, dodging sports cars, fleeing ill-tempered dogs, breathing polluted air. They run in rain, cold, and broiling heat. They do it in sickness and in health.

Outside Fairfax, Virginia, a bearded runner named John Heidbreder approached a steep hill. In the chill and windy gloom, the hill looked like a swell way to get a coronary. A state trooper offered the runner a ride to the top. He refused, fearing that if he stopped, he wouldn't be able to get loose again. "About ten feet from the peak," described Boehner, "John went into his Rocky act. He threw up his arms and danced around in a little circle. He knew he would make it."

The cadre runners would average eight miles a day, and every seven days a by-now tired group of runners would be replaced by a new team.

Boehner was an exception; over the course of the entire relay, he ran more than a thousand miles total. His partners on AT&T's relay management team, Lou Putnam and Kate Washburn, each covered hundreds of miles.

It was pleasant, even from a distance, to observe the teamwork, the gentle interplay, between Boehner, Putnam, and Washburn. The three were to be major figures throughout the relay planning, and during the run itself. Responsibility for managing much of the actual work ultimately and inevitably fell on their shoulders. For them, the emotional stake was greatest—and the hardest to shake when it was all over.

They earned their livings in office jobs at AT&T; running was their common escape and their passion. When none of the three had miles to do, they huddled with their clipboards or peered over the shoulders of the com-

puter operator. They were working with numbers that would be brought to life by hearts and legs.

They joked about how little they slept. They averaged three hours a night. Kate once fell asleep on one of the buses, standing up.

On the simulation run a bunk had been reserved for me on the motor home occupied by Dick and Lou. My interest in this arrangement lasted right up until the moment I learned that they rolled out of bed at 5 A.M. Writers are a civilized breed who prefer to go through life leaving a wake-up call for noon.

Boehner was responsible for the two alarm clocks that went off each morning. The clocks were positioned on a chest of drawers between the two

When the relay began, no one knew what the road foreshadowed. The American media, as its reputation dictates, was cynical. But the summer's sleeper would soon turn the cynics meek.

Whatever it was that happened, whatever powers the relay possessed, the effect could be seen in expressions of ardor and elation —before or after being drenched in a rainstorm.

One carrier of the flame said she held her torch high because, to her, "it represents freedom."

double bunks. Dick set the clocks and was the first to rise, rousting the others like a wagon master. One night the clocks were missing. Three days later the clocks were discovered under Boehner's pillow. Both of them. Not fully awake, he had reached across his bunk, shut off the clocks, slammed them under his pillow, and gone back to sleep. This was a modern, Olympic version of "The Princess and the Pea."

In vital statistics Dick and Lou seem to be almost clones. Both are five feet eight, welterweights at 145, Dick a year younger at 37. But the packaging

definitely comes from different stores. Dick is wound tight, chesty, a college wrestler who still spends hours a day running and pumping iron. His hair is blond and wispy, and he has a smile that is wide and cheery. But it is the intensity of Dick Boehner that people notice most. A friend who had not seen him in months caught up with him on the tenth week of the relay. Deep sun-squint lines framed his eyes. He was bleached and bronzed and burned hard-dry. The friend said he looked "Wagnerian."

For pure natural ability Kate Washburn may have been the most gifted athlete of the three relay managers. (In the field, to their teammates, they were viewed not as bosses but as playing captains.) At St. Lawrence University, in upstate New York, she was a star in swimming and cross-country

skiing. By 1981, she had a master's degree in cardiovascular fitness, from Michigan. And a new interest in cross-country running.

Slender, blue-eyed, with brown hair, Kate, at 29, has the look of a sweet Mary Decker.

If Lou Putnam were an actor, he would always be cast in the role of "best friend." People sense in him a mildness, a balance that can't be faked. He is the product of a big family, four brothers and four sisters, including two sets of twins. The patience he may have learned at home made him a cross-country runner in college. He captained the team at Oakland University, near Rochester, MI.

Lou's wife gave birth to their second child, a daughter, eight days before the simulation run was to take place. It was a big month.

Late on the first day of the March simulation run, a young YLK runner handed his torch to Boehner, who

now had two. When Dick tried to explain that carrying the torch was part of the honor, the young idealist replied, "That's your problem." In truth, it was only one of his problems. The route had been changed slightly, and the next shuttle was late. The relay had gotten behind schedule, and the new kid seemed hell-bent on making up the lost time.

Boehner made a quick round trip to the security car to drop off the extra torch. Then he raced back to escort the sponsored runner. After two miles or so the pace caught up with him. When

the security car drew alongside, he opened the door and threw himself in. He looked like he was going into oxygen arrest.

Putnam replaced him, giving up his seat in the security car. Lou had gone a mile when it dawned on him that he was running in his street clothes. He had not even packed a bag because with a week-old baby at home, he hadn't planned to stay. Six days later he was still on the caravan, wearing a borrowed sweater and slacks.

One day I agreed to drive Putnam's beige Ford station wagon, so he could

help with the schedule and possibly plan his escape. The weather was clear that morning when he left Romney, near the West Virginia border, and it was enjoyable to look out the window at the homes spaced miles apart and wonder what the people did at night.

Rain began to fall, then hail, and in a span of time that seemed about as long as the snap of a finger, I was in the middle of a blizzard. Now I was hunched over the wheel of a borrowed car, with a sheer mountain drop to my right, petrified. I had never before driven in snow, which doesn't exactly fall like teardrops on the humid Texas coast, where I live.

I drove as slowly as I could without actually killing the motor, maybe five miles an hour. At any moment I expected a runner to pass me. The visibility was so poor that I did not notice, until I was beyond them, an occasional van or car from the relay, pulled off to the side of the road. I was afraid to hit

A fine athlete, soft-spoken and lively, Kate Washburn kept the spirits high among the AT&T cadre runners. She was one of a troika of relay managers, along with Boehner and Putnam.

the brake or turn the wheel, for fear of putting the car in a skid.

Even without the snow we were in mountain roads that promised endless thrills. Signs in the form of an arrow winding like a corkscrew indicated the position of the next turn. Strange thoughts filled my mind: If I went over a cliff, would my insurance cover Lou Putnam's car?

Finally one of the motor homes loomed straight ahead, and with a heart that leapt like a fawn, I followed it through the worst of the mountains and the fiercest of the storm. We made it across the West Virginia line into Maryland and took refuge in a log-cabin café in a town called Red House. A sign outside advertised barbecued sausage links.

The highway patrol had shut down the run at the start of the storm. One by one the vehicles came in, and the passengers poured into the café, stamping their feet and blowing on

their hands. There was a lot of banter back and forth, but behind it was a real and persistent fear. A good deal of window watching went on, until everyone was accounted for. The look on Lou Putnam's face was especially heartwarming when he saw me there and realized that his car was safe.

The snowstorm had been mean enough that patrol cars from both states had pulled up at the café. Inside, a kind of celebration was going on. A bonding process had started.

Kate Washburn was the subject of one of the more memorable and telling anecdotes of the relay—telling, because of the sense it gives of the relay as a giant, moving cocoon.

Passing through Lake Tahoe, Kate heard someone mention that Walter

Mondale was waiting at one of the exchange points to greet the caravan. Kate had been on the relay for ten weeks, had not seen a newspaper or watched television in all that time. She was in an orbit all her own. But she admired Walter Mondale. She jumped off the bus and greeted the Democratic nominee for president with a handshake and a quick, "Hi, Mr. Mondale." Then she shook the hand of the lady standing at his side and said, "Nice to meet you, Mrs. Mondale." Later that day, she saw in a newspaper a picture of the woman whose hand she had shaken, and that was when, and how, Kate Washburn learned that Geraldine Ferraro was the first woman to be nominated for the vice-presidency of the United States.

OF FLAGS AND FLAMES

While maidens in ancient costume paraded in the ruins of Olympia, a young Greek runner lighted a torch and began the first leg of a twelve-day run through Europe, bound for Berlin. The date was July 20, 1936. A tradition had been born.

For all the doomsaying, all the suggestions of how or if the Games should be saved, the Olympic spirit has somehow proven to be hard to extinguish. It has survived two World Wars, two superpower boycotts, sex tests, drug scandals, and murder. While old men argue and governments choose sides, young people play. And on the evidence of the 1984 Games—higher and brighter than ever.

It should be pointed out here and now that those who would keep politics out of the Olympics are fighting a war without end. They might just as well try to keep ants out of a picnic or parents out of the Little League.

Of course, it could be done. As Pierre Trudeau, the former prime minister of Canada, once put it: "All you have to do is eliminate the flags and the national anthems and let each athlete compete on his own. Then you could hold the Games in a YMCA somewhere." It is worth noting that Canada is still paying off a billion-dollar debt from the 1976 Games.

Or, if we are to return the Olympics to true amateur purity, the athletes should be required to compete in the nude, as they did in the days of ancient Greece. Science has established that nudity does not improve performance, but it does help attendance.

Without radical social change, but with an echo from the past, the Olympic ideal—and America itself—made a comeback in 1984. The turnaround started with the run across the continent. Yankee pride and ingenuity came together with a spark that had fizzled since the 1950s. We had, in that time, lost ground in the arena and grown tired of the constant political intrusions, even those of our own creation.

So large did the torch loom on the winding road to Los Angeles that it comes as a mild surprise to learn that the flame did not appear, in this century, until the summer Games of 1928, at Amsterdam. The Torch Relay came along eight years later, in Berlin, the usual starting point for a political history of the modern Games. Before we reflect on that coincidence, we pause to recall two famous examples of American self-expression.

In 1908, when the U.S. team passed by the reviewing stand, a weight-

At the altar of Hera, near the stadium where the first Olympiad was held in 776 B.C., Greek actress Katerina Didasklou holds the torch aloft after it was lit at a May 7, 1984, ceremony in Olympia, Greece.

thrower named Martin Sheridan refused to dip the flag in a salute to the king and queen of England. "This flag," he declared, "dips to no earthly king."

In 1912, another monarch, Gustav of Sweden, watched in wonder as Jim Thorpe accomplished what no man had done before or since: win both the pentathlon and the decathlon. As he handed Thorpe his medals, he said with admiration: "You, sir, are the greatest athlete in the world."

To which the Sac and Fox Indian clearly agreed. "Thanks, King," he replied.

This kind of chauvinism and confidence were reflected in the celebrations of 1984. That they represented

some kind of release or rediscovery, not many doubted. But how deeply the feelings ran, what bars of music had been struck, may be tied to whatever people saw in that seductive flame.

In 1928, the torch burned for the duration of the Games, as it has since. But the tradition of the torch races can be traced back to the ancient Greeks. In Olympia, a sanctuary dedicated to the goddess Hestia, was housed the glowing embers which, every four years, would be fanned into flame by the winning athletes. To preserve the purity and power of the fire, it had to be moved with speed. Soon competitions developed to see which individual or group—a relay—could move the torch the fastest. The winner won the honor of lighting the fire in the name of the patron deity of the city or the god in whose name the festival was being held.

The races were on foot or horseback,

with as many as 48 members on a team. The distances ranged from 800 to 2,500 meters (approximately 1.5 miles.) Runners competed wearing only leather or metallic crowns. The races were usually held at night and so fascinated the Athenians that Plato described them in *The Republic*, making him arguably the first track and field writer.

In Berlin, in 1936, the dimension of the Torch Relay was added to the modern Games. Dr. Carl Diem, a former runner and *chef-de-mission* for the last four German Olympic teams, was moved to create a Torch Relay ceremony from a model portrayed in the writings of Plutarch, the ancient Greek writer and philosopher. An all-

Before departing from its birth site at the Olympia ruins, an Olympic flame is shuttled in a ceremonial procession to the nearby memorial of Baron de Coubertin, founder of the modern Olympic Games. Here the flame is carried to the memorial in a vase before leaving for the London Olympiad in 1948.

The pageantry and the history of land and region have blended in every torch relay, as here the runner leaves ancient Olympia through a tunnel of flags.

weather magnesium torch, weighing 1.5 pounds, and 2.25 feet in length, was developed. A special concave reflector was made to focus the sun's rays and create fire. A grove in Olympia, Greece, was designated as the starting point.

The relay began on July 20, 1936, traveling from the temple of Zeus at Olympia in Athens, then through Bulgaria, Yugoslavia, Hungary, Austria, and Czechoslovakia. The route was one the Germans had traveled before but in the opposite direction, when they followed the Kaiser into World War I. This time 3,000 runners covered 6,000 kilometers in twelve days. Fritz Schilgen, a former Olympic athlete, ran the last leg of the relay down a series of steps and onto the stadium

floor to the resounding music of Beethoven's Ninth Symphony.

What else was notable about 1936 was the simple fact that for the first time the United States made a venture into the true spirit of the Olympics; that is, winning. The instrument was the grandson of a slave, a sharecropper's son from Alabama named Jesse Owens. Raised in Cleveland, a great track star at Ohio State, his role became clear to the American sporting public when the German propaganda machine began calling the ten blacks on the U.S. team "The African Auxiliary." The story gathered momentum after a real or coincidental snub of Owens by Adolf Hitler.

Owens dominated the Games. On August 3, he won his first gold medal

by holding off a late bid by teammate Ralph Metcalfe, also black, to win the 100 meter. He had set an Olympic mark in his heat, defeating a German rival, and it was here that Hitler had supposedly snubbed him. In truth, the Olympic committee had warned the Führer against congratulating *any* winners, lest he discriminate against blacks or Jews or any other prejudice of his choice.

The next day Owens won the broad jump. On Wednesday he captured the 200-meter title—his third gold medal. Before the Games closed, he also ran on the victorious U.S. 400-meter relay. American athletes, black and white, had captured twelve of the thirteen track events.

No matter what else they did or did

In 1936, the Games were perverted as a political instrument, and a pattern of pain and mischief would follow through the years. The torchbearer, Fritz Schilgen, chosen for his "aesthetically pleasing" form, climbs the steps to receive Hitler's salute.

not do, the 1936 Olympics set a trend of American involvement. The events leading to World War II wiped out the next two Olympiads. It wasn't until 1948 that the sportsmen of the world got together again and something new was added. The Soviet Union was getting ready to poke its nose through the Iron Curtain. There were Soviet photographers, coaches, athletes, newsmen. They were everywhere,

hovering around like fruit flies, watching, filming, taking notes.

The Torch Relay for the 1948 Games, in London, began during a Greek civil war, striking echoes of another time. The first runner was Corporal Dimtrelis, of the Greek Army. He appeared fully dressed in uniform, laid down his rifle, changed into running attire, and began his run. The torch passed through eight war-torn coun-

tries of Europe. The last leg was run in Wembley Stadium by British middle-distance runner John Mark, president of the Cambridge University Athletic Club.

The 1952 Games were held in Helsinki, and for a long time there was doubt whether Russia would compete. They had spurned the Winter Games in Norway. They even refused to let the Olympic torchbearers cross into Soviet territory at Talinn, thereby lengthening the journey from Athens to Helsinki by 2,000 miles. But in the end they came.

For Helsinki, the Olympic flame went airborne for the first time. It was flown from Athens to Copenhagen, then transported by ferry to southern Sweden. A relay of runners, bicyclists, and motorcyclists brought it to the stadium, ending in the hand of Paavo Nurmi. There were 70,000 fans packed into the Olympic Stadium, even as rains threatened to wash away the

Games. But the enthusiasm was genuine when Nurmi, who had brought world honors to Finland as a long-distance runner of another era, trotted slowly down the track with the torch in his hand. The spectacle was curious —the fire below and thousands of wet pigeons fluttering overhead.

The Russians did not win a single gold medal that year, losing their best chance when America's Horace Ashenfelter brought off a huge upset in the steeplechase, beating the Russian, Vladimir Kazantsev, the world record holder. A 29-year-old Penn State graduate, Ashenfelter had gone to work for the FBI. He had not run the steeplechase more than eight times in his life and had never run it in less than nine minutes. Thirty-two years later he would run one of the special kilometers during the 1984 Torch Relay.

The 1956 Olympics were the wave of the future. Egypt, Lebanon, and Iraq walked out in protest against the Suez War. Spain and the Netherlands quit over Russia's treatment of Hungary. Red China quit when somebody slipped inside its compound in the Olympic Village and raised the National Chinese flag on its pole.

At Melbourne the torch was carried into the stadium by Ron Clarke, a national junior-distance record holder, a future Olympian and one of the early four-minute milers. From Down Under, by land, the torch reappeared in Rome in 1960, transported on the sailing ship, the *Amerigo Vespucci.*

America waited for 1960 with some apprehension, knowing that its dominance in international sport was threatened. John Thomas was the symbol of American hopes that year. He was, without a doubt, the best high jumper in the world on the day he left for Rome. As a student at Boston University, he had made a shambles of both the indoor and outdoor track seasons.

During a workout in Rome, shortly before the opening of the Games, Thomas was preparing to test the high jump bar at 6'8" when he noticed a group of Russians approaching with cameras. In a stage whisper loud enough to shatter glass, he asked his trainer to raise the bar to seven feet. He cleared it twice with little effort and the Russians murmured "zamechatelno" (wonderful). Valeri Brumel was one of those watching. He looked grim. "He is unbeatable," said the

Yoshinori Sakai, a 19-year-old student born the day the atom bomb fell on Hiroshima, circles the track before lighting the fire to open the 18th Olympiad in Tokyo.

Russian coach, Gabriel Korobkov, about Thomas.

What happened to John Thomas in 1960 would bruise the ego of American track fans as no individual defeat had up to that time. They expected to lose to the Russians in gymnastics and canoeing and the like. They even conceded that the Russians might dominate the "unofficial" team scoring.

Thomas finished third, behind two Russians, failing three times to clear 7'1", the winning height. The setback was compounded on a day when the U.S. failed to qualify a single man for the 800-meter run, an event it had won every year since 1932. In the 100 meter, the U.S. lost the gold for the first time since 1928.

A year later Valeri Brumel, Russia's

third-place finisher in the high jump, came to the United States for a series of three matches. He won them all by large margins. On the way home the Russian coach criticized American training and techniques.

The relay for Tokyo in 1964 was distinguished from all the others by its all-encompassing flight routes. The airplane carrying the torch stopped in eleven countries on the way to Japan. The relay lasted 49 days, and although the distance traveled was only 7,500 kilometers, a record was established for sheer numbers: 100,000 runners. In each country a mini-Torch Relay took place from the airport into the capital city and back to the airport. It then toured the Japanese Islands before Yoshinori Sakai, a Japanese boy born

in Hiroshima the day the atomic bomb fell, ran into the stadium with the flame.

The history of Christopher Columbus and his route to the New World were the focus of Mexico City's Torch Relay for the 1968 Olympics. The torch traveled from his birthplace in Genoa, Italy, to Barcelona, Spain, where he was received by Queen Isabella after his historic voyage, and finally to San Salvador, the exact site of his landing. Eduardo Moreno became the first athlete to convey the Olympic Torch over water when he swam with it to shore from a ship that docked in Vera Cruz, Mexico. For the first time a woman ran the final leg. Enriqueta Basilio, 20, a

In 1968, the torch followed the route to the New World of Christopher Columbus, stopping at Vera Cruz. An escort of seventeen swimmers brought the flame to shore, and 20-year-old Norma Enriquetta Basilio became the first woman to carry the torch into the opening ceremony.

Mexican national champion, carried the torch up a long stairway to light the fire.

The year had been a turbulent one, and the Games followed the pattern. The Mexican government vowed to keep order, and soldiers used force to put down a student riot, leaving forty dead. Two American sprinters, Tommie Smith and John Carlos, raised their gloved fists on the victory stand and bowed their heads to protest racial injustices in the United States. In the context of the times the protest did not seem undignified, but Smith and Carlos were expelled from the U.S. team and for years afterward had trouble finding jobs.

Smith eventually went into coaching and was briefly on the staff at Oberlin College. Carlos turned up in 1984 on the staff of Los Angeles Olympic Organizing Committee (LAOOC) and ran a kilometer on the Torch Relay. He prefers not to talk about the 1960s and the so-called Black Power salute at Mexico City.

That was also the Olympics when burly George Foreman, a product of the Job Corps created by Lyndon Johnson, won the heavyweight boxing title. In reaction to anti-American feeling over Vietnam, Foreman circled the ring waving a small red-white-and-blue flag.

The Munich Torch Relay of 1972 traced the same footsteps as the 1936 Berlin run. But the Bavarian Games were intended to erase for the rest of the world the grim memories of another Germany. Planned and staged with meticulous care, the Games

■ 31 ■

Two 15-year-old runners, Steve Prefontaine and Sandra Henderson, were the final torchbearers at Montreal in 1976. They were the youngest so honored, the first to carry the flame jointly, and, in a romantic postcript, were married several years later.

ended under a man-made rainbow and to the buoyant mood of the song "My Sweet Lord," while away from the TV camera soldiers bearing submachine guns patrolled the grounds. The system had broken down, and dead in the wake of it were eleven Israeli athletes and coaches, a German policeman, and five terrorists.

Munich was the subterranean low point in the matter of Olympic hopes and ideals. And it is against this depression that the distance we had traveled to 1984 could be measured. Sports had been the last sanctuary. Athletes were special people. Like the Olympians from 121 other nations, those from Israel would have caught the eye of any parent who had raised a son in sports, watched their muscles grow, lived with their anxieties, saw them lose and cry. Such recollections

drifted through your mind as you thought of them, lying dead from machinegun bullets and hand grenades and the flame of fire. It had happened at the Olympics, where countries gathered to celebrate peace and fellowship and understanding.

In the aftermath of the massacre at Munich, the whole concept of staging international sports events began to change, leading to security measures on a scale never thought possible. Security forces at Montreal in 1976 added $100 million to the cost. And all because it was proved one day in Munich that sports can't be detached from earthly madness. Up until then we lived in the fantasy that it could.

Barbed wire and armed guards were in heavy evidence at Montreal. The athletes, most of them, favored these conditions—it kept the press at a dis-

In a moment of irony that did not go unfelt, Sergei Belov, the Soviet basketball star, runs with the torch past the Olympic team from Afghanistan during the opening ceremonies of the 1980 Games in Moscow. The USA led a boycott of over forty countries.

tance. At the 21st Olympiad, the parade of teams to the airport was nearly as long as the one around the track. Taiwan was forced to return home because of pressures applied by Red China, a country that did not then recognize the Olympic Games. A total of twenty-two African nations walked out to protest an appearance by the New Zealand rugby team in Rhodesia.

Timeless hatreds were in flower, but the technology at Montreal was new. The torch was lit in Athens by a sensor, which coded the energy of the flame and beamed it to a satellite. The satellite transmitted the signal to Ottawa, where it ignited the torch used to light the Olympic cauldron at Montreal.

At Moscow, in 1980, the Games featured a Relay of Champions. Goldmedal winners from six sports ran the torch from Greece, across Bulgaria and Romania, and into the Soviet Union.

Sergei Belov, a member of three Russian Olympic basketball teams, carried the torch into Lenin Stadium as giant telescreens flashed pictures of Soviet cosmonauts circling the earth.

It is accepted today that the most secure and the most efficient Olympiad in modern times was staged by the Russians. There were no labor problems, no voters banding together to withhold funds, no organized protests on the part of environmental groups worried about fish eggs. Before the Games, every dissident, anyone considered to be a troublemaker, was pitched into prison. Every child in Moscow under the age of sixteen was sent to a summer camp. The crowds were extremely well behaved. A city empty of teenagers may be joyfully re-

ceived by teachers, pedestrians, and even many parents, but something called the American way of life argues against such tidy and simple solutions.

The United States kept its Olympic team at home in 1980, to protest the Russian occupation of Afghanistan. The boycott cost the Russians the worldwide television coverage they craved, and millions in tourist dollars. The decision by President Jimmy Carter was not a popular one, but it made a point. You do not allow the Soviets to reap a financial and propaganda windfall when you are trying to get the Russian boot off another nation's neck.

One way or another, the stage was set for 1984.

THE MUSIC MAN

Some say that the country needed a spectacle, a grand display of American pride and attainment. One man heard the call.

Since the Berlin Games of 1936, the torch had been sent by air, sea, and foot to ignite the opening ceremonies, carried by one runner or many, a few miles or across several borders. America thought it had a better idea. The goal would be to give, for the first time, most of a country a chance to be part of the Olympic and Global Village. The torch would go farther and stay longer than ever before, passing through 1,200 cities and towns, not all of them listed on the map. It would be seen in 82 days by 30 million people, making it the most visible spectator event in history.

The flame would be passed hand to hand by 200 trained runners/employees of the corporate sponsor, AT&T, the American Telegraph and Telephone Company. For charity, another 12,000 would run a single kilometer, for each of which they or a sponsor donated $3,000. These would be an Olympic first, the Youth Legacy Kilometers, the YLKs. The money would

benefit the YMCA, the Boys' Clubs of America, the Special Olympics (for the handicapped) and other youth groups around the country.

But for all the good intentions, this selling of the torch pitted the Los Angeles Olympic Organizing Committee, whose idea it was, against the government of Greece. The Greeks argued that the torch was a symbol of peace. To allow people to buy a kilometer would focus attention on the runner, rather than the symbol. "The flame is for us a sacred thing," said Spyros Foteinos, the mayor of Olympia, where the ancient Games were first held. "It is not for sale."

As guardians of the flame, the Greeks threatened not to release the holy fire. Someone had gotten their history wrong. Where in the *Iliad* does it say the Greeks should beware of Americans bearing gifts?

The dispute led to delays that caused the route of the relay to be shortened, from an original plan that

would have taken the torch through all fifty states. As the clock ticked closer to the start of the Games, the issue grew thornier for Peter Ueberroth, head of the Organizing Committee. He turned to a longtime crony and ex-business partner, Dick Sargent.

On the LAOOC staff, Sargent was the designated troubleshooter. Of medium height, with the kind of permanent suntan only the wealthy could once afford, he did not fit any conventional mold. Out of college in California, he did what many dream of doing: he moved to Tahiti where he lived for several years. After his return, he teamed up with Ueberroth, four years his junior, to form a travel company that would become the second largest in the country and make them both multimillionaires.

Sargent had first negotiated with the Greeks to have the flame officially transferred to the Americans. Tough and resourceful, he was at his best behind the scenes. The original deal he

The original route of the Torch Relay. It would have journeyed through every state; flames transported to Alaska and Hawaii would have returned to Los Angeles for the opening ceremonies.

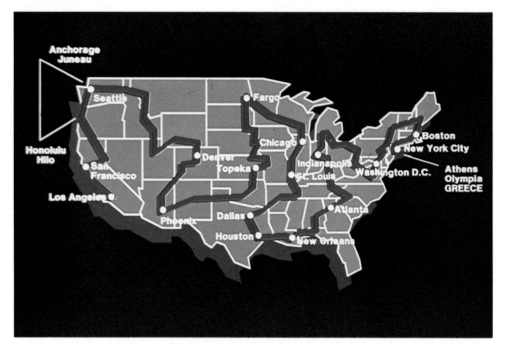

cut was uncomplicated. The Greeks would turn over the flame to the Los Angeles Olympic Organizing Committee for a $25,000 fee, most of which would fund a traditional torch relay in Greece. Sargent also agreed to provide outfits for all of the Greek runners.

The plans to pick up the flame moved ahead. AT&T chartered a plane from United Airlines, another of the Olympic sponsors. The flame would burn in three miners' lamps sealed in a safety box custom-designed by an engineer at United. (The box would ride in the plane's no-smoking section.) Eight hundred uniforms were shipped to Greece for their portion of the relay. Permits were obtained to transport a flame through international gateways.

It all seemed cut and dried, the fun part of the project. The flight to Greece and back would be a transAtlantic tailgate party. Officials from LAOOC and

executives from many of the Olympic sponsors all volunteered to accompany the flame.

Ueberroth agreed to shut off the YLK sales at 4,000, in the hope that the Greeks would not sabotage the ceremonial lighting of the flame. No matter how elusive the idea seemed to his critics, Ueberroth thought the rewards were clear. "It doesn't just have to go to charity in terms of raising money for kids," he said. "It could be used in a poorer country to buy a blanket or a basket of food." Yet in Western Europe the relay was being described as some kind of honky-tonk parade.

Again negotiations broke down. The Greeks wanted LAOOC to do away entirely with the sale of sponsored kilometers, even though the money would go to charity. Neither side was willing to give in. "Right up to the week the relay began," says Sargent, "we never knew what the

Greeks would do: if they would or wouldn't give us the flame."

The charter flight was canceled. Then Sargent made a final demand: Release the flame or LAOOC would bypass the tradition of lighting the torch on Greek soil. Further, the Greek team would march into the Coliseum in their alphabetical position, instead of leading the procession, an honor which has been theirs since the start of the modern Games.

Within hours the Greeks replied. The Americans could pick up the flame. However, the Greeks would provide no security. They would cancel their relay from Olympia to Athens and return the 800 uniforms.

Now a new element was added to the exchange of the flame: the fear of a terrorist attack; from what quarter was never made clear. AT&T declined, not wishing to risk the safety of its employees. But Sargent volunteered. It took some courage. He called the White House and arranged for an Air Force jet to carry him and three others to pick up the flame.

The jet landed secretly in Europe on

America's idea was to give anyone the opportunity to take part in the Olympics. By donating $3,000 to a local youth group an individual could carry—or sponsor someone else to carry—the flame for a Youth Legacy Kilometer.

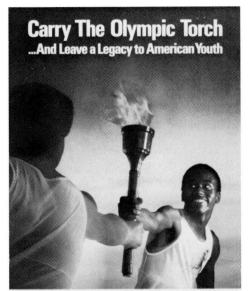

Carry The Olympic Torch
...And Leave a Legacy to American Youth

Olympic Torch Relay
New York City to Los Angeles
May 8–July 28, 1984

Contact Your Local Boys Club, Girls Club, YMCA or Call 1-213/Go-Torch

The Greeks, always considered guardians of the flame, saw the selling of kilometers as an unacceptable commercialization of the Games. Later, the Soviet Union made similar claims.

May 7. Two helicopters were rented through a Greek airline to fly them to Olympia. The airline gave him instructions to have $2,400—$1,200 for each chopper—in hundred-dollar bills. He was to pay before boarding. Sargent didn't know it, but the negotiating wasn't over.

The next morning he slipped twenty-four crisp hundred-dollar bills into an envelope and stuffed it inside his jacket pocket. At the airport a commotion developed between a representative of the airline and Sargent's Greek envoy, Peter Kalerleros. Sargent was told that the price was now $2,800. There they stood, twenty-four hours and an ocean away from the start of the Torch Relay, haggling over $400.

Sargent told his man to tell the airline agent there was no more money. They could take the $2,400 they had agreed on or he would turn around and go home. The Greeks didn't believe him. Sargent turned around and

walked away. He had not gone many steps when they called him back. They would fly his party to Olympia.

The two helicopters landed in the middle of a soccer field adjacent to the ruins. Sargent and his team walked over to the Altar of Hera, where, at high noon, the vestal virgins performed the ceremony of kindling the Olympic flame with a concave reflector and a piece of film filament. Once ignited, one of the torches was lighted. The vestal virgins then laid a wreath on the crypt that contained the heart of Baron de Coubertin, the founder of the modern Games, who once said that his "mind and body will always be with France, but my heart will always be with Olympia."

At the end of the ceremony Sargent accepted the flame, lighted the miners' lamps, climbed aboard one of the helicopters, and headed for home.

This was the most public of several threats to the smooth conduct of the Torch Relay. Still, the relay was shaping up as one for *The Guinness Book of World Records,* if there is a category for the longest and biggest torchlight parade. More than 10,000 volunteers

would be involved. A convoy of 41 vehicles would burn some 52,000 gallons of gasoline. The cooks would serve 15,000 dozen eggs and 5,000 pounds of meat, poultry, and fish. It would be, in short, a production number, a mobilization, seldom seen in this country in peacetime.

At the outset no one could be really sure of what to expect from an Olympic Torch Relay. The first and most obvious question was: Who needed it? With all the headaches inherent in staging an event to which the immediate world was invited, why take on a project on such a scale, so laden with risks? The torch would be out there for 82 days. For the runners it was a long stage and a naked one. If anything went wrong, no one could hide.

But Peter Ueberroth, impresario, risk taker, and president of LAOOC, sensed that the country needed, or wanted, a spectacle, some grand display of American pride and attainment. It was like Robert Preston in *The Music Man,* knowing that River City needed a band and promising that the town would have one. There were

The flags of Greece and the Olympics wave in the breeze outside this modest municipal building in Olympia, where the Greeks threatened to block the departure of the flame.

Olympia Mayor Spyros Foteinos took on officials at the Los Angeles Olympic Organizing Committee: "The flame for us is a sacred thing. It is not for sale."

polls that showed Americans losing interest in the Olympics and questioning the meaning of Olympic ideals in a world torn by timeless hates.

Ueberroth was virtually unknown to the public when he accepted, after twice turning it down, the job as president of LAOOC. The concept for the relay was his, and the stakes were large. The passage across America would set the tone for the Games.

Ueberroth won big. His success in producing the 1984 Olympics led to his selection as the commissioner of baseball. This move was worth noting, if you think becoming commissioner of baseball is a good thing to have happen to you. After his Olympic experience Ueberroth was confident he could handle the hard-nosed baseball writers he would encounter in his new job. "I've been vilified in twenty languages," he said. "It's nice to have it reduced to one. They've already complained about my name. They've just

gotten to the point where they can spell Yastrzemski, and now I come along."

Ueberroth quickly became one of the more interesting and enigmatic figures to land on the national scene in years. He seemed to come out of nowhere, or a little to the right of there, when a head-hunting firm proposed him as the president of the LAOOC. That was in 1979, five years before the Games.

He has a young face, blue eyes, thin lips, soft features. He worked his way through San Jose State pumping gas, selling shoes, collecting eggs at a chicken ranch, and working as a ramp attendant for nonscheduled airlines. He eventually made a small fortune with the Ask Mr. Foster travel agencies. He is the embodiment of that staple of nineteenth-century American fiction, the self-made man.

His management style has been described as based on the theory of "cre-

ative tension." If we read that code correctly, he doesn't object to conflicts among his staff. Or between agencies. There was certainly a sense of rivalry, and competition, possibly more, between LAOOC and the Olympic Corporate sponsors, including AT&T.

Nothing about Ueberroth seems forced. He is not a glad-hander, a quality sometimes taken as coldness. Nor does he shrink from people. He has the capacity to make hard decisions, in the spirit of the old Russians in winter, throwing each other off the back of their sleighs to slow down the wolves. He approved the firing of one associate who had been a friend for twenty-five years.

That Ueberroth felt some special, proprietary interest in the trans-America torch run cannot be in doubt. But he never saw the relay in person, nor any film of it until near the very end—except for clips on the nightly news. Daryl Walker, one of the attorneys for

LAOOC, was in Ueberroth's office discussing a legal matter one day when a visitor brought in a videotape of the event. "I don't remember Peter saying much," said Walker. "Didn't have to. I just looked at him, and I could tell what the relay meant to him."

Ueberroth had tried to beg off seeing the videotape, pleading that he didn't have time. Besides, there would be plenty of footage for him to view later; AT&T was filming the run. The visitor said he didn't think the Olympic boss had seen any film quite like this. Ueberroth gave in.

Soon on the screen was a nine-year-old girl waiting for the next runner to reach her, on a highway in a little town in Kansas. Ueberroth studied the nine-year-old. "She was handicapped and she had her head down, and I wondered, 'Gee, why is he showing me this—is this another complaint?' So I felt bad about this girl, and then the runner, a full-grown man, came with the motorcycle escort and lit her torch, and she started to move.

"She could hardly get one leg in front of the other and she was suffering, and I thought, 'Why am I seeing this?' There was a motorcycle policeman who was getting angry, and he had one of those big plastic shields over his face, and he was gunning the engine. It was just a bad moment. Finally she got one leg in front of the other and slowly started moving, and then her head came up and there was a smile that was this wide . . . she was so determined and she kept going.

"Her kilometer was uphill, which helped, because, with her handicap, she could move against the gravity of the pavement. I watched as she went. All along the roadside there were people with signs saying, 'Run, Amy. You Can Run, Amy," to this nine-year-old girl in Kansas. Somehow people had put up $3,000 so she could do it. I watched the TV cameramen with their cameras down all along the way, and that's why I never saw any footage. ABC, NBC, CBS—all these hardened people, they aren't taking the photos. Then when she finally got to the end, it was exhilarating. To me she looked like she was ten feet tall. She lit the next torch and the runner slipped off,

Participation in the Olympic Games seemed one of those goals destined to remain forever out of reach for Amy Haas. Since birth she has been handicapped by cerebral palsy.

The 8-year-old daughter of avid runners, Amy carried the flame for one kilometer near her hometown of Stilwell, Kansas. She was raring to run: "I made up my mind to do it."

Amy's courage touched Time *magazine's 1984 Man of the Year, Peter Ueberroth, who viewed a videotape of her run the following day: "She was so determined and she kept going," he said.*

and I noticed the motorcycle policeman didn't go. He had his plastic shield pushed up and had his handkerchief out and was wiping his eyes.

"I knew then that this was a special country and the Torch Relay had worked. That was our first victory in the Olympic Games. The second came in the opening ceremonies, when one hundred and forty nations took part after every kind of political pressure, every kind of emotional pressure, every kind of threatened pressure."

The reference was to the Soviet boycott and the fear that most of the Eastern bloc would follow, in announcements that would be dragged out for maximum effect. One-a-day bitter pills, Ueberroth called them. Although stunned by the action, which followed by four hours the lighting of the torch in New York, Ueberroth was quick to react. He dispatched his envoys around the world—to China, East Germany, Cuba—and eventually

chartered planes to bring in athletes from forty African states. His strategy was based on limiting the damage, not on the futile hope that the Russians would reconsider.

Red China competed for the first time in its history. Ueberroth could count other victories, high among them the presence of Romania, a country he called the poorest in the Soviet bloc and probably the least understood by the West. "We can't lump them all together," he said. "Romania wanted to make a statement, wanted to come to the Games. They came in. It took all kinds of courage."

If you ask him about the significance of the 1984 Summer Games and the Torch Relay that was its prelude, Ueberroth will tell you crisply that the system of private enterprise works. "You get corporate America, you get leadership, you get the government, you get everybody together and say, 'Let's get going and get something done,'

you can do it." Indeed, it was an effort that spread around the country and beyond. The '84 Games were held in twenty-nine cities and three states of the Union. They were billed as the Capitalist Games. Never before had the Olympics been produced, in any country, by the private sector.

How the 23rd Olympiad was so structured is a tale in itself. The Games are owned, in effect, by the International Olympic Committee, based in Switzerland and the last bastion of *noblesse oblige*. The average age of the delegates is 72. Controlled by a European coalition with the Soviet bloc, the IOC has always awarded the Games—and will in the future—to a city government backed by the financial credit of its country. Montreal had the Games in 1976 and Canada wound up in the soup with a billion-dollar deficit.

"So they awarded the Games to Los Angeles," said Ueberroth, "and the

It was minutes before the relay began at the United Nations Plaza when the heavens opened. Nick Kilsby (LEFT, IN RAINCOAT) of Burson-Marsteller and cohort Al Schreiber (RIGHT) discuss expectations. One of Kilsby's many relay duties was to assist the national and local media in covering an event on wheels and feet.

city government took it. Jimmy Carter signed the paper giving the full faith and credit of the U.S. government. And *then* the people spoke. Of those who voted in Los Angeles, seventy-three percent said, 'No, you don't—you're not going to put on a sporting event with taxpayers' funds, with society's need to use that money in a better way.' So they rejected the Games and they were handed back to the IOC. But at the time, because of the terrorism in Munich, and the deficit in Montreal, nobody would take them. No city around the world. Maybe Teheran. But Teheran was going through a management change.''

That was when a private group was formed in Los Angeles, with the avowed objective of staging the Games. They had no money. No employees. No office. Ueberroth put up the first thousand dollars to open a bank account. All they had, really, were the ghosts of Olympics past. They had the tragedy of Munich, the financial disaster of Montreal, the traffic problems of Lake Placid. (The

1932 Olympics, in Los Angeles, had shown a small profit. It was a different world. The United States team made its final selections five days before the opening ceremony.)

Ueberroth had developed three concepts he felt would provide an underpinning for the Games. Each applied as well to the Torch Relay and, in fact, was tested there. "First thing we said was, we'd take no money from the government—not a little bit. None. Because the government could help you, but if you're asking for money, you have to do business their way. That's the way it should be in a free society. But if you're in the private sector, you can move a little faster and, some people believe, a little smarter. I'm included in that group. So we took no money from the government.''

Nor did they accept donations, figuring correctly that churches, synagogues, hospitals, and cultural groups needed funding, and to compete with them would endear the Olympics to no one. In Montreal, charities had suffered. But the key to

the plan was the third concept: to finance the Games on television rights, ticket sales, and corporate sponsorships. "We never asked the corporations for a penny in donations,'' Ueberroth says. "We told them, 'Work with us to find a way you can participate in these Games, and ring your cash register and promote your business at the same time. Too many people go to corporate America with their hands out. Give them a chance to be a partner, give them some incentive, and the corporations of Amerca can do about anything.''

The relay was to become a model of corporate teamwork. One of the things that unified the different parties was an absence of over-confidence. Burson-Marsteller, the largest public relations firm in the world, was retained to keep the information flowing. One of the company's vice-presidents, Nick Kilsby, put the task into focus: "My initial reaction was fear, rather than excitement. The variables were scary and the logistics unprecedented.''

A LONG-DISTANCE CONNECTION

Bill Higgins (LEFT) *and Charles Mitchell* (RIGHT), *two "behind-the-relay-scene" executives for AT&T, often weighed the rewards to the risks—to the tune of $10 million.*

In the early months of planning, Peter Ueberroth had a recurring bad dream. He could see himself in the Coliseum, checking his watch. The athletes of the world were on the field. In the stands, 80,000 necks were craned. Around the globe, millions waited in front of their television sets.

And Ueberroth could hear himself saying: "I'm sorry, the torch is in Fresno."

It was irony enough that the first threat to the peaceful journey of the torch would come from Greece, not Russia. But this much the planners understood: if the run across the continent succeeded, few would know or care what obstacles were overcome along the way.

You recalled the story of the banana boat that sailed from South America to unload its cargo in Florida. There, the captain of the boat tried to tell the cus-

tomer what they had endured to bring him his bananas. The boat nearly sank. They had to battle pirates and a typhoon and raging seas. They had no food and water for a week. The crew came down with diphtheria . . . And the customer replied, "Just sell me the bananas."

All the public expected was for someone to bring them the Olympic flame, and to have it in Los Angeles on time. In short, this was the challenge Ueberroth and his team faced in early 1982. They had the concept—a Torch Relay across all or most of America. Now they needed what horse traders call a willing buyer.

Dick Sargent recalls sitting in a staff meeting, trying to decide what to do with the Torch Relay. "Most of the people," he said, "wanted to fly it into San Francisco four days before the Games, run it down to Los Angeles,

make it simple, be done with it. Peter offered some other ideas. He said he wanted more people to participate. He wanted it to symbolize the unity of the country in terms of the Olympic movement, and more so, to give people across this country an opportunity to physically see something having to do with the Olympics."

This was indeed a novel and generous approach. Although television would carry the Games to sixty million homes here, few families could afford the cost of a trip to Los Angeles, or the price of tickets when they got there. Even if they could afford tickets, people tend to jump up and down a lot inside the stadium, so you wouldn't see much unless the person in front of you has pierced ears.

The Torch Relay, then, was a good idea, a big vision. All Ueberroth needed was a corporate sponsor to un-

The concept of a cross-country torch relay had merit. But could the flame be kept moving without hassles and delay?

The vastness of the country, the possibilities of things that could go wrong, and the disaster that could lurk from uncontrollable Mother Nature made the challenge grandiose.

derwrite whatever the expense might be. First the company had to be willing to ante up $4 million—the corporate sponsor's fee. Ueberroth had adopted an aggressive marketing strategy, wildly inflating the price while reducing the number of sponsors to 30 (there had been nearly 400 at Lake Placid in the winter of 1980.) In reality, the Games were no more commercial than in the past. They were, however, more elitist—and more expensive.

Next LAOOC needed a company with national resources and manpower. As the LAOOC staffers reviewed their lists they saw what appeared to be a perfect marriage. AT&T (then still the Bell System) had committed to a sponsorship but had not yet pinned down a specific proj-

ect. AT&T may not have been the only company equipped to take on this task, but it didn't take long to call the roll. LAOOC asked, and AT&T, in the role of corporate good citizen, agreed to sponsor and manage an event that would become a watershed in the sporting and civic life of this country.

"At the same time," said Dick Sargent, "AT&T was going through their divestiture. To stay with this project through that upheaval really showed a lot of class. They were really the only people that could do it."

More had taken place than the partial dismantlement of one of the world's most powerful companies. When commentators referred to the passing of Ma Bell, the phrase was not merely a glib topical aside. In a nearly

literal sense the action marked a death in the family for one million employees and the division of twenty-two operating companies. The Bell System had been part of our history, an institution that had the ear of virtually every home in this country. Some mourned the passing of an America that once was and might never be again.

On January 1, 1984, AT&T emerged as a company with one-fourth of its former assets, and just under 380,000 employees. The future seemed unpredictable, if not unpromising. It was a company confronting new competition and new opportunities. What the new AT&T did not seem to need was a project as complex and distracting as the Olympic Torch Relay. Yet the

event took on an unexpected importance: during a critical transition, the run across the continent helped hold the new company together in spirit and became a rallying point for the successors of the old Bell System.

Even in the shadow of its divestiture, AT&T had a priceless asset: an established network of people who were service-oriented. Somebody had to obtain permits to travel through 1,200 cities and towns. Somebody had to drive every mile of the route to check for safety and road clearances. Somebody had to drive, act as marshals and pathfinders, help disabled runners, and operate the ham radios that were the lifeline of the convoy.

Those somebodies were the Telephone Pioneers of America, most of them working on their own time, without pay. Its members, more than

a half million active and retired telephone company employees, live in almost every county in America. The only requirement for membership is eighteen years of service with a telephone company. The first honorary member was Alexander Graham Bell in 1911.

The Pioneers lend their resources wherever a national disaster strikes. They raise more than $5 million annually for service projects, the latest of which is the restoration of the Statue of Liberty. In fact, as well as symbols, they pass the torch.

AT&T and the Pioneers made for an incredible team, but Ueberroth didn't have much to do with either. He had a reputation as a big picture man. The little things—air, food, water, blood— he generally left to others. When he did get involved, Peter could be a bit of a martinet. His decisions were often arbitrary, his rules rigid. And he had

no time for people he did not understand.

As this related to Lou O'Leary, Ueberroth was not the sole licensee. O'Leary, then a senior AT&T public relations executive, was initially AT&T's principal contact with Ueberroth and LAOOC. A hard charger, rotund, an intellectual, a writer of sorts, O'Leary had seemed to some a slightly overage 1960s flower child. A trauma in his personal life—the death of his wife—led him to reshape himself. He became a runner and, at 50, competed in his first marathon. The drive that some admired, others found abrasive. Soon to retire, O'Leary moved out of the picture. In a gentle twist, he reappeared in the tenth week of the Torch Relay as a cadre runner, after he had taken his retirement.

In the belief that negotiations with Ueberroth's staff might be improved, the project was shifted to the office of

The Telephone Pioneers handled a myriad of backstage jobs from driving the Torch Relay vehicles to handling the distribution of runners outfits.

Walt Cannon, vice-president of public relations for AT&T's long-distance division.

Cannon was AT&T's top-ranking executive on the relay, a patient man with the reassuring air of a country lawyer. A graduate of Southern Methodist University, Cannon had started out at street-level journalism, as a reporter for the Associated Press and the Dallas *Times-Herald*. He has a reputation for not losing his poise and for remaining a gentleman under fire. He is also known as a shrewd negotiator. Because of these strengths, the company felt Cannon could deal with Ueberroth.

Cannon delegated the responsibility for bringing in the right people to someone he knew and trusted, Charlie Mitchell, a director of public relations

An organization bred on a Bell System adage internally known as "A Spirit of Service," the Pioneers have more than 600,000 members.

and Cannon's second-in-command. The "Reach Out and Touch Someone" campaign, one of advertising's great success stories, bears Mitchell's imprint. Serious and attentive, he still has, in early middle age, a youthful, scrubbed look. As a veteran ad man with an instinct for what will play, Mitchell saw quickly that the relay would not lend itself to easy listening.

It ought to be noted that right up to the opening of the Games, tensions between the corporate sponsors and LAOOC remained fairly consistent. As their cash investments mounted, and many of their questions went begging, these men who ran companies as big as some countries found Ueberroth an elusive figure who had this strange capacity for inspiring people without actually seeing them. He was a presence felt more than seen, a kind of invisible hand. The hand, however, did not often reach for a phone and return calls. With what whimsy this indignity was received by his partners at AT&T, one can only guess.

The burden of this frustration fell largely to Bill Higgins, who, on the day of his appointment in April 1983,

as project manager for the Torch Relay, found himself responsible for 10,000 volunteers, 200 runners, and an office force of four. It was a little like being out front, leading the bulls through the streets of Pamplona, and trying not to get trampled under their hooves. He also had a budget that would be badly under-clubbed at $7.5 million.

Higgins inherited a small but resourceful staff. They impressed him. Three—Dick Boehner, Lou Putnam, and Kate Washburn—were not only good managers but also superb runners. Another, Cathy Basinski, was an information planner. They would be joined later by Karen Steiner, who turned out to be a kind of supersecretary.

As an orchestrator, Higgins was a fine choice, modest and self-effacing, with a core of iron. He is a problem solver, a good evaluator of people and their abilities. Of Mitchell he says: "He's as straight and ethical as anyone

At every exchange point Telephone Pioneers acted as marshals, there to give instructions on handling the torch and to assure a smooth passing of the flame.

Nearly 10,000 Pioneers nationwide worked on the relay; over three times as many volunteered but were turned down.

I've ever known. Very energetic. One of the few surviving Calvinists in the business world today. He figures if it doesn't hurt, it can't be going right."

In fact, it was Charlie Mitchell who had hired Higgins, years earlier, away from an ad agency whose clients included the AT&T long-distance division. "I was put on the account," says Higgins, "because they were sure I'd get along well with a workaholic advertising director named Charlie Mitchell." Clearly he did.

In the area of public relations Higgins had some of the best training a man could have. At 26, he had been the youngest sergeant on the Philadelphia police force.

That experience proved invaluable,

because AT&T needed someone able to handle trouble, who dared to sit in the middle and take the slings and arrows. That was where Higgins came in: "They needed somebody who didn't mind getting beaten up. There were these various powerful groups. The Pioneers felt it was their caravan. The committee in Los Angeles knew damned well it was theirs. As a department, AT&T public relations felt it belonged to them."

Higgins was not an early or easy convert to the cause. He first heard the full proposal at a lunch meeting with Mitchell and Dick Boehner. "As I listened," he recalls, "it sounded like a ticket to oblivion. Like something you could not possibly do well with a po-

tential to turn out badly for everyone. But Boehner seemed to have the whole thing figured out. He was sketching on napkins, on the tablecloth. He had an answer to every question. I could see our being an Olympic sponsor and putting up big bucks. What I couldn't see was the logic in our being responsible for pulling it off. But Dick was sure we could do it and do it well."

His friends say, only half jokingly, that Boehner saw the Torch Relay as almost a video game. You had to handle it with sophisticated electronics. You had to program it. On Higgins's first day on the job, Boehner dropped on his desk a thick black notebook containing a business plan and a bud-

A vice president for AT&T, Walt Cannon took a "hands-on" turn in the relay. He ran with the flame in Bedminster, New Jersey.

get. It contained figures for the worst case and the most likely case; for relays ranging from six weeks to fourteen. The costs were broken down to the number of jars of Vaseline needed to grease the heels of the runners so they would not get blisters.

The budget moved up the corporate ladder. When the $7.5 million outlay was approved, Mitchell called in Higgins and told him, point-blank, that they would both be fired if the budget was exceeded. Higgins nodded and then said: "Charlie, just indulge me for a moment. We have exceeded the budget. We are now fired. What does the company do next? Does the torch stop in Indiana or what?"

Mitchell grinned and said, "Get out of my office."

You have been told before, no doubt, that "while victory has a thou-

sand fathers, defeat is an orphan." Higgins knew within a month that the budget would be blown, the only question being by how much. By then he had put down a brief rebellion by the Pioneers and had experienced his first clash with the Ueberroth staff.

It was the original understanding of the Pioneers that the Torch Relay was to be their baby. How this conclusion was reached no one is sure, but the Pioneers assumed that they would organize, manage and *run* it—all 9,000 miles. Higgins had to tell them that their assumption was wrong. He did so at the first opportunity, a meeting with Gib Eggen, Pioneer national coordinator, and his regional directors. The room was filled with temper and threats to walk out. A student of body language, Higgins noticed that one of the Pioneer officers kept brandishing her steak knife, jabbing the table or the air.

But Higgins held his ground. On

the decision to recruit the 200 most qualified runners in the company, there was no room for compromise. It went to the heart of his first objective: "Do not get anyone killed."

"This was always on our mind," he said. "If you didn't have competent runners in superb condition, you could kill someone running them through the deserts and mountains. You didn't want a semiretired telephone company employee running across the Arizona desert in the middle of the afternoon in July. And you didn't want them running up and down hills. I didn't want to leave white markers with people's names on them all across this country."

Higgins knew there was pride and a sense of self-reliance involved here. There was one thing he could do. He could purchase a number of the Youth

Bringing together players and resources was a critical first step for AT&T. Meetings with other Olympic sponsors like United Airlines, Levi–Strauss, and others, determined how each could contribute to the cause.

Legacy Kilometers and assign them to the Pioneers. "How much of the relay would you have to run," he asked, "to stay in?" No one had a figure. "If you want a thousand kilometers," he said, "that would cost us $3 million, and I can't do that." What he could provide was 100 kilometers—one for each of their 88 Pioneer chapters and 12 regions.

"That's the best offer I can make," said Higgins. He looked around the table and added, "Now, if there is anyone here who has less than a total commitment to this event, just get up and walk away now, because we don't want you here."

Gib Eggen stood up and said,

"Make no mistake. We're in this to the finish, and we're in it because we want to make it work, not for what we're going to get out of it. Whatever deal we can get, that's fine. But our goal is to make it succeed." The deal was done. Higgins looked around the table. The lady with the steak knife had laid it beside her plate. The kilometers took $300,000 out of AT&T's budget, but Higgins called it "the best $300,000 we spent."

There is no way to exaggerate the contribution made by the Pioneers. In all, they devoted more than 300,000 man-hours to the project. Their basic responsibility was to see that a multitude of strangers got to the right place at the right time safely. If there was a fork in the road and no sign a few miles outside a city, how would the drivers know which fork to take? So a

Pioneer would stand there with a sign that read, TURN THAT WAY.

Gib Eggen reflects the kind of people the Pioneers are. An Iowan, salt-of-the-earth, patient, ethical. An astute manager, he had worked his way up to an assistant vice-presidency of one of the Bell operating companies. He was the highest-ranking person in the company who worked on the relay full-time. He had a knack for taking a complex task and making it look not only easy but also fun. This was, in fact, the spirit of the Pioneers: to work together, have fun, do good.

Differences with LAOOC often took longer to resolve, and friction was sharpest in matters that seemed not so crucial. When the time came to hold a press conference to announce the availability of the Youth Legacy Kilometers, AT&T, which was to pick up

the tab, wanted to hold it at the Pierre Hotel in midtown New York. The word came back from Los Angeles that Ueberroth had selected a Boys' Club in lower Manhattan. There were three immediate problems with this location: 1) the club, at that point, was not represented in the Torch Relay; 2) the basketball gym, on whose floor the news conference would be held, was not air-conditioned; and 3) the plumbing in the rest rooms did not work. These facts would have been known to LAOOC if anyone had checked it out.

Memoranda flew like missiles from coast to coast. A little problem had escalated into a big one, touching on deeper issues. At one point Higgins recommended that AT&T withdraw from the relay, arguing, "We cannot carry out operational responsibilities

for an event of this magnitude without having the authority to make practical decisions. . . . I recommend that we cut our losses, thank the Committee for their confidence to this point, but tell them if we can't have control, we respectfully bow out."

Shortly, a response from Ueberroth was relayed by one of his assistants: "Let them go. I'll get Lee Iaccoca and Chrysler to take it over." In a similar flap the Walt Disney Studios had withdrawn as a sponsor. AT&T did not withdraw. The diplomatic Mitchell smoothed some ruffled feelings, and the word went out that the company would keep its commitment.

The press conference was held as scheduled at the Boys' Club, and almost no one came, for a reason that had nothing to do with the positions on either side. That was the day Lee

MacPhail, the president of the American League, picked to announce a decision in the famous case of the Pine Tar Bat. MacPhail upheld a decision by an umpire that disallowed a home run by George Brett, the Kansas City third baseman, whose use of the sticky substance had exceeded the legal limit. Only the most religious baseball fan could have known that such a rule even existed. But most of the press chose to go hear MacPhail's announcement, proving again that nothing is too trivial to become a national controversy.

The affair at the Boys' Club cost nearly $120,000 for the food that went mostly uneaten, air-conditioning for the gym, a tent on the roof where the food that was to go uneaten could be served, and repairs to the rest rooms. The next day an item appeared in a New York newspaper, quoting an un-

Evan Goldsmith, 7, carries the torch with the assistance of an AT&T runner in New Rochelle, New York. When the cadre runners weren't moving the flame, they ran along side of the YLK runners, often lending a helping hand.

The criteria to qualify for a berth on the AT&T cadre of runners were almost as demanding as those for the U.S. Olympic team itself. Several thousand applied, but less than two hundred made it. Dot Farley (RIGHT) is one who made it.

named LAOOC official as saying that the AT&T brass had wanted to hold a champagne reception at the Pierre, but Ueberroth forced them instead to spend the money on repairing the johns at a Boys' Club in lower Manhattan. The reason for the press conference, the news of the special kilometers, came out garbled, implying that runners from around the country would be selected in contests or whatever.

In retrospect, which is often the best way to view such matters, Higgins could see the absurdity in the whole episode. But below the surface was the issue of how much say, if any, a sponsor should expect to have in the way its money was to be spent. "What we learned," he said, "was that Ueberroth would have things his own way. You could either live with it or get out. We chose to live with it."

The experience, by indirection, led

to a decision that helped to eliminate some of the lost-in-space feeling that went with the deal. In an unusual arrangement, LAOOC proposed that AT&T hire a special coordinator who would work on Ueberroth's staff. Two firms were interviewed. Wally McGuire was the candidate of Joel Fishman, who had worked for him when Fishman was just out of college.

Higgins saw this as a logical step to get more access to the decision-making process. He had found no direct way of making a case to Ueberroth. "I resented the fact that our company was involved in something," he said, "for which it had the responsibility and almost no authority. There were people in our company who had the same resentment. They were not judging the event itself. They were judging the terms under which we had become involved."

Observers would later agree that the

genius of Ueberroth, in his flawless staging of these Games, could be best seen in the contracts he had negotiated up front with the sponsors. He had delegated virtually all of the expense and kept almost absolute control. In the language of New York's Seventh Avenue garment district, he had kept the vest and sold the armholes. Yet it had been a hard pitch to resist. He was peddling American and corporate pride and the veiled threat that companies who took a pass might be left in the dust.

McGuire turned out to be the answer. He was tough and unemotional, and it did not trouble him to say no.

■ 51 ■

He said no to special requests from the Reagan White House and the governor of Massachusetts. He was, in fact, no more willing to be dictated to than Ueberroth, which won him a certain respect and a measure of independence. "McGuire was able to negotiate with Ueberroth," says Higgins, "on a basis that was effective and fair to both sides. If we made a request that had no merit, he stopped it right there. But now we knew if our viewpoint was getting to the top or not. It was McGuire's integrity that made the arrangement work. Everybody, including people in our company, was used to special privilege. People who are mayors of a city or a chairman of the board, they figure they have the right to have it done their way. McGuire was willing to be the guy who said no, the villain. He never made a decision based on who got what. No matter who came to him with any kind

of personal viewpoint, he put that second to the event."

Although AT&T paid his salary, and that fact was generally unknown, McGuire was not a double agent or even necessarily AT&T's advocate at the court of "Czar Peter." But Higgins admired him as "a guy who literally saw this as an opportunity to work around the clock and not eat regular meals. Wally is an unreconstructed liberal from the sixties generation, who believed anything is possible if you suffered enough. He was on the road with the relay when his new baby was born."

In a curious way, there was a lack of skepticism within his company that made Higgins nervous about the fate of the Torch Relay. He was nervous because no one else seemed to be. He expected more doubts. After all, this was a company that had employed a million people, had been until recently

the biggest in the world. Its embarrassment could have been in proportion to that standing.

AT&T had invested heavily, more heavily than had been intended, and would have to measure its return on a vague thing called product exposure. Says Higgins: "AT&T saw the Torch Relay as an important, onetime business activity that had potential risks for the company. Period. In my view, the risks were considerable. It could have been an 82-day comedy of errors. You know, 'Where have the buffoons taken the torch this morning?' That was the horror story that kept flashing through my mind. And it would have gotten great press: 'THEY GOT LOST AGAIN, FOLKS.'

"In a way we were all betting on Ueberroth. I think he saw the Torch Relay as the one event that gave the Olympics a grass-roots appeal. In a sense, the Olympics are the most elitist kind of activity. You have to be one hell of an athlete to get there, and

Wally McGuire (BELOW), *a seasoned advance man with several presidential campaigns under his belt, led his "A-Team" in the task of continually reworking the route with the Pioneers. He also hired Ruth Berry* (ABOVE RIGHT) *and Jim Suennen* (BOTTOM RIGHT), *as trip directors; both had worked with McGuire on the Jimmy Carter and John Glenn campaigns. Alternating their days as director, the two made sure that the core caravan kept to its schedule.*

probably most of the fans are the hard-core, track-and-field freaks. People who know all the intervals and fractions. Ueberroth saw this as having potential beyond that relatively narrow audience. He saw the relay as a way of widening that appeal and as a great preliminary to the Games."

In the end, two factors influenced the time and length of the Torch Relay: when they could receive the flame from Greece and how many Youth Legacy Kilometers would be run through which cities. The numbers would change, and AT&T's project office would be out of the loop for days or weeks, working with schedules that were meaningless.

Though he chafed at some of the problems created by their dependence on LAOOC, Higgins gained a certain respect for Ueberroth. A little grudg-

ing, perhaps, but no less real. He recalls flying out to Los Angeles to attend an ABC Television meeting at the Beverly Hilton. Ueberroth spoke. "He was talking about the Olympics," recalls Higgins. "Characterizing it to all the sponsors. He asked them, 'What's the most popular sporting event in the world? Answer: The New York marathon. The reason: You run through the toughest city in the world, all areas of it, and nobody ever throws a rock! Now, how can we give the Olympics that kind of acceptance?' That was the challenge. When you think about that, his frame of reference, you see where the Torch Relay fit in."

For AT&T, however, there was a new discovery, or a crisis, every day. "AT&T provided all of the manpower," said Dick Sargent, "and all of the planning for the Torch Relay.

When we overlaid that with the benefit kilometers, it added a logistical nightmare. But they accepted it."

After a simulation run in March, AT&T spent $35,000 on custom hardware so the cooks would not fall as they tried to get in and out of the diners. One cook had fallen off a ramp and knocked himself out. The security budget was doubled, to half a million dollars. Professional drivers, ex–state troopers, were put behind the wheels of the four or five cars that formed the protective pod around the runner. After the simulation runs, the planning team's attitude toward security changed. Before March the idea had been: How much can we afford? Now it was: whatever it takes to get the job done.

An ex-Secret Service agent, Bill Mattman was responsible for crowd

Responsible for the security and safety of the relay, Bill Mattman called upon the assistance of hundreds of local law-enforcement agencies along the route.

A scene out of The Dukes of Hazzard. *Mississippi State troopers Steven A. Thompson and M. C. Graddy stand guard with AT&T runner Christy Sepsas minutes before her first run with the flame.*

control and security on the relay. His staff included a former captain with the California Highway Patrol, so hefty that he broke the springs in a Buick just by sitting in it; and a Japanese-American who was a qualified samurai warrior. He owned the proper swords, although he did not bring them, and he knew all the grunts. As far as is known, no one asked him to show his credentials.

They were well chosen to run interference for the torchbearers. There was always a problem to be knocked down. At one point the Texas Highway Patrol refused to provide any protection for the runners, although city police would escort them through Dallas. Higgins reached for his stock answer. He instructed Mattman to tell Texas that when they crossed the Oklahoma border, the runners would pile into their buses and the Highway Patrol could explain why the Olympic Torch went through the state at fifty-five miles an hour. The word quickly came back: "You're clear for Texas, y'all."

There was a story behind the Lone Star reluctance. In late 1983, a large toy company had sponsored a skate-a-thon across the country. Two skaters were killed in Texas, one when the motor home trailing a few yards behind ran over him after being clipped by an eighteen wheeler. The second, a passenger in the motor home, was thrown through the window. The skate-a-thon was canceled on the spot.

The Federal Highway Safety Department had serious reservations about issuing permits to the Torch Relay. An agent for the bureau called Higgins and grilled him for an hour on what safety measures AT&T planned to take. At the end of the conversation the agent, clearly impressed, had only

one other suggestion—a crash attenuator. Although the name implies something high-tech, a crash attenuator is a dump truck with an arrow on the back, equipped with flashing lights and a loudspeaker. The driver can tell drunks and leadfoots, "Hey, turkey, slow down," or he can radio ahead and tell the caravan to get off the road.

Each day Bill Higgins talked with the people around him, and his bosses, and he worried a little about the budget and a good deal more about security. But gradually the checklist began looking better to him. How could he not have confidence in the team that had taken shape?

He knew there was no resource quite like Gib Eggen and the Pioneers. Many of them were accustomed to

Kate Washburn and Cathy Basinski ride the security vehicle running boards usually used by ex-secret service men hired by Mattman. Although there were several threats to the relay, none surfaced to bring about danger.

working in emergency conditions, restoring phone service and setting up field procedures in areas devastated by storms and floods and tornadoes. They made it work because they were good managers, and you couldn't replace them with 10,000 Kelly Boys or Girls.

Meanwhile, Wally McGuire was cutting through a lot of red tape. He didn't care whose idea it was if it was good. It may have helped that the project had gone far enough and encountered enough rough spots, that now Ueberroth was getting nervous. Higgins welcomed the company. If McGuire did not exactly have the key to Ueberroth's office, he received the time he needed. There were senior vice-presidents who met with the Olympic impresario each day for three minutes, said their pieces, and got out.

"In most cases," says Bill Higgins candidly, "in most big companies you tend to be conservative. In a big company it hurts you to be associated with failure. One way to protect yourself is not to take any strong positions. Implicit in this is the assumption that nothing you are doing is worth so much that you should risk much to make it succeed. In the beginning I thought about this project in the same terms as any other corporate activity. Along the way I began to come around. I saw Dick Boehner and Lou Putnam and Kate Washburn putting their hearts and souls into this, and I decided it was not fair to them just to play it safe.

"One of my main roles was to authorize bills to be paid. In theory, anytime anything had to be done that cost money, I had to make a decision whether to spend or not. Then the March simulation run came along and I fell in love with the event itself. At the end of that week I resolved not to deny them what they needed, or hold back, because it involved sticking my neck out. I told myself, I didn't care if I got fired. This one was worth the risk."

One torch, one goal, two hearts and hands: Bill Thorpe and Gina Hemphill represented the spirit of Olympics past. Behind them, AT&T chairman Charles Brown.

The date was May 8, 1984, and the omens were not exactly friendly. A steady drizzle pelted the spectators and turned the streets slick and oily. A layer of fog added a touch of gloom and the wind whipped at women's skirts.

A few hundred curious New Yorkers paused on their way to work, trying to get a peek at the dignitaries and runners huddled under a canopy, waiting to light the Olympic Torch and send it on a broken-field journey across America.

The weather inspired two predictable New York reactions: street vendors appeared from nowhere, hawking umbrellas out of a box; half the cabbies in town flipped on their off-duty lights. From somewhere in the crowd pressed against the fence, a distinctly British voice muttered: "Wouldn't you know it? This great American event and this bloody British weather."

The ceremony proceeded smoothly. The mayors of New York and Los Angeles (Ed Koch and Tom Bradley) both spoke, a hands-across-the-country sort of thing. So did Peter Ueberroth and Charles Brown, chairman of the board of AT&T. All remarks were brief, with the clear approval of the moistened crowd and the relief of the waiting runners. Rafer Johnson, the former Olympian, dressed in a dark three-piece suit, touched a spark to a cauldron and flames licked at the air.

Now Gina Hemphill and Bill Thorpe, Jr., touched a torch to the fire, raised it, and awkwardly began to walk-trot toward the street. They gripped the torch together, and as the crowd caught a glimpse and cheered, they held it higher, heading up First Avenue on the long and twisting road to Los Angeles.

In the joining of these two there was an echo of old glories and hardships not forgotten. America has produced no heroes quite like Jesse Owens, the black man who embarrassed Hitler, and Jim Thorpe, the Indian whose athletic records still exist after seventy years. But their achievements bore bitter fruit, and in their prime they were both cheered and neglected. Now a

■ 57 ■

Peter Ueberroth, organizer of the Games, lends a steadying hand as Gina Hemphill dips flame to cauldron. He donated the kilometer Gina ran.

debt was at last acknowledged. A new generation, the black granddaughter and the Indian grandson, were inheritors of the flame.

The invitation for Bill, Jr., to take part in the Torch Relay came in an elevator after the ceremony clearing Jim Thorpe's slate. A passenger in the elevator happened to be Peter Ueberroth, the ramrod of the 1984 Olympic Games. "He saw my name tag," recalls Bill, "saw that I was one of the Thorpes, and asked me questions about Granddad. This was in the Biltmore Hotel in downtown Los Angeles. Later, his office called when I was out. My folks took the call. I was invited to come to New York for the press announcement of the Torch Relay. I was proud to be there to represent Granddad. I didn't know until I got there that I would be running it."

It is an interesting twist of fate for a young man who would not have carried the torch if a seventy-year-old injustice had not been corrected in late 1982. That was when his grandfather's gold medals, won in 1912 at Stockholm in the decathlon and pentathlon, were restored to Jim Thorpe's family.

Bill wound up losing his job because of the time he had to take off to prepare for the relay and the trips to New York and Los Angeles. He was in charge of the field department for a pest control company, and he didn't seem to take the loss as a major life setback. "At first they said it was okay," he explains, "then they flat refused to give me the time. I'm not sure if I was fired or quit. It was a little of both."

After the relay Bill worked part-time as a carpenter and began a crash course in bobsledding. His coach thought he was a natural. Odd as that

may sound for a young man who lives in Grand Prairie, Texas, near Dallas, and has rarely seen or been attracted to snow, the grandson of Jim Thorpe was introduced to bobsledding while returning on a bus after he had run his special kilometer in New York.

"I met the manager of the 1980 bobsled team, Bob Nelson," he remembers. "He sat down next to me on the bus. He had run the fifth kilometer that day, after Gina and I ran, and he knew from the publicity and interviews who I was. We got to chatting. He asked me if I ever considered bobsledding. I told him I enjoyed it on TV but never tried it and had no idea how to get involved.

"I thought he was just making conversation. He told me about the different things he had done in the sport. The U.S. team had finished sixth in

A drizzle of rain didn't dampen their parade. Thorpe and Hemphill hadn't been in the public eye until they led off the Torch Relay.

A drizzle of rain didn't dampen their parade. Thorpe and Hemphill hadn't been in the public eye until they led off the Torch Relay.

1980 at Lake Placid. I'm a pretty good-sized fellow, and strong, and Bob told me that was what you needed, that and quickness, a good start. You need to be a sprinter and strong, not a real easy combination, because the sled weighs so much and you need a certain strength just to push off. A two-man sled weighs approximately four hundred and thirty pounds or so, and a four-man sled can go up to seven hundred. Everyone pushes initially. It's a team effort to start, everyone runs as far as they can, then—ideally —the driver gets in, then the number-two and -three men, and then the brakeman. The last man has to run about fifty meters. That's the distance of the start. The farther you run, the faster you get the sled going.''

The upshot of all this is that Bill Thorpe, Jr., checked it out, trained

with Bob Nelson at Lake Placid toward the end of 1984, and fell in love with the sport of bobsledding. He is now a candidate for the U.S. Olympic team in that activity for the 1988 Games. It isn't pro football, and it isn't the big track in a major stadium, but it offers a link to the past, to his grandfather's Olympic heroics, and he is elated at the prospect.

He never knew his grandfather. Jim Thorpe died of a heart attack in his house trailer in Lomita, California, a suburb of Los Angeles, in March of 1953—two months before his sixty-fifth birthday. He was not a pauper, as many believed. He lived in a trailer because he liked the mobility. But he was not a moneyed person, and there is no question that he never found a way of exploiting his name or his fame.

Bill Thorpe, Sr., was one of four

sons born to Jim and his second wife, Freeda Kirkpatrick. Bill, Sr., has vivid memories of the man who was called the greatest athlete in the world. ''We lived in California when I was a boy,'' he says. ''Dad would take us hunting and fishing. He loved the outdoors. He loved to coon hunt, to get the dogs out at night and listen to them run. He was not much of a storyteller. Once in a while he talked about his family, how he grew up, the things he did as a kid. I think baseball was his favorite sport. He encouraged us to play it. He used to back me up against the garage door and pitch to me. I was a catcher in semipro ball.''

The reference was not without irony. It was because Jim Thorpe played semipro baseball in the summers of 1909 and 1910 that his Olympic medals were later stripped from him. He received either $2 a game or

With a backdrop of blue highways—a map showing the route of the run across America —Hemphill and Thorpe are introduced to the press by Ueberroth.

$25 a week, according to most accounts. It was a common practice in those days for college athletes to pick up money playing pro baseball or football. Unlike the other players, however, Thorpe used his real name. Either he was ignorant of the rules or he had no intention of returning to the Carlisle Indian school in the fall of 1910, to continue his amateur career.

His semipro baseball stint was only a faint memory when Thorpe went to Stockholm in 1912. The big pregame American hope, in the two multiple events, was Avery Brundage, later the president of the International Olympic Committee for twenty years. Brundage finished sixth in the pentathlon and fifteenth in the decathlon, as Thorpe won both tests, a once-only performance.

Many track fans hoped, over the years, that it was not pettiness or prejudice that led Brundage to resist the reinstatement of Thorpe's medals all through the years. The story had surfaced in 1913 that the Sac and Fox Indian had played baseball for pay. The AAU voted to demand the return of his medals and to immediately strike his records from the books. And it was done. The move was an injustice by any moral or legal standard. The rules required that a protest had to be filed within thirty days of competition. The story didn't appear until six months after the Games. But the action stood. The medals were returned, the records expunged. The controversy continued for seventy years, and then one day in 1982 it was resolved in two hours.

Jim Thorpe never issued a public complaint about his mistreatment, if indeed he perceived it as such. But his son and grandson, the Bill Thorpes, are insistent that his life would have been considerably brighter and richer without the shadow cast by the denial of his medals.

There is pain in Bill, Jr.'s voice when he recalls the story. Nothing in his own time has been made easier by the blood he shares and honors, and you sense that there is still a cultural clash in America, in 1985, for those of Indian heritage. All the Thorpes have been natural athletes, or so they feel, and for the most part the gift has gone unused.

Bill, Jr., a sturdy prospect at 6'1" and 215 pounds, showed promise at football and track. But he injured both legs in motorcycle accidents in high school

Out of the friendships he made on the torch run, Bill Thorpe (BELOW AND RIGHT) developed an interest in a sport his grandfather never tried—bobsledding.

and gave up football after his sophomore year. He was a low hurdler in track, until the day he and another runner collided. He hit a hurdle, went sprawling, and spiked the other boy. One of the coaches screamed at him, "Now I understand why the Indians always lost." Billy never went back.

So if he feels an empathy for the grandfather he never knew, it is not hard to trace the line. "Until his medals were returned," says Billy, "I was never really tuned into sports the way I might have been. I still had bitter feelings about the way my granddad was treated.

"I always liked to hear my father talk about him. I've always looked up to him, and he has been a proud part of my life. One thing Dad told me,

Granddad was such an exceptional athlete, you could name your game, and he could watch it one time and beat you at it. Track, boxing, bowling, anything.

"When I was asked to carry the torch, the first thing I thought about was getting back some of the recognition Granddad didn't receive. That day I felt a kind of bliss when I ran. It was cold and drizzly, forty degrees or so, but the people on the street were cheering the torch on, hollering, *'Go, U.S.A.!'* The torch brought people together in spite of their differences, and for that one moment we were all one."

When Bill, Jr., refers to his grandfather, he does so with a kind of for-

mal respect that brings to mind a remark by the poetess Marianne Moore. A very long time ago she taught a course in commercial law at the Carlisle Indian School, in Pennsylvania, and one of the students was Jim Thorpe. She watched him play football and do it all in track and field, but what she remembered was, "He was a gentleman. I called him James. It would have seemed condescending, I thought, to call him Jim."

Jim Thorpe had loped out of the plains of Oklahoma, streaked across the campus of Carlisle, and went on to become one of the first good Indians in American lore. The legend of Thorpe had all the qualities of a fairy tale. He led tiny Carlisle to victories over the giants of that era in football:

■ 61 ■

Jim Thorpe, who was once, literally, a one-man track team at the Carlisle Indian school, became the only man in history to win the pentathlon and decathlon—in the 1912 Olympics.

Yale, Harvard, and Army. *The New York Times* once reported that "trying to stop his progress was like trying to clutch a shadow."

When he was in his late forties, he gave an exhibition at Soldier Field in Chicago. He stood at midfield and drop-kicked the ball through the goalposts. Then he turned, faced the other direction, and drop-kicked the ball through that one.

Once, Thorpe and his coach showed up for a dual track meet, and the opposing coach inquired: "Where's your team?" The Carlisle coach pointed to Jim Thorpe. "He's our team," he said. And so he was.

It is the least bit poignant to hear Bill Thorpe, Jr., describe as his greatest sports thrill a third-place finish in the discus in junior high. Now he has carried the torch, for himself and for his grandfather. "Anytime you do something like that," he says, "it changes you. Maybe it has given me a newer way to look at myself and to look at the world in general. I could never accomplish what Granddad did because his kind come along once every hundred years. But now I want to make the Olympics. Now I have a

goal. Not only for the story it might make, but as something I want to do for myself."

For Hemphill, a graduate of Arizona State with a degree in broadcasting and marketing, her life, too, would not be the same after the day she carried the torch. "If I ever had a normal routine," she says, "I'm out of it now." In the first six months after the Olympics she attended twelve to fifteen banquets, made new friends, established some interesting contacts, and changed jobs twice. At one dinner she met her current boss, the presi-

dent of WLS-TV, the ABC-owned station in Chicago, where she now works as a production assistant. At another she was seated with Suzette Charles, then finishing a rather complicated term as Miss America.

Gina was working with the family services office of the Olympics when Peter Ueberroth's secretary called with an invitation. Mr. Ueberroth would like her to be his guest at a luncheon in New York to announce the arrangements for the Torch Relay. A few weeks later the secretary called back and said that Mr. Ueberroth would like to sponsor Gina as a runner to

carry the torch—in fact, the first kilometer. It did not sink in until later what the request involved. "I was very cool about it," she says, "very calm. I didn't know then that it was a once-in-a-lifetime thing."

Well, actually, a twice-in-a-lifetime thing. Two days before the opening of the Games the speculation had reached a peak over the identity of the runner who would bring the torch into the Coliseum and light the flame. In fact, there would be two runners.

"The ceremonies were on Saturday," she said. "On Wednesday,

David Wolper, the Hollywood producer, said he needed someone to run with the torch so they could time it to music, and would I stay around after rehearsals. I had on a skirt and nylons, no sweats or tennis shoes, but David said it didn't matter. So I practiced running into the stadium with the torch and fantasized about it. But I never imagined I would be the one. I was initially one of the flag bearers.

"At Thursday's rehearsal they told me they were going to skip my place in line for the flag but not to worry about it. I thought, 'Uh-oh, what's this?' Then David called me aside and

Gina Hemphill enters the Coliseum in Los Angeles carrying the torch. Her grandmother, the widow of Jesse Owens, was in the stands.

said I was going to bring the torch into the tunnel and give it to the final runner. I didn't know yet that the runner would be Rafer Johnson. That's how secretive it was.

"That evening I saw Peter Ueberroth in the office, and I gave him the biggest hug. He said, 'You know, you have to keep it a secret.' I said, 'I will, I will.'

"I have never been so nervous in my life as I was waiting in the tunnel. Some of my friends on the American team passed by and asked me what I was doing there. I said, 'You'll see.' Then I was out of the tunnel and into the light, and when I heard the first cheers and felt the first flashes of the cameras, it was such a high. Friends

were yelling at me. One said, 'You're on cloud nine . . . don't come down.'

"Then I thought about my grandfather. I know this sounds conceited, but I knew he was watching me. My grandmother was in the stands. I hadn't told her about it. Her reaction was so touching. It sent chills through me. She saw me start around the track and she said, 'Golly, that looks like Gina.' Then she jumped to her feet and shouted, 'My God, that's my grandchild.'

"So then the people around her knew who she was, and they got excited: 'Oh, my gosh, this is Jesse Owens's widow.' "

Her grandfather died of cancer at 66, in 1980. They had been close. "I

knew him as a person," she says, "rather than an athlete or celebrity. I knew him as somebody who liked Western movies and popcorn and all kinds of jokes. We went to track meets and Phoenix Suns games. They lived in Phoenix when I was in college. I used to love to hear him speak. He was the grand marshal of our homecoming one year. He was just wonderful. I sat there overwhelmed. He didn't talk much about his experiences. He just used them when he

Poised in front of a microphone, Hemphill tells a crowd in downtown Chicago that the Torch Relay "has been the most exciting time of my life."

Bears running back Walter Payton, who broke Jim Brown's record for career rushing yardage, said he was afraid he might drop the torch.

wanted to make a point. He talked about things like having a good outlook on life."

There was a nice symmetry to Gina's involvement in the Torch Relay. She shared the first run and the last run and, in the middle, stood on a platform in Chicago with Walter Payton of the Bears. "He kept fidgeting and pumping his legs," she said. "He'd had arthroscopic surgery on both knees and he needed to get warm. He asked me what it was like to hold the torch, and I said, 'You can break all the NFL records there are, score as many touchdowns as you

want, and this will still be special for you. It only happens once.'

"I told him he gets to keep the torch and he said, 'Do you really?' Then he told me he was nervous about running with it. I said, 'With all you've done, and the records you hold, how could you be nervous?'

"And Walter said, 'Because it means so much.' I hear he keeps the torch in his living room."

The largest crowd in the history of downtown Chicago, according to police estimates, 125,000, turned out to watch the torch, Payton, the runner

they call "Sweetness," and Jesse Owens's granddaughter. Gina is still not sure why she, among the five grandkids of the hero of the 1936 Olympics, was tapped by Ueberroth.

"I asked him once," she says. "I told him that I would probably get that question from people. Peter said, 'Tell them you were the one I wanted.' And that's the only explanation I have. But I have the greatest thanks and admiration for that man."

As a senior at East Technical High in Cleveland, Jesse Owens (LEFT) *was already breaking world records in the sprints and broad jump. Whenever or wherever Jesse Owens ran, records usually fell. As the star of the Ohio State track team* (BELOW) *he competed in four events—the 100- and 220-yard dashes, the broad jump, and the low hurdles.*

She never heard a bitter word from her granddad about his life after Berlin. It wasn't the style of Jesse Owens to complain or sulk. He returned home with his degree from Ohio State to consider an offer to teach at an all-Negro college for $2,700, or to earn whatever promoters were willing to pay to have him run against horses and whatever other sideshow attractions they could generate. In his lifetime Owens never dwelled for long on the paucity of his options.

One story he might have told his granddaughter has become a part of Olympic legend. It concerns the polite rivalry between Owens and the blond-haired hero of the Germans, Luz Long. When Owens was going for his fourth gold medal in the broad jump, his chief rival was Long, a German national hero.

Owens fouled on his first two qualifying jumps (by stepping across the takeoff line). He had one try left, or else he would be eliminated from his biggest event and Luz Long would be the sure winner. But Long drew Owens aside. He suggested that Owens draw another line in the dirt, several inches short of the official line, and use that for a takeoff point. Long placed his warm-up jacket next to the line as a marker for Owens.

Owens qualified easily and went on to win the finals, beating the German

No athlete is so identified with one Olympics as Owens is with the 1936 Games in Berlin (LEFT). He won four golds and made Adolph Hitler uncomfortable. The years after the Olympics were a struggle, but Jesse Owens became a successful Chicago public relations man (BELOW) and was in demand as a speaker.

on his last leap. This wasn't Super Race against the African Auxiliary. These were two athletes in the fellowship of pain.

Owens and Long became friends. They toured Europe for some post-Olympic meets. Owens was cheered everywhere, the greatest sports hero of his day. They corresponded after Owens returned home, but a few months later Luz Long was in uniform, fighting on the Italian front.

In 1951, Jesse Owens returned to Berlin for the first time since his Olympic triumph. The occasion was a German track meet. For a little touch of sentimental pageantry, Owens put on his old Olympic track suit and jogged slowly around the Berlin Stadium while 75,000 roared in recognition.

As he left the field a teenager asked for his autograph. Owens signed the book and handed it back. Then he stopped the boy. "That book," he said. "May I see it again?" He looked at an old picture pasted on the inside page. "That's a picture of Luz Long," said Owens.

"My father, sir," said the boy. He told Jesse that his father had been killed in the war. Owens put his arm around the boy's shoulder and they walked off the field together, an ex-Olympian and the son of a man who might have been his enemy but who wound up as his friend.

TORCH YES, RUSSIANS *NYET*

With the Capitol as a symbolic backdrop and agents clinging to open doors of security car, caravan leaves Washington, DC, and renews passage across America.

At Fifty-seventh Street in New York City, Gina Hemphill and Bill Thorpe, Jr., handed the torch to 91-year-old Abel Kiviat, a silver medalist in the 1,500-meter race in the 1912 Olympics, and a roommate of Jim Thorpe's. They shared a cabin on the boat going over to Stockholm. Kiviat didn't remember Thorpe having much to say. A great-grandfather, and America's oldest living Olympic medalist, Kiviat is a spry elf at 5'1". He took up middle-distance running in 1909.

"Don't compare us with the athletes of today," he warned. "They live in Colorado Springs and have their medical and food taken care of. We had nothing. Training was much simpler then." He jogged the first block of his run and walked the rest of the dis-

tance. Then he lit the torch of 12-year-old Timothy Towers, who had won the honor in a raffle, and urged, "Carry on."

There was no way to anticipate at this otherwise scenic moment the bitter irony and melodrama then at large. On the day the Olympic Torch came to New York and the United Nations Plaza and was re-ignited and began its safari across the continent, the Soviet Union announced that its team was staying home, as ours had in 1980.

As the twenty-second runner, Nicole Zell, age 13, started her kilometer outside City Hall shortly after noon, the teletype machines began to chatter with the grim news from Moscow.

In the lobby of the Intercontinental Hotel two of the AT&T executives re-

sponsible for the Torch Relay ran into each other. "Did you hear the news?" Walt Cannon said to Charlie Mitchell. "The Russians have pulled out."

"I know," said Mitchell. "I need a drink."

New York City's Mayor Ed Koch would say later, "I think the Russians have it wrong. They should go to Los Angeles and withdraw from Afghanistan."

The first reaction at the higher Olympic levels was one of depression, if not panic. Ueberroth issued a statement hoping that the Soviet decision was not final. President Reagan issued a statement saying that it wasn't nice to mix politics with sports, and if it was security that troubled them, no problem, we would make them feel

Unaware that Russians aren't coming, three Olympic presidents give torch a U.N. sendoff: Samaranch and Ueberroth stand at podium; former Treasury secretary William Simon (SEATED) headed U.S. Committee.

secure. But we couldn't make them feel loved.

And everyone over the age of four thought back to 1980, when President Carter had canceled the U.S. team's trip to Moscow to protest the invasion of Afghanistan. The chess match continued.

Although this was not a time to look for deep and underlying reasons, to think about the brotherhood of man and the meaning of the universe, we were reminded again that the Russians, like the very rich, are different.

At Innsbruck a few years ago, the Russians forced the officials of the Winter Olympics to cancel the credentials of a network called Radio Free Europe. The Soviets argued that if *they*

had sponsored something called Radio Free America, bringing news of Eastern Europe to the United States, we would not want such an agency accredited, either.

Of course, that just shows how poorly the Russians understand the American nature. Such a network actually might do well in America, especially if it played top-40 tunes.

But in the arena of sport there is an energy at work that has little to do with our different approaches to freedom of expression. It must have dawned on the leaders of the Soviet Union that weekend exactly how many people, how many groups of people, hated them.

Just running down the list of groups

that planned to make life miserable for the Soviet team in Los Angeles was to get a lesson in political geography. It was a thumbnail directory to the survivors and victims of forty-five years of Soviet repression—and a few crackpots who just enjoy a brawl. Included were Lithuanians, Poles, Czechs, Hungarians, Estonians, Cubans, Afghans. An umbrella organization called the Ban the Soviets Coalition claimed to represent a total of 160 separate anti-Russian and German groups urging Communist athletes to defect. Safe houses were to be set up to hide defectors from Soviet authorities. An airplane was going to tow a sky-sign

They forged a human chain from coast to coast, and here, blind Joseph Pardow carries torch on Church Street in New York, linked by metal chain to cadre runner Susan Mink.

The rain above and the fire below: While spectators huddle under umbrellas, former decathlon champion Rafer Johnson leans across cauldron to ignite Olympic flame.

over the 135 miles of game sites, listing a twenty-four-hour telephone number that defectors could call.

These activities, it ought to be noted, are all legal in our system, and the U.S. government rejected Soviet demands that they be suppressed. On the other hand, the Soviets suspected, maybe correctly, that the Reagan administration was not exactly eager to discourage the protesters.

Once again certain values were called into question, and the Olympics —as a spectacle, as an institution— were assailed as too big, too political, too costly, too commercial. The next day's headlines would hammer at the theme of defeat and disappointment:

"THE RUSSIANS AREN'T COMING, THE RUSSIANS AREN'T COMING."

"NYETS TO YOU, TOO."

"A DEATH BLOW FOR THE OLYMPICS."

"GAMES WILL GO ON BUT AT WHAT PRICE?"

"TIME HAS COME TO DOUSE OLYMPIC FLAME."

But ten miles outside of the city limits of New York, the convoy behind the torchbearers would spot a sign that put the matter in a different context: "SCREW RUSSIA. GO U.S.A."

While the Russian withdrawal dominated the news and the shock waves spread, the torch was moving—off camera, so to speak—like a contestant on one of those television scavenger shows, sent off on some vast or whimsical quest while the studio audience waits for the next act. No one then had much reason to expect the Torch Relay to be much more than a one-day story. It had left New York, would disappear for eighty-two days, and then show up in time to light the fire for the opening ceremonies in Los Angeles. But something would keep attracting the people—hundreds, and then thousands, until the total was in the millions.

The first day, May 8, was a test of no small proportion, however. The rain. The Russians. The uncertainty. But the AT&T relay managers didn't

Photographer perches on back of car to snap Mike Walsh, arm extended, as relay passes an American landmark, St. Patrick's Cathedral. Walsh, a media director for an advertising agency, won his kilometer in a drawing held by Sports Illustrated.

This street scene was repeated endlessly in cities large and small; a young boy, encouraged by his mother and envied by spectators, looks up in awe as he grips the torch offered by a sponsored runner.

let that dampen their spirits. Lou Putnam had provided the honor guard for Hemphill and Thorpe and then Kiviat. He was the beaming figure on their left in the first-day photos. Dick Boehner slept little the night before, felt like squirrels were dancing in his belly, and ran ten miles before the opening ceremony. Kate Washburn was on the communications bus, checking and rechecking the schedules for the first day's shift, excited, talking a lot.

On board the buses and around the relay itself, there was little talk of the Russians or the political distractions that marked this first day. Just the sheer effort and excitement of getting the torch to move was enough to oc-

cupy the caravan for the trip to the Connecticut border. No one wanted to deal with the bigger and unspoken question: the fear that all of this might be in vain. Would there be an Olympic Games by the time they carried the torch into the Coliseum on July 28 for the opening ceremonies?

Cancel the Olympics? Unthinkable. It would be like canceling Christmas.

It would take most of the day to run through Manhattan. The spectators were sparse in Central Park, and there was some annoyance among motorists who found the intersection blocked by police cars. Inside and outside the park, a few people applauded as the relay passed. Many stared blankly. A

Trump Tower doorman in a long red coat watched, hands on hips, obviously bored.

From Church Street, across from the World Trade Center, Joseph Pardow, who is blind, carried the torch to Avenue of the Americas. He was able to keep a straight course because he held one end of a short metal chain. Susan Mink, an AT&T cadre runner, held the other end and ran alongside him.

From the first tentative steps when Hemphill and Thorpe had delivered the flame to Abel Kiviat, the design, the soul of the relay had been clear. This was no elitist event, no demonstration of the new American man or woman. It was a celebration of the di-

CONVENTRY, CT

Tom Sawyer would have done no differently than young Jason Garick, who decides to skip school to catch a glimpse of the Olympic Torch Relay: "There's something about the Olympic flame—it's a feeling you just can't explain."

Press photographers jokingly referred to their flatbed truck as "The Cattle Car." Exposed to the weather, with New York traffic behind and around them, moving at an average speed of eight miles an hour, they captured the event on film.

versity of this country and its people, all shapes and sizes, all ages and shades, the known and unknown.

Some had names that seemed too good to be true, or a story to match. Marilyn Polite, a former president of the Girls' Club of New York, walked her kilometer in Central Park. Five days earlier she had stepped off a curb and twisted her knee. It hurt just to walk, but she wouldn't give up her turn at the torch.

The caravan passed the Bronx Zoo at 4 p.m. and crossed the Connecticut line by nightfall at Greenwich. Rain had fallen off and on during the day,

and the air was damp and misty, but the residents of Greenwich waited on the Post Road three and four deep to catch a glimpse of the torch.

There the owner of a local motel, the Showboat Inn, Joe Keating, donated a bus and filled it with 800 balloons bearing the torch insignia. They were distributed to children along the route.

As the torchbearer ran up the hill to Pickwick Plaza, a Dixieland band, heavy on the drums and banjo, swung out with such suitable favorites as "I'm Beginning to See the Light," "My

Old Flame," and "Smoke Gets in Your Eyes."

In Greenwich, native son Jeffrey Urstat arrived with the flame as blue-and-white helium-filled balloons whipped in the wind, some breaking free from the parking meters to which they had been tied. They didn't soar any higher or faster than the heart of Jeff Urstat. In Hartford, a YLK runner, Warner Depuy, charred a few pieces of wood for children standing along the roadside, a permanent memento of the Olympic flame. A 33-year-old lawyer, Depuy read to them the Latin

Fighting ships left from this Connecticut port in the Revolutionary War, and generations of whalers and clippers have called Mystic Seaport their home. The runners kept going, past the Maritime Museum and the quaint shops and a shipyard little changed in two hundred years.

Her muscles tensed, a grimace on her face, an AT&T runner shows the strain of carrying the torch as the caravan leaves Mystic Seaport.

words inscribed on the rim of the torch: "*Citius, altius, fortius* (swifter, higher, stronger)." Added Depuy: "That's really what it's all about."

Bill Kelleher, the track coach at the University of Connecticut, stood beside his pickup truck with a U.S. flag hoisted above the fender as the procession continued. "You see this flame," he said, "and you know that the Olympics is greater than any one country."

A police officer, Marvin Kasowitz, of West Haven, heard about the torch's passing as he was ending his shift at 11 P.M. "I called my wife right away and told her to wake up the kids," he said. "I didn't think twice about it." His wife and three daughters, all clad in their pajamas, waited

inside the family van for the torch to appear.

In the first twenty-four hours a pattern was set. Strangers had come together, touched, waved, made eye contact, and gone their own way, filled with a peace or pride they could not fully explain.

New Haven was the first overnight camp. It was nearly 2 A.M. when the runner swung onto the campus of the University of New Haven, and the security cars and medical bus found their parking places. It is fair to say that no one slept very soundly that first night, which is just as well, because most of them had to be up by 4:30 A.M., to get to the staging area. They were tired and edgy and excited, working on nervous energy, giddy at

just being under way, drawn together by the pressures of the previous day. The relay was an investment in the future and maybe the past. No matter what happened in their lives, this they would always have: the summer they carried the torch to Los Angeles. They could see the pictures in the scrapbook and hear themselves telling stories about it forty years later. They were not always strangers, of course. Barry Feinberg, 44, of Orange, NJ, ran one of the first kilometers of the second day along Howard Avenue. In front of the Yale–New Haven Hospital, he passed the flame on to his father, 73-year-old Murray Feinberg.

One of those in the crowd when the torch came through New Haven was

In the shadow of the statue of Paul Revere, Boston's Mayor Raymond Flynn prepares for his leg of the Torch Relay. The location is Boston's historic North End. For the messengers still to run, the symbolism was hard to miss.

Greg Haslinger, who would join the relay as a cadre runner a few weeks later. A veteran of seven marathons, a runner for ten years, Greg's running career had almost ended a month after he applied for the relay. "My wife and I were in a severe automobile accident," he said, "on our wedding anniversary. I had a collapsed lung and had to have four hundred stitches in my head." His shoulder was still sore from the crash, but he had not told anyone with the relay for fear they would not allow him to run.

Eastward across Connecticut the runners pounded, crossing a bridge over the Connecticut River from Old Saybrook and into Old Lyme. The wind was so blustery that there was some concern about the AT&T torchbearer, 33-year-old Paul Squires, a wispy figure at 135 pounds. A motorcycle policeman who was escorting the torch was reluctant to drive over the bridge in the high winds. He took one look at Squires and said, "You must be expendable if they make you run over this bridge. You'll probably blow off." Runner and torch made it safely.

Paul Squires was not atypical of the cadre runners who performed the first week. Having started at 14, he ran track in high school and college and was accustomed to the competitive pressure. But this was different. It wasn't a race, yet the cheers of the crowd caused his adrenaline to rush in the same way.

In some ways the first week was clearly the hardest. Squires noticed that the press kept returning to the same two subjects: the Russian pullout and the commercialism of the Olympics. This kind of emphasis made the

In Bristol, Connecticut, the school bus stopped to let the children wait for the relay to pass. Others lined the street, waving the torches they had made out of crepe paper as a class project.

runners wary about what kind of reception they could expect as they moved across the map.

The runners were aware of the dispute with Greek officials over the merchandising of the special kilometers. But the fine political points were mostly lost to them. What it meant to the cadre runners was that they would now cover much more territory, roughly 70 percent of the entire route. They considered this a promotion.

In spite of the weather and the early, skeptical press coverage, the crowds were larger and more spirited than expected. On the second day Squires was running his leg in Providence when he passed a traditional white church. On the front lawn a choir was singing "God Bless America."

In Rhode Island, one of the state's twenty-seven YLK runners was 19-year-old Jimmy Walsh, who had battled back from leukemia in 1981 to win a spot on his high school football team. He was now a freshman at Boston College.

Waiting up the road for the torch was Janet Stone, who in 1952 won a gold medal in Helsinki, Finland, as a member of the U.S. women's 400-meter relay team. Residents of Barrington, where Janet teaches physical education at the middle school, had flooded the office of Congresswoman Claudine Schneider with letters, urging that the former Olympian be assigned one of the kilometers sponsored by twenty-two Rhode Island companies.

Schneider herself carried the torch to the Statehouse, arriving at 11:15 P.M., to the sounds of a fife and drum corps, through streets lined with onlookers holding lighted candles.

The flame reached Boston late on the morning of May 10. Governor Michael Dukakis greeted it on the steps of the Capitol, and Mayor Raymond Flynn ran with it through the city's historic downtown streets before hoisting the Olympic flag at City Hall. Cake was served to the assembled spectators, at least to those who could get to the serving tables. It was a little like a very large wedding reception.

John Thomas, 43, who won bronze and silver medals in the high jump

One headline described the run as "miles of smiles." The faces of this towheaded YLK runner and his escort make the point as the caravan approaches West Point.

The rain-slicked road winds through the campus of the U.S. Military Academy at West Point, past stately brick homes where the likes of Lee and Grant, MacArthur and Eisenhower lived in their faculty years.

during the 1960 and 1964 Olympics and once held the world's record, ran a kilometer in memory of his high school trainer, William (Doc) Linskey, who had died two weeks earlier. "This means a lot to me," said Thomas, now an account executive with AT&T. "Every athlete in the Cambridge school system knew Doc."

Tens of thousands had turned out to see the torch in Boston. There was no doubt now in the minds of anyone on the caravan that something special, something rare, was taking place. Thomas, who had lost to the Russians and whose Olympic dreams had fallen short, savored the moment. "Today belongs to the Torch Relay in Boston," he said. "That's the only thing that matters. Let's everybody be positive today. The political thing will go on and on."

On the Statehouse steps, Governor

Dukakis alluded to the Soviet pullout. "My people had a tradition," he said, referring to his Greek ancestry. "I hope one of these days we can restore the Olympic idea—that international conflict and politics can be stopped [during the Games]."

The trip to, and on through, Boston was to be a scenic and colorful one. A miner's lamp was lighted from the torch and placed inside the Statehouse, there to be kept until the Olympic soccer games began on the Harvard campus, at Cambridge, the last Saturday in July. A mini-Torch Relay, run entirely by former Olympic medal winners, would open the soccer competition.

At another spot, a local high-school

track team curled out of the practice field and jogged alongside the runner. When the caravan stopped at the University of Connecticut, they learned that the New Christy Minstrels were staging a concert on campus. The runners asked to meet them. To their surprise, the Christy Minstrels wanted *their* autographs.

From Boston the torch began to move westward and southward. The tempo picked up. The crowds became more involved and more creative as the relay crisscrossed from town to town, twice reentering Connecticut and then New York State.

Cool weather followed them 'into Peekskill and to an overnight encampment at West Point, on Armed Forces

In Far Hills, New Jersey, the flame dances against the dark of night while onlookers applaud and a tentative youngster gets a sendoff from an AT&T cadre runner.

Balloons provide a splash of color, and Philadelphia makes its message clear in big, bold letters. Tight schedules had to be met for ceremonies in major cities, and runners referred to such occasions as "hot spots."

Day. The chaplain for the military academy led a prayer for the runners and their cargo, as cadets in their dress grays stood by and a sense of timelessness settled over the banks of the Hudson River. Through Storm King and the Crow's Nest mountains, the caravan had a view of the countryside that extended for miles.

The relay headed south to New Jersey, into Mahwah and down Route 202 into Oakland. There one of the first scheduling conflicts occurred: The town of Oakland had planned, for the same day, to hold its annual Fireman's parade, one hundred strong, along the same route and at the same time the torch was to travel there.

The Pioneers' state coordinator placed a call to the mayor and did some fast and serious talking. He pointed out there probably would not

be another Olympic Torch Relay in America for many, many years. They needed to keep the highway clear. The mayor agreed to delay the Fireman's parade until the torch had passed. And so it was done. The torchbearer ran through the open flanks of the firemen while the sirens of the engines wailed and the volunteer firefighters sped him on with their cheers.

They were welcomed to Bedminster with fireworks and a fifty-foot banner strung across Route 202, wishing the runners "Godspeed." Somerville was celebrating its seventy-fifth anniversary as the caravan arrived.

The relay continued south to Princeton, into the halls of ivy. Besides being the seat of one of the world's great universities, the town is rated among the most desirable places to live in Central New Jersey. The cost of real

estate in recent years has skyrocketed, in part because of the physical charm and beauty of this colonial town, but also in part because of the reputation of the public school system. So prestigious is the Princeton mailing address that there is a long waiting list to get a box at the town post office. Princetonians know they have a good thing going for them, so it should have come as no surprise to the organizers of the Torch Relay that they ran into a brush with city government.

The mayor and town council insisted that a special insurance policy was required, protecting the town and its property holders from any damage caused directly or indirectly by the procession. There was no time to arrange an alternate route, and the only one available offered a narrow, unlighted road with deep ravines on

All along the route there were runners who ran with their hands: this torch, held in a wheelchair, was lit in Baltimore. It was hard to watch such scenes, said the cadre runners, and remain a cynic.

each side. As the torch rolled through the center of town, 10,000 people lined the streets with American flags in one hand—and many with a drink in the other. The next day, after the Relay had moved well on down the road, the coordinator for the Pioneers received a final letter demanding to see an insurance policy.

The relay continued to a campsite Saturday night at Rider College, in Lawrenceville. Noted Al Novell, one of the cadre runners: "I saw more patriotism in four days than I have seen in my entire life." Novell recalled running in the town of Branford, when he spotted on the side of the road "a very old man in a wheelchair. I stopped for a minute and handed him the torch.

You should have seen his eyes light up."

The week was over before Squires knew it. He said his good-byes to the Pioneers, the drivers, and radio operators, all the support people he had gotten to know so well in so short a time. He said he hoped they would all get together again sometime for a reunion. Even as he said it Paul felt self-conscious. Only a week. But it was a week that would last a lifetime.

The torch left Rider College in a special holder attached to the wheelchair of Mike Lione, a native of West Orange. Out of Lawrenceville, one of the drivers was Pioneer Eleanor Dicker-

son, who spent her first night aboard the motor home numbered "Torch 19." With the changing of the shifts it went unnoticed that no one had replenished the vehicle's water supply. That morning Eleanor brushed her teeth with the only liquid available—grapefruit juice. The key to coping with eighty-two days on the road, clearly, was an ability to adjust.

The crowds grew larger. Stories were collected like seashells. "There are twenty tearjerkers a day," said Gib Eggen, the national coordinator for the Telephone Pioneers. He did not say it cynically. People had overcome handicaps and rearranged their lives

There was a traffic jam three miles long in the nation's capital. The torch caused it, but a pretty face didn't help speed up the pace.

Two imports from Canada, who established their sports fame in the U.S., share the joy of carrying the fire. Gordie Howe's career in ice hockey lasted past his fiftieth birthday. When Craig McFarlane left home, he lived with the Howes in Hartford, Connecticut. Described as the world's best blind athlete, Craig has competed in wrestling, golf, skiing, and surfing.

to take part in this movable feast, and no one who went along for the ride ever seemed to grow immune to it.

As the relay headed south through Trenton toward Philadelphia, there was a dramatic change in the roadside scenery. The manicured lawns and stone walls of New Jersey's prep schools gave way to the vintage World War II aircraft perched atop Amelia's Bar, and the twenty-foot grinning giant standing guard over the discount store across the street. The relay slipped into Philly while most of the city was serving Mom breakfast in bed, or standing in line outside restaurants featuring Mother's Day buffets.

George Pilz, a blind telephone repairman from Norristown, Pennsylvania, mimicked a dramatic scene

from the movie *Rocky* as he held the torch high and bounded up the steps of the Philadelphia Art Museum. Pilz is a well-conditioned athlete who runs an eight-minute mile. He described the experience as "the high point of my running career." The only thing missing was the music crashing to a crescendo as he reached the top step, arms flung upward in a gesture of triumph. It was Mother's Day and his mother was waiting at the top with open arms.

Pilz passed the flame to an 11-year-old named Trevor Farrell, who had gained national attention a few months earlier by waging a one-boy campaign to feed and clothe the homeless in downtown Philadelphia.

Now the relay moved on to Annap-

olis, where Ellery Clark, Jr., 74, a retired Navy captain and track coach at the Naval Academy for thirty-eight years, took the torch at the seawall with two gold medals around his neck. They had been won by his father, Ellery Clark, Sr., at the modern revival of the Olympic Games in Athens, in 1896.

He had dedicated his kilometer to "the memory of my father and the other nine track and field members of the first [modern] Olympic team."

Another YLK runner, Robin Woolford, brought the torch to the harbor and tears to the eyes of those in the crowd who knew him. Nine years earlier, the 28-year-old Woolford was shot in the neck and paralyzed during a robbery at an Annapolis dry

At the end of a White House ceremony President Reagan watches gymnast Kurt Thomas light the torch of a Special Olympian. Thomas was one of the American athletes who remained home in 1980 because of the boycott of the Moscow Games.

cleaners. "The doctors told my parents I wouldn't last till morning," he said. "I've been surprising them ever since." He still walks with difficulty. Asked what he was thinking during his one-kilometer trek, he said, "I was thinking, 'Don't fall. Don't fall.' I tripped in my office the other day and skinned my elbow. I said to myself, 'I hope this is my fall for the week.' "

Nearing the end of the first eastern leg of the relay, the flame, after winding its way through New England, pointed south, and paused at the most famous address in America—the White House.

There was always a schedule to keep, a clock to race. On this day the White House had asked that the runner be on the grounds at 5 P.M., in order to get footage of President Reagan receiving the torch in time for the evening news. The relay had been slated to arrive after 7 P.M., when most of the traffic had cleared from government workers heading home.

When word of the schedule change reached Lou Putnam, one of the co-managers, the runners were not quite twenty miles out of town and had less than three hours in which to meet the deadline. Putnam called in the next relay and gave them the message: The President of the United States was waiting and they had to turn it on. This portion of the trip became a race, not a run or a jog. No one held back.

They made up the ground and the time, and were a bare three minutes late when they reached the gates of the White House, where gymnast Kurt Thomas stood waiting for the torch with Dick Boehner. Thomas presented the torch to the President, whose words were carried to a thousand White House workers and several times that many standing in the streets. There was an embarrassing pause while several attempts failed to ignite the next torch. Boehner finally stepped in and the flame caught. The runner, Charlotte Pearson, a special Olympian, moved off to the approval of the crowd.

Boehner bolted toward the driveway when, to his surprise, Mr. Reagan called out to ask for his autograph. "I'm sorry, sir," said Dick, leaving the startled President standing there, "but I don't have time." The torchbearer was already around the curve, pulling away and almost out of sight.

"I think," said Boehner, "he was making one of his jokes about the autograph. At least, I hope so."

LONG, WINDING ROAD

Traffic slows to a crawl as the caravan reaches the outskirts of Seattle. Motorcycle police flank the runner.

The caravan pinballed its way across the country, seeming to ricochet from state to state. An observer tracing the path on a map might have wondered about the sobriety of those who had charted this pilgrimage. At best, it could be described as circuitous.

Three times the route was redrawn, and even the last and shortest one led them through areas that contained 55 percent of the population. "You started with what you knew was certain," said Wally McGuire. "The two dates, May 8 in New York and July 28, when we had to be in the Coliseum. Just like when you drop in a maze, you start with those things you know for sure and work your way out. We

figured what we could do each day— long days. We usually ran about 18 hours a day."

In every region there is a favored saying that describes the loyalty of a certain kind of person. In Texas they say, "He'll do to ride the river with."

There may be more delicate ways to pay a compliment. But whatever the form, the Pioneers earned the praise that kept coming their way. McGuire, whose job on the road was that of a wagon master, could not imagine the relay being done without them.

The preparations for this endurance test had begun, in earnest, two years earlier. Throughout 1982 and 1983, the work proceeded on four tiers. There

were the AT&T relay managers, working with the original blueprint drawn by Boehner and Putnam.

Meanwhile, the Pioneers were combing the country, checking out underpasses and lifting manhole covers, obtaining fire and parade permits. Bill Mattman and his agents did their security sweeps, logging in with city cops and sheriffs and state troopers. Much of the hard digging had been started when McGuire came aboard, and his advance team fanned out to pin down the endless details.

The AT&T operating plan weighed six pounds, more than the torch itself. But the work could not be measured in pounds or even tonnage. The plan

Onward and forward, the relay moved closer towards Los Angeles like clockwork. More than a year of actual footwork produced a meticulous schedule.

ran the gamut, setting "milestones" and deadlines for any number of things: selecting the Olympic sponsors to participate in the relay; leasing or buying the motor homes; drawing up legal contracts; enlisting the team of cadre runners; or determining toiletry needs. In fact, the number of activities and subactivities (not to mention the "what-if" assumptions for each) became countless. The compelling part was the way in which the units and the people worked, moving on separate tracks but pulling into the same station.

The really interesting case was Mattman, because his work is in that twilight zone of public safety and

sabotage that has preoccupied us so much in recent years. To begin with, the numbers fed into the computer told them that there was a 3 percent chance of a terrorist attack. The figure may seem low. But in Munich, in 1972, there were no projections at all. The threat of violence was always there.

In his thirteen years with the Secret Service, Mattman planned security for state visits by Lyndon Johnson and Richard Nixon and for Henry Kissinger's many trips to Paris in the 1970s, to negotiate a truce to the war in Vietnam.

"From a planning point of view," said Mattman, "this was much more

complex than a presidential visit. Everything stayed so fluid. They were selling kilometers practically up to the last minute, and details changed constantly. Eighteen-hour days were the norm, and toward the end I'm sure no one had more than two hours of sleep at night."

When AT&T hired his firm, Mattman Security, he proposed that the torch be treated "like a highly visible VIP. At the time no one could foresee the enormous crowds that would come to see it."

At first, AT&T officials had esti-

Serious and watchful, security men (ABOVE) *ride on running boards of trail car. Early in the relay you could identify them by the bandages on their aching thighs from jumping off the vehicles.* (BELOW) *It wasn't Lindbergh or MacArthur or an astronaut back from the moon, but a stranger carrying a torch. What drew them, what did the crowds see when they saw the runner and the flame?*

mated that perhaps a million people would turn out to watch the torch pass through their towns. Mattman and his staff were the authority for the final crowd count of 30 million, a number he insists is "conservative." That number was the basis for the description, often quoted by Mattman, of the Torch Relay as "the largest single sports spectator event in the history of mankind."

Disbelief at the size of the crowds that would turn out was a frequent stumbling block in the planning. "Our biggest problem," he said, "was convincing local police departments before the torch got there that this would be the biggest thing that ever happened to their cities." In California they would encounter crowds so large that the torch literally could not move through them. The police tried to push the crowds back, but there were so many people that there was nowhere for them to go.

Mattman traveled 20,000 miles crisscrossing the country. For a while it must have seemed that everyone connected with the Torch Relay was qualifying for frequent-flyer trips to the Orient. They were all on the road again.

The selection of the towns and cities for the final route remained almost to the end a subject of high puzzlement. In many cases the choice of a town depended on the number of Youth

From the planning office in New Jersey, known as Torch Central, Cathy Basinski and Karen Steiner were in daily, even hourly, contact with runners, support people, sponsors, press, and LAOOC. Karen's record was putting ten calls on hold at the same time.

Engineer Gil Farnham (RIGHT) and his assistant, Abed Zantout, check a handle fitting at Turner Industries' plant at Sycamore, Illinois. The company produced more than 6,000 torches.

Legacy Kilometers sold there. The path of the torch often depended on where it could not go: on poor roads, over shaky bridges, or through low tunnels.

As one Pioneer later put it: "Sometimes the kilometers in the open country had rather strange 'addresses'— twenty paces past the entrance to the junkyard, thirty-five feet before the bridge or across the road from the graffiti-covered rock . . ."

Less mysterious was the process by which the runners qualified for the AT&T cadre. In September of 1983, Lou Putnam directed a massive distri-

bution of application forms throughout what had been the Bell System. They went by direct mail, desk to desk, and in newsletters.

Criteria were established: an applicant had to be able to run ten miles a day; men had to have run a 10-kilometer race in just over 37 minutes, women in 43 minutes. Although the times were based on recognized U.S. running standards, complaints were heard that few in the company could qualify. But some 2,000 applied and 1,500 of them met the criteria. Two hundred were selected, a quarter of them women. "The runners," said

Putnam, "had to be able to make up time lost to traffic tie-ups, crowds, detours, and a variety of natural phenomena."

The AT&T cadre runners were tested twice in simulation runs, the first from Dallas to Little Rock in January. Twelve runners covered the 300-mile distance in two days, supported by ten vehicles. In March they stretched the run to eight states and 800 miles in seven days. This time they used sixteen runners and tried out twenty of the vehicles. The motor homes were so new that the microwave ovens were still taped shut. Both

The torch was treated, as one writer put it, "like a visiting Greek god." People clamored to hold one and to be photographed with it. Indeed, the torch belonged to them in all its splendor. (Below the Olympic motto, etched around the bowl, are the peristyle and arches of the L.A. Memorial Coliseum.)

The mood of patriotism and festivity was neatly captured by this "Aunt Sam" and her bright balloons.

times the bottom line was what Putnam said it was: "The torch moved."

Even before the trial runs, a huge map of the United States was tacked to the wall of "Torch Central," AT&T's relay management center in Bedminster, NJ, so the Relay could be tracked as it passed from state to state. The colored thumbtacks stayed in the box they came in. The people who worked there never had time to put up the tacks.

Among other things, they were inundated with requests from vendors who wanted to put the AT&T logo on their products. "Balloons, garbage bags, you name it," recalled Cathy Basinski. "Cups, mugs, wallets. Anything and everything."

It was a full-time job just to coordi-

nate their needs and schedules with the other sponsors involved in the run: United, Buick, GMC, Converse shoes, ARA Services, Levi-Strauss, and Turner Industries, the company that manufactured the torches. All did their share, and often more, but the product that attracted the most interest was clearly the one with the flame.

The torches were twenty-two inches long, made of spun aluminum with an antique bronze finish and leather grip. Turner produced more than 6,000 of them, well short of the popular demand. One runner said a spectator shouted out an offer of $10,000 to buy

his torch. He didn't stop to ask if the man was serious.

One of the runners, it turned out, actually helped make the torches—at the plant in California. Paul Joseph O'Neil, a machinist, worked on the valves that controlled the flame. His name was drawn out of a hat.

"We added a flame enhancer to the torch," said O'Neil. "What it is, is a piece of perforated metal that has been cut and rolled to the right diameter to fit into the cup of the torch. It is then packed with ceramic fibers and soaked in Coleman fuel. So if we didn't add something that has a higher carbon

For some runners time stood still. But all had a schedule to meet, day and night. Two simulation runs helped fine-tune the relay and keep it on target.

No matter how many ways the route was checked or the schedule timed or the plans traced in colored markers, the test came on roads, not on paper.

content, you wouldn't see the flame as they ran by. The people would be very disappointed. In the cadre torches we actually added almost two pounds of weight, by adding a large Coleman burner under the propane burner. That's why their flame is so visible."

The torch was molded in Sycamore, Ill. and shipped to California for the final assembly, plating and the etching of the bowl, on which appears the Olympic motto.

Keeping the torch on schedule and the runners secure was what all the planning and traveling had been about. Observed McGuire: "We started off in a situation where we had

a tremendous amount of muscle in the Telephone Pioneers and the AT&T staff. Then there were two very critical points: first off, the assumptions we had all been working on, in terms of the timing of the caravan and the method of setting it up. Could we get the runners out ahead, both the cadre runners and the YLKs? We found out that it worked. We could keep to a schedule. We could hit it within three or four minutes of when we wanted to be somewhere. That was critical because you had to let people know you were coming.

"The biggest thing we had to do was just to time all these runners, who run different speeds in different weather conditions. Then we had handicapped runners assigned to different grades of

road. To make all that fit into a schedule that would keep us on time was mind-boggling."

The route was mapped and charted and measured in inches. The AT&T planners and McGuire's advance team had to know that a line on a map was really a road that the runners and the armada of buses behind them could navigate. They had to avoid railroad tracks and drawbridges and tunnels too low for the motor homes to clear. They did this in a thousand towns, whose very names echoed from deep in the American soul and character.

Who could resist places called Mystic Seaport, CT or Amity, Economy, and Freedom, in Pennsylvania; on to White Pigeon, MI, and Flat Lick, KY;

These were the high-tech Olympics. Computers and sophisticated telephone and transmission systems showed how far we have come since 490 B.C., when Pheidippides reported the news of an Athenian victory over a larger Persian army. He ran the equivalent of a marathon, collapsed, and died. The news was much easier to deliver in 1984.

to Festus and Knob Noster, in Missouri; and then a name collector's utopia in Texas: No, there wasn't a town named Utopia, but they did discover Aubrey, Agnes, Olney, Vera, Idalou, Muleshoe, and Progress. Across the great divide, the towns suggested grandeur and open spaces: Empire and Dinosaur, CO; Bountiful, UT; Othello and Olympia, WA, and Cascade Summit, OR. In California, Pismo Beach made the final cut, but none of the famed train stops from Jack Benny's old radio show: Anaheim, Azusa, and Cucamonga.

During the relay the advance team traveled a day's ride ahead of the main caravan—150 miles, tops. It was their job to clear any last-minute wrinkles and arrange a detour if needed. Whatever space was selected for the two daily stops, at lunch and overnight, one major test had to be met: the parking area had to accommodate the two sixty-foot-long tractor-trailer rigs, redesigned as a galley and mess hall. They were the length of two six-story buildings and they needed room in which to turn around.

The command vehicle, known as Torch One, was the mobile communications and computer room. In there, occasionally, Doug Jeffcoat, an AT&T computer operations manager, could be found bent over his computer, a white towel under his red-and-white AT&T cap and draped across the top of the terminal, to block out the light. Every Saturday, the day of the weekly briefings, Jeffcoat would be surrounded by Kate Washburn, Cathy Basinski, Karen Steiner, and Jeffcoat's assistant, Sue Manassa, giving or waiting on information. It didn't take long for someone to put together the white towel and the circle of ladies hovering around Jeffcoat and hang on him a nickname: "The Sheik."

More than 200 pages of printout would be needed to keep track of the

Lou Putnam (LEFT) and Dick Boehner, in their running shoes, confer with Pioneer Roy Potter on a route through Durango, Colorado, a town spawned by the Rocky Mountain gold rush. (The town was later bypassed.)

At 13,000 feet above the Colorado timberline the "switchbacks" of Engineer Mountain offer one of the more panoramic—and rigorous—stretches of road.

daily schedules. The slightest change in plans had a domino effect. From New York to California they had pinpointed hospitals, gas stations, campgrounds, even convenience stores where the motor homes could refill their huge water tanks.

The information came largely from on-site work, much of it done by the Pioneers. Typical of the advance work was a trip Dick Boehner and Lou Putnam made to Colorado, eight months

before the Relay left New York. They were joined by Roy Potter, a Pioneer based in Denver, the manager for that segment of the route. Out of Durango, past black-faced Angus cattle grazing on scrubgrass, they drove slowly out on Highway 550 into the Rockies. When they reached a place called the La Plata Fairground, Putnam suggested that it might be a good parking area for a meal stop.

Potter shook his head. "They'll be

having a rodeo there when the flame passes through," he said. "But I know a campground a little farther on." Here the word *logistics* took on a fresh reality.

It was the dead of winter when the trio of Boehner, Putnam, and Potter checked out the Rockies. The peaks were carpeted in snow above the timberline. The highway hugged the mountainside, and the road began twisting back on itself, with S-turns

The sight of a public pay phone on the long, open road often reminded individuals on the relay support crew to phone home. For some, news of a newborn son or daughter was heard in a lonely roadside phone booth.

talked to the Colorado Highway patrol?'' he asked Potter.

''We're going to ask them to escort us through the state,'' Potter responded.

''I'd like to see a patrol car in front of us and behind us all the way,'' said Putnam.

Now and then one would bend and squat and study something in the road. Another would whip out a camera and snap pictures. The road across the Rockies twists down from Red Mountain into a tunnel carved out of the rock. ''Can we make it with the tractor-trailers?'' asked Boehner.

Potter nodded. ''It's thirteen feet,

and figure eights to lessen the steepness of the grade. In Colorado they are called switchbacks. ''It's the same as when a sailor tacks into the wind,'' said Potter.

Just twenty-two miles out of Durango they were at nearly 11,000 feet. Boehner, who was born in the state, and whose parents live near Denver, was no stranger to the difficulty of running on such terrain. ''Have you

nine inches, and thirteen-feet-six will do it.'' Potter has hunted, fished, and camped in the area. Thirty years ago he had begun his career there, laying phone lines to Rocky Mountain villages. After three hours Dick and Lou were on their way to the airport to catch a flight home.

The irony was that the Relay didn't follow the route they had covered. That part of Colorado was scratched

David Thurston was so caught up in the spirit of the relay, he had his wife, Linda, also a runner, fly out to meet him. There were moments, many of them—this one in Boise, Idaho—when the runner had the look of eagles.

In the words of Copernicus, "I caught the fire from those who went before" . . . this time in Mountain Home, Idaho.

when the final distance was cut to 9,000 miles.

The Pioneers were like the tinkers of old, riding through with their carts, tools, and pans banging against the side. No job too big or too small. Whenever anything knotty turned up, they were there to solve it. Take the matter of the uniforms.

Levi-Strauss was the official outfitters of the Games and the Torch Relay. (As an interesting aside, they were awarded the 1984 sponsorship even though other manufacturers had outbid them. In 1980, when the U.S. boycotted the Games in Moscow, Levi-Strauss went ahead with the order, finished the uniforms for which they would get no publicity and delivered them to the athletes who no longer would wear them. Ueberroth took note.)

Cathy Basinski remembers trying to figure out a system for getting the clothing to all the people involved: a shirt and a pair of shorts and socks to each YLK runner, 4,000 of them. Then 10,000 Pioneers had to be issued slacks, T-shirts, windbreakers, and caps. Cathy received word that a chapter in Albuquerque, New Mexico, had volunteered to pack and ship the gear. "I thought, 'My God, that's in the middle of nowhere.' But they did it. They collected boxes from local supermarkets and they sat on a floor of a high school gym, working weekends, packing the boxes and mailing them to the individuals. And they didn't get paid for it."

Ultimately there was a flame to be

passed—from one end of the nation to the other. Over and over a scene would be repeated: an AT&T cadre runner holding the torch for the first time. It was a prideful moment and the feeling was palpable: excitement mixed with shock.

The runners had been instructed to work with weights, up to four pounds, and many did, for months at a time. Some ran with rocks or bricks or barbells, one with an ax, stirring who knows what terror in the hearts of his neighbors. The training was essential, but a barbell is compact and it isn't on fire. And those differences were crucial.

On the caravan it became a point of pride among those entrusted with the torches that the flame be kept alive "at the source," the same flame that had been brought from Greece was nurtured in six "mother" lanterns carefully guarded by the Pioneers. Rain, high winds, rough road, and occasional clumsy handling snuffed out various torches, but a determination that bordered on piety kept at least one flame alive . . . the eternal fire.

"It was very important," said Steve Cross, AT&T's spokesman on the relay, "that the people know that what they were seeing was the original Greek flame."

This was really what the cross-continent run could be reduced to: Cross, with AT&T public relations, and thousands of others, clocking eighteen-hour days and using a state-of-the-art communications system, all to move and protect a few tiny tongues of flame.

★ ★ ★ ★ ★ ★
GREAT LAKES: ROCKWELL COUNTRY

Lights on against the gathering dusk and framed by the camera beneath the girders spanning the bridge over the Allegheny River, the long convoy of cars and buses trails a lone runner into Pittsburgh.

The torch passed through West Virginia and in Morgantown posed for a picture with a 90-year-old matriarch in a wheelchair. She was part of five generations waiting for the flame. All through the region a kind of "Family Week" atmosphere prevailed—the world of Norman Rockwell brought to life.

A day later they headed north to Pittsburgh, where one of the cadre runners, Donna Jean Harper, casually mentioned that she wished her parents could see her run. They were at home in Norfolk, Virginia. Two of Donna's running mates quietly placed a call to her mother and father and arranged for them to catch flights to Pittsburgh.

When her parents arrived, the con-spirators had only to figure out a way to transport them to the intersection where their daughter would be running. They were to meet at a Pittsburgh hotel, and Donna's friends decided that the quickest way to get there would be to run. They had to negotiate their way through a tunnel and planned to use the catwalk. At the entrance to the tunnel, however, they encountered a problem. A blue-suited problem with a badge. They were advised that no one was allowed inside on foot. Whereupon they explained where they were headed and why. Based on the white runner's togs they were wearing, there was no reason to disbelieve them. The officer promptly flagged down a van—a Pittsburgh citizen just driving through the tunnel—

and directed the driver to take Alex and Jay through the tunnel.

As matters developed, the man had just come from watching the Torch Relay and was on his way to see it again. He not only carried them through the tunnel but stopped at the hotel to collect Donna's parents and drove the group to the crucial intersection.

The Harpers watched Donna run, then were driven to Three Rivers Stadium for ceremonies and lunch with their agreeably surprised daughter.

In many ways Pittsburgh is the essential American city, a symbol of where the country has been, moving through urban renewal into the future. Pittsburgh was built around coal mines, steel mills, and the joining of

■ 95 ■

The rains in Pittsburgh didn't dampen any spirits, as this torchbearer in a wheelchair proudly holds high the flame. Of the four thousand YLK runners, a fourth were handicapped.

three rivers. A city of brick and cobblestones, people who stop to talk on the sidewalk, Iron City beer, and the polka. John Wayne and Marlene Dietrich starred in *Pittsburgh* the only movie most people remember about the city.

They waited in the rain, under their umbrellas, to watch Franco Harris, the former Steelers halfback, carry the flame for one downtown kilometer. Just as were others across the country, many in the crowd in Pittsburgh were surprised by the armada that rolled in behind him, the six vehicles and a flatbed media truck that stopped traffic in Market Square. The rest of the convoy was moving around the city. One onlooker remarked, "I don't think that's the way they did it in Greece."

The caravan hugged the Ohio River north to New Castle, PA, where the teenagers along the roadside wore tuxedos and party dresses. It was prom night in New Castle. But Jim Singer had to wait. His date was otherwise occupied. They all cheered as she came into view. Barbara Baynham, sixteen years old, ran her kilo-meter with a big smile on her face, then went home and changed. She arrived at the prom a little late. "My date was real understanding," she said. "He thinks this is really great."

The relay moved due west into Youngstown, Ohio, through the iron and steel pits of Akron, before crossing into Cleveland. There was a story behind the coming of the torch to this city hard by the shores of Lake Erie, the story of one man's refusal to take no for an answer.

Ed Crawford was on a business trip to California when he first read of the

The runners, young and old, grown male and young female, black and white, often met as strangers and parted sharing a bond as firm as the grip on the torch they held. They were a cross section of America.

Many of those who carried the torch looked as fit as athletes or attractive enough to be models posing as athletes. The kilometers often began with a handshake or a high five or, as did this one in Detroit, with a hug.

Olympic Torch Relay and the plans to allow anyone willing to donate $3,000 to carry the torch. The owner of his own small business in Cleveland, he wanted his son to have the honor, and he made a few calls to arrange it.

He was told that the Olympic Committee was thinking of dropping Cleveland from the route because of the slow sale of the YKLs. If his son wanted to run, it might have to be in another city. Dejected and a little irritated, Crawford decided to act. Returning home, he rounded up some of the city's business leaders and formed a committee to sell the kilometers.

Inspired by Crawford, the committee set its own rules—above and be-

yond those set by LAOOC—as to how a sponsor could use the kilometer. Among other steps, they decided that the ten kilometers through the center of the city would be run by Special Olympians only. The sponsor of any of those YLKs would have no opportunity to choose a runner, only the obligation to contribute the three grand to charity.

The committee not only sold the ten sponsorships in the center of Cleveland but *all* the kilometers within the city limits, a total of 71. Along with Los Angeles and New York, Cleveland was one of the first three cities to sell out its available kilometers.

Crawford brought the Olympic Torch to Cleveland. But he didn't stop

there. He had a twenty-foot replica of the torch designed, built, and displayed in public. Seven days before the relay was to travel through Cleveland, a special ceremony was held to light this tower of a torch to celebrate the coming of the relay. The replica stayed lit for one week, after which Crawford donated it to the city in honor of the ten Special Olympians who carried the flame in the city. Later the torch was moved to the Soldiers-Sailors Monument in the public square.

Although big cities often meant big crowds, and the excitement and confusion that were their companions, the AT&T cadre runners consistently expressed their greater pleasure in the

The pace was brisk as this runner on wheels carried the flame into Cleveland, hugging the middle of the road. The faces of those behind him tell a story of approval and pride.

The caravan rolls past Tiger Stadium in Detroit during a summer that saw the Tigers lead the American League from start to finish and win the World Series. Lou Putnam, one of the relay managers, escorts the YLK runner.

reception of the smaller towns and villages of America.

An example was Vermilion, down the road from Cleveland, where the street was lined with a thousand flags and the townspeople dressed in the fashions of the 1800s. Banjo music filled the air—it is hard to be unhappy when you're playing a banjo—and two American Legion posts presented their color guards. They greeted the runners with a flag twenty-five feet long by fifteen feet wide, and the mayor declared: "The idea is to show America what a small town feels about the Olympics. We have strong feelings of patriotism in the inner part of this land—the deep roots of America—and we want to display that for the runner as he passes by."

But sales around the rest of Ohio were thin. LAOOC had decided not to advertise the sales in deference to the complaints of the Greek government, relying instead on news items and word of mouth. Sometimes the word was slow to reach the hinterlands. The officials knew they had a problem—the YLKs were scaled down to 4,000 runners, one-third the original estimate. "But we wouldn't peddle it like detergent," said one committee staff member. Ohio had been allocated 455 kilometers. Only 123 were sold, over half in Cleveland.

This seemed to confirm what the relay's vagabonds had been saying: Until the people saw the torch move, knew what it was and what it meant, there was no way for the public to gauge the sweep of the task.

A meteor shower brightened the skies over Ohio as the flame crossed the border into Michigan, at Erie Township. There was rain in Lansing, wall-to-wall people in Flint and free enterprise in Pontiac. There, the Done Right Engraving Shop cranked out hand-lettered T-shirts that featured an eye, a saw, and other symbols to create the message: "I Saw the Olympic Torch Runner."

The shirts sold for five dollars each, and the first hundred moved briskly. The motive, said the owner of the shop, Ron Bohmier, was need, not greed. "What we're trying to do," he said, "is pay for another silk-screen machine and open another job here. We're hurting for jobs in this town."

Michigan, one of the great melting-pot states, clearly connected with the moving flame. At the Trinity Lutheran

In the city of wheels, one of Detroit's finest leads the torchbearer down a flight of steps. In the background is the distinguished Renaissance Center.

School in Monroe, that old school spirit financed a kilometer for two sixth-graders. What took place was a burst of energy that may have been duplicated all over America. The students held a bake sale, a run-a-thon, two "dress-down" days, during which students paid a buck to wear blue jeans, and a carnival where in one booth they got to throw wet sponges at teachers for a quarter.

A fifteen-foot replica of a torch, used decades earlier when the city of Monroe took part in an annual Torch Drive —now the United Way—was rescued from a warehouse, raised, and lighted in the middle of downtown. "The torch looks like it came out of the hand of the Statue of Liberty," said Jim

Alban, director of the Family YMCA, the recipient of $24,000 in sponsorship fees from the eight Youth Legacy Kilometers run through the city.

There, in a package, the action and symbolism and benefit all came together.

For Chris Amolsch, one of the chosen sixth-graders, it was literally a dream come true. "My twenty-six-year-old brother called me from London, England, before the drawing," he said, "and told me he dreamed I had won."

The torch drew thousands on a sun-

drenched day in Detroit, as tourists and office workers streamed into Hart Plaza on the Detroit River. The torch came through the parking lot of Tiger Stadium, on through the smaller towns and greener fields.

In Greektown, actually an enclave of shops and eateries in Detroit, Vaso Margilaj watched from the window of the café where he worked as a cook. An immigrant from Yugoslavia, he had come to this country ten years ago, at eighteen. A few doors down, Basil Lukos, 73, had taped Greek and American flags to the parking meter in

■ 99 ■

VERMILION, OH

An article in the local paper, the *Photojournal*, boasted that "neither rain nor snow nor dark of night" could stop the town from supporting its local athletes.

So it was that one out of every four residents turned out to brave a downpour and see the passing of the Olympic Torch. Mayor Hobart Johnson compared the event to the annual "Woolybear Festival," which attracts each fall 100,000 tourists, ten times the town's population.

As tradition has it, each year the festival's weather sage journeys into the woods to "read" the coat of the Woolybear, a small caterpillar popular to the area. Depending on the colors of the animal's fuzz, the sage can determine if winter will be long or short, cold, colder, or snowy.

The runners often wondered as they came over the crest of a hill or made a turn if anyone would be there. They nearly always were, sometimes looking as though they had been recruited from Hometown, U.S.A. In East Lansing they waited in the rain.

There was always one moment of expectancy and intensity, when the previous runner passed his or her flame to the next. The seriousness with which they performed this task, as a marshal looks on, tells you that they were not playing with fire.

front of his Athens Book Store, which he has owned for forty-five years.

Hildred (Hildy) Nielson put down her lead pipe when she carried the torch through Pontiac. She had trained with the pipe on her daily three-mile runs in the underground tunnels of the St. Joseph's Mercy Hospital. A gift from her coworkers in the maintenance office, the pipe was another of the varied and sometimes exotic instruments people adapted to

prepare them for the torch. Doctors and nurses in surgical gowns stood outside the hospital, waving and cheering, as Hildy brought the torch up Woodward Avenue.

And in a neat rounding of one circle, the relay passed the General Motors Worldwide Truck and Bus plant in Pontiac, where the sidewalks were lined with many of the autoworkers who helped build the trailers, vans, and trucks that accompanied the run-

ners on their journey across the U.S.A. In Flint, Wes Bartlett ran through the access road to the Buick plant, whose special cars were engineered to be driven on the relay at speeds under ten miles an hour. As Bartlett pumped the torch the workers cheered and banged on the sides of the metal buildings, which must have been fun for those still inside.

The fellow who kept all those vehicles humming was Tom Smith. Relay

In Edwardsburg, Michigan, where the spirit of being American burns strong, the torch-bearer is given a two-flag salute by members of the American Legion.

workers spoke with reverence about a time when the stocky mechanic coolly climbed into his rig and pushed to safety two motor homes that had become disabled in a tunnel traveled by logging trucks. On a contract with General Motors, Smith and his assistant both maintained and repaired the fleet. He also stopped to fix the cars of a couple of strangers he passed along the way.

For someone who spent most of his adult life immersed in engine cowlings, the reception to his brightly marked Torch Relay vehicle left Smith bemused. "The people seem just as happy to see us as the runners," he said. "They stand up and cheer and holler and wave. It's nice to be a part of that."

The license plate on the back of Smith's truck read: DR. GOLDEN TOOL. Inside was a complete auto repair shop on wheels with some plumbing and electrical tools thrown in for good measure. Some of the support crew may have mistaken Smith and his assistant, Paul Carter, for Mr. Goodwrench. They kept knocking on his door to tell him their microwave oven didn't work, or the air conditioner was acting up. Smith, his hat covered with the small enameled pins the people on the caravan traded with each other, would get out his golden tools and fix the problem.

The enthusiasm for the crowds in Michigan left AT&T runner David Tahan with a voice cracked and hoarse. He got in the habit of shouting and cheering right back at his well-wishers along the road. He was bowled over by what he saw. "I just get excited right along with them," he said. "When people yell, the torch goes up. This just makes me want to wrap my arms around America."

After four joyous days in Michigan, the relay headed for Chicago.

There former Olympian Willye White carried the flame to Walter Payton, while the Fort Sheridan army band provided the background music. Broadcaster Jack Brickhouse emceed a program that included the governor of Illinois, James Thompson; Chicago mayor Harold Washington; and Gina Hemphill. Payton looked at the torch and announced to the crowd, "I'd just like to say I hope I don't drop it." He didn't.

The AT&T cadre runners were pleased when they heard that Walter

With the orange-red flame shooting to the sky, reflecting the color of her hair, an expression of near rapture lights the face of the next runner, in Chicago.

Payton, preparing to run his kilometer, admitted that he was nervous. It was the honest pleasure of any sportsman, when a star from another orbit acknowledges that your game is hard.

Some of them bantered with the great Bears halfback who had broken the career rushing record of Jim Brown in 1984. They kidded him about whether he could run a kilometer (six-tenths of a mile). True, he had gained over 12,000 yards in his career. But the most Payton could run at one time was one hundred yards, and in a full year he would be pressed to gain a mile.

By the end of week three of this expedition in sneakers, the runners had seen the great variety of American landscape and sensed the American fascination with the open road; no matter television, fast food, or discount air. They were part of something hugely ambitious, a production that stretched from one coast to the other. This was no quaint adventure, a solitary character walking backward or rolling a pizza from sea to shining sea.

The flame was passed from torch to torch during an eleven-hour run through Chicago and its suburbs to the south, before cutting back on the same route to Indiana. The torchbearers were on a schedule that brought them into Indianapolis as a prelude to the traditional Indy 500 Festival parade.

They reached the horsepower capi-

Resembling life-size pieces on a chessboard, the runner and a security man jog across the checkered starting line of the Indianapolis 500 parade. They arrived the morning of the annual five-hundred-mile auto race and became part of that day's parade.

In Flint, Michigan, the rain was so severe and the lightning so threatening that the relay had to be stopped and the torch retired to a security van. Still, people turned out for a glimpse of the Olympic flame.

tal of the world under sunny skies, while 200,000 racing fans flooded the streets. They were due for a major adjustment, from watching the torch glide by at maybe eight miles an hour, to the Indy cars zooming past at speeds up to 250 m.p.h., passing in a blur and an opera of noise.

The clear weather was in sharp and welcome contrast to the turbulence that had stopped the relay the night before in Flint. "Friday was supposed to be an easy day for us," said Tony D'Andrea, one of the AT&T cadre runners. "But the weather got so bad, we had to bring the flame into the van and stop running because the lightning was so fierce. We were supposed to reach our overnight stop around nine-thirty P.M., but instead it was well past midnight."

D'Andrea ran two miles in a hard, pelting rain before everyone took refuge from the lightning. He carried the flame to the parade ground, relaying it to Gary Romesser, 32, the winner of the 500 Festival Mini-Marathon.

The fans were already moving toward the Speedway, when the relay took U.S. 31 south toward the John F. Kennedy Bridge and on to Louisville. Slowly, quietly, the flame went forward, while behind it thirty-three cars ran in circles all day, at speeds faster than most people can think.

The exchange of the torch sometimes took place among crowds. Sometimes in silence. Here in Knoxville, Tennessee, they are two with the flame.

Rich, rolling pastures, shady lanes; long, green rows of burly mansions nestled among towering oaks and maples—and everywhere the echoes of history. This is Kentucky—bluegrass country.

Black-fenced horse farms line the tree-shaded roads. There is a feeling of continuity here. So much of the past survives in the land of bourbon and fine horseflesh. Along the Paris and Winchester Pikes—where else do they still call roads "pikes"?—the gray stone walls border the rolling land. Slave fences, they are called, because most were built by slaves who picked the stones from the fields and fitted them together into fences of useful beauty.

Bluegrass thickens into a dense mat of dark green, suggesting a more lei-surely time, when horses were loved not so much for themselves but for a way of life they represented. It is not farfetched to say that once, in parts of the state, and maybe still, horses lived better than people.

The flame entered Kentucky across the Clark Bridge at Louisville at one in the afternoon, on Sunday, May 27. Two kilometers across the bridge, they handed the Olympic Torch to Muhammad Ali, three times the heavyweight champion of the world, now 42, in less than robust health, puffy-faced and overweight.

"When I was asked to run the kilometer," he said to the reporters and photographers around him, "I wanted to find out how much, how far that was. I'm in no condition. So I take my jacket—it's cool out—and I'm going to try to make it. And in case I don't, promise me, if I fall on my face, you won't take pictures."

There was a plaintive note in the former champion's voice. The old Ali would have been jiving us, but now one can't be sure. He has been ill with a form of Parkinson's disease, also known in boxing circles as left-hook disease.

Ali shuffled his six-tenths of a mile along a street where, in the high noon of his indestructible youth, the city had held a parade in his honor. The kids were still with him. They were everywhere. And you recalled a story Ali told out of his own childhood, a story about how he would psych himself for a fight.

When he was 12, Ali, then Cassius Clay, worked all one summer sacking

A handful of settlers from a town that calls itself "a spot on the road," Hazel Patch, KY, turned out to chant, "U.S.A., U.S.A.!" The runners would hear that chant from millions of voices all along the route.

Bless the children: Wearing a shirt honoring another timeless American hero and waving two flags, this youngster sits on top of a car, waiting to salute the passing of the torch.

groceries so he could buy a second-hand red bicycle. A week later the bike was stolen from behind the market. Ali spent the next several months walking all over Louisville, looking for his prized possession. He never found it. But later, every time he fought, no matter who his opponent or how tough, he would look across the ring and tell himself, "That's the guy who stole my bicycle."

At the end of his run—he didn't fall down—Ali passed the torch to Melinda Warren, a housewife who had baked and sold cookies door to door to raise the $3,000 she needed to buy the right to run one kilometer. Ali told the crowd: "It's been some time since 1964, when I was twenty years old, since I won the Olympics. If you had told me twenty years ago that I would still be participating in the Olympics, I would've said you were crazy. But I'm here, and time really flies. Yesterday I won the Olympics and it's already been twenty years."

Ali's memory had tricked him slightly. It was in 1960 that he won the Olympic light-heavyweight title. He was 18, not 20, and he turned out to be an eloquent defender of the American way of life. After he received his gold medal a Russian reporter in-

quired whether he did not find it ironic that he still would not be admitted to many public restaurants back home.

He looked down his nose at the reporter and replied, "Russian, we got qualified men working on the problem. We got the biggest and the prettiest cars. We got all the food we can eat. America is the greatest country in the world, and as far as places I can't eat goes, I got lots of places I *can* eat—more places I can than I can't. Lookee here, Russian—there's good and bad in every country, and if there weren't . . . we wouldn't have to be talking about Judgment Day."

On his way to the gold Cassius/Ali

The runner beside him seems to be saying, "You're looking good, Champ," as Muhammad Ali, an American original, carries the torch along the boulevard in Louisville that carries his name. Fans on bicycles follow him.

No longer light of foot and, at the time of this picture, recently tested for a form of Parkinson's disease, Ali still awakened the memories of the crowd. Thousands turned out to see and hear him as he circled the Louisville Civic Center.

had defeated a Russian, Shatkov, in the quarterfinals. As usual, he had found inspiration in his own wild imagination, pretending that the United States, in the person of Cassius Clay, was at war with Russia. "If I lose, our country will be *lost,*" he told himself. "Everybody at home be blown up. I gotta give it everything I got and bomb him out and win the war for the Yew-nited States."

A few months later, in a fit of pique at a racial insult in Louisville, he flung his gold medal into the Ohio River. It was never recovered. He went on to win his first fight for money against a part-time cop named Tunney Hunsaker. A year later, less than three years after his return from Rome, he confounded all the boxing experts by beating Sonny Liston for the heavy-

weight title, beating him so badly that Liston refused to come out of his corner for the seventh round.

One could not miss the symbolism of that moment in 1984 for Ali. Once he had mocked everything he thought white America stood for; he had changed his name, refused to be drafted, beaten the best white fighters in the world. Now, white America had seen him go down, his health uncertain, and . . . well, they hurt for him.

Now he was carrying the torch, and the crowds cheered them, Ali, and the flame, both part of this unique American pageant. Ali had outlasted his critics and had come to stand for something. He no longer needed to tell us how great he was—we had

found out for ourselves—and we appreciated what he had always been: the most accessible athlete of his time. You ran into him in airports, in coffee shops, at the crap tables in Las Vegas (where he would kibitz, seldom playing). As a coffee shop orator he had no equal, pulling up a chair and delivering speeches to startled guests trying to eat their eggs.

But in truth, Ali was no more the star of this day in May, or this expedition, than the nameless, mostly faceless citizens who helped move the torch along, step by step, hand to hand.

The torch was the star. The runners, especially the 200 who formed the official cadre, were the supporting cast.

Gently, with guiding hands, the AT&T cadre runner nudges this bright-eyed Lexington youth onto the road. The scene recalls a Boys' Club motto: "No man ever stands so tall as when he stoops to help a child."

Whatever their role or their feelings, or whatever they understood about what was going on around them, they knew that nothing like it had happened before, not in their lifetimes.

As for the people running the YLKs —the youth legacies—they were everybody's next-door neighbor. How they got there, and sometimes why, was an unending story of American ingenuity.

Nearly a year in advance, Sue Feldkamp, a gym teacher and coach at a small college in Berea, Kentucky, had heard about the plans to send the torch across the country. "I knew about the torch in 1980," she said, "when they were taking it to Lake Placid. I wanted to do it then, but I

was busy teaching and not running that often, and I knew it would be in the middle of winter. So I watched and figured they'd have to do something in 1984.

"Well, I heard rumors about this relay, that they were going to work out a way where many people could participate. I started writing out a practice letter on how I would raise the money, because I didn't have $3,000 sitting around that I could donate at the time. I invited support from friends and family and acquaintances, anybody I had an address for. I mailed out these letters, asking people to donate to my fund, which I called S.O.R.F., which stood for Sue's Olym-

pic Run Fund. I started getting contributions through the mail and by Christmas, of 1983, I had a thousand dollars. But I needed three. So I borrowed $2,000 from the bank and sent in my check before the January deadline. I continued letting people know that I was running. I promised them a picture." A letter postmarked Denver brought her a check for $200 from an unknown benefactor.

She raised part of her money by staging a play, a "Christmas melodrama," at the community theater in Berea. As the stage manager, Sue held up the signs that told the audience when to boo and hiss. She received

tographs. But, despite the hoopla, the runners never lost sight of the truth: The flame —and the torch that held it—were the real stars.

press coverage from TV stations in Lexington and from newspapers in northern Kentucky.

Some of her friends and family were puzzled by all this effort, this determination to take part in an event that seemed remote or esoteric. "My nieces asked me why I wanted to do it, and I said it was important, a chance to participate in an historic event, and I was going to go for it. To me it was like a dream. As a child I wanted to be a swimmer, and I couldn't afford it. So this was my chance."

At the end of her kilometer a writer asked Sue Feldkamp how it felt to carry the torch. "It was just running and smiling," she said. "I feel as though I have a permanent smile stuck on my face."

Wherever the torch passed on its magic-lantern kind of journey, there was a story, an anecdote, a piece of character exposure that went with it. In Knoxville the torch emerged from under a railroad bridge and, a few blocks later, reached the campus of the University of Tennessee. Students were gathered along the curbs, closing in behind the runner as the caravan moved along. The wife of the governor of the state, Honey Alexander, took the flame from a high-school coed and carried it out of the campus.

In Seiverville, a town of about 27,000, both sides of the main street were lined with people for nearly a mile. Each spectator held a large American flag, the kind displayed on the fronts of homes. As the torch caravan approached, the people closed to allow a single line of traffic, enabling the caravan to pass through an arch of American flags.

The torch stopped at Gatlinburg that evening. The next day it would pass through the Great Smoky Mountains

■ 109 ■

The flame became more visible after sunset —and looked ever more threatening to those who carried it. Several flame bearers ended their runs with burned skin and singed hair.

and would wind up in the hands of Steve Streater, a celebrated high-school athlete in Sylva, North Carolina, later a star defensive back at Chapel Hill and a 1981 draft choice of the Washington Redskins.

Streater had flown home to the Raleigh-Durham, North Carolina, airport after signing his contract with the Redskins, on April 30, 1981. He was driving home alone when his car spun out of control and careened into an embankment. Steve's neck was broken, leaving the young football prospect paralyzed from the waist down. His world, which had seemed so filled with promise, was suddenly vacant.

Three years and one month later, Steve Streater carried the Olympic Torch. He held it high as he steered his electric wheelchair into the downtown area of Bryson City, not far from his family home in Sylva. Walking alongside were his sister, father, mother, and an uncle. His best friend sat on the rear bumper of a flatbed truck preceding the runner, clapping and cheering for him.

He entered the city to a giant roar. Dreams die hard, and Steve Streater will never recapture what he lost that day on a dark road heading home. But the torch and the crowd gave something back to him. "Why the accident happened," he said, "I'll never know. I think about it every day. But holding the torch, I felt as though I was touching the whole world. It was outstanding, a feeling I didn't think I'd ever have again."

Steve returned to football, in his wheelchair, as a coach of a local semi-professional team. In February of 1985, he was appointed the state co-ordinator of public service programs for North Carolina.

The author John Steinbeck once took his dog and embarked on a tour of this nation to check the pulse of its people. He could not have enjoyed, or possibly imagined, some of the sights provided those on the Torch Relay. In the town of Cherokee, Indians danced, and by a stream in Nantha-hala, kayakers lined both sides of a mountain road and formed an arch with their paddles, under which the torch passed.

If you were in Atlanta the night before the torch came through, you were treated to four hours of continuous entertainment, sponsored by AT&T,

Through the mountains and across the Cumberland Gap on a mild day in late May the torch moved into the Volunteer State— the land of cotton, Daniel Boone, the birth of the blues, and the resting place of Elvis Presley. The state line looms ahead.

The Gap is the break point in the mountain range where Virginia, Kentucky, and Tennessee converge. For the settlers rolling west, the Gap was a path across the wilderness trail in the 1800s. The runner is Debbie Weeks.

Coca-Cola USA, Colony Square, and a local radio station, WSB 99 FM. More than 20,000 people packed the Colony Square area to watch two dozen ethnic groups perform, including a national championship clogging team.

The next day, on the same spot, the president of Coca-Cola, Brian Dyson, exchanged the torch with Andrewayne Thunder Sun Forsythe, a musician and artist and, at twelve, the next to youngest of five adopted Indian children. "I wanted Andrewayne to run as a way of enhancing his self-

image," said his father, Peter. The kilometer was sponsored by the International Children's Institute.

The exchange took place at 9 P.M. Restless and excited, Andrewayne held his 7-year-old sister, Anja, while he waited for the torch to arrive. High-intensity lights beat down on him. Police motorcycles patroled the area and kept the crowd back. Fireworks lighted the sky and camera bulbs popped as the young Indian boy began his run. At the end of his kilometer he ran into the arms of an older

brother, Aric, 16, who had helped coach and train him for this moment. They still clung to each other as the torch moved on, in the hand of another runner, toward Los Angeles.

Another heroine of the run through the south was a 10-year-old charmer named Nancy Nix, from Gainesville, outside Atlanta. She is a fifth-generation descendant of a man named Benjamin Parks—her great, great, great-grandfather—who started the first American gold rush, in Delonega, in 1828. As the story has been

To some, simply carrying the torch was a challenge, a test of courage, and an accomplishment. This kilometer started on the outskirts of Atlanta.

handed down, he was deer hunting near Yellow Creek and stubbed his toe on a piece of quartz. Angered, he picked it up and threw it hard against the ground. When he did, the rocklike object broke open and revealed a yellow streak of gold—"as yellow as an egg yolk," according to the local newspaper. And so began the first gold rush in the United States.

Now, more than a century and a half later, Nancy Nix had decided to take part in another kind of gold rush. Her third-grade teacher at River Bend School, Maxine Partin, had told the class about the Torch Relay. She read

to them one day from the Scholastic bulletin an item that said they would be needing runners through Georgia. Mrs. Partin remembers Nancy, "a serious child, saying, 'I'm going to do that.'"

At breakfast a few days later, Nancy announced her plans to her mother, who reacted as any parent would: with disbelief. "Just out of the blue, at seven A.M., she said she would like to be in the Olympics. I had a friend in Alabama whose daughter was in training as a swimmer, and I knew that they put in many, many hours in the gym and in the pool every day. So when she said that, I had mixed feelings. I was excited for her and, well, wondering if I could support her to

the extent that would be needed. So rather than squelch her idea, I just said, 'Well, Nancy, what would you like to do?' She said she would like to carry the torch. At that time I didn't know about the relay run. So I said, 'Nancy, when you get home from school today, we'll test your running. The person who carries the torch and lights the torch is probably the fastest runner in the United States, so we'll see how fast you can run.'"

Of course, what they had here was a small problem in communication. Nancy was not exactly thinking about challenging Mary Decker. But, at the moment, the goal of Mrs. Nix was to let her daughter down as easily as she could. "When she got home that after-

CUMMING, GA

For Renata Whitmire the parting was sweet, even though she may never see one of her life's treasures again.

Born and raised in Germany, Whitmire had won two victory wreaths while competing in national track-and-field events in West Germany during the 1950s. As an AT&T cadre runner, Earl Owens, carried the torch through her town, she welcomed him by placing one of the laurels on his head.

A future long jumper hopscotches across a sidewalk stamped with the Youth Legacy logo, in Berea, Kentucky.

noon, we put her outside in the neighborhood and let her run. I checked her time and measured it roughly by car for about a mile, and her time was pretty good. So I thought, well, that made her happy for the moment and we could just quietly dismiss it. She had not been involved in any kind of sports until this year."

Two weeks later Mrs. Nix was packing for a family trip. "I took out a newspaper to polish my husband's shoes," she said, "and when I opened it up, there was this write-up, the first

one, about the Olympic Torch Relay. That's when I knew that this was what Nancy had been talking about. That afternoon I asked her to tell me how she found out about the relay. She said her teacher had mentioned it in class."

The next step was to raise the entry fee. They decided to bake cakes on a pay-now, eat-later, plan. "We prepared an order form," said Mrs. Nix, "and people would mark the type of cake they wanted and give me a check for it and the date they wanted to receive the cake. I think the people who got the cake were very happy. Most of

them were delivered hot because we didn't have time for them to cool." Mrs. Nix had written a poem called "A Window to God," and Nancy handcolored the personalized copies and sold them for whatever people cared to contribute. Finally they worked together on handmade gold jewelry, a fairly big ticket item that was sold on consignment in the Cornerstone Christian bookstore in Gainesville.

"That's how we raised the money," said Mrs. Nix. "It took a week and a half."

SEE HOW THEY RUN

A Pioneer stands in the middle of an armada of custom-built trucks, buses, and motor homes used to carry, feed, and bed the runners and support teams.

It was in a very real sense like moving a city. The challenge was herculean. Forty-one vehicles moved, fed, housed, and cleaned 100 runners and support people at a time. You needed an overhead view to really grasp the dimension of this community on wheels. The caravan curled behind the runner like the tail on a kite, averaging 125 miles a day, most of it in first gear.

Picture the scene. A protective pod has formed around the runner. State and local police cars are at the site, sirens wailing. Directly behind the runner is a security car, a Buick with flashing lights. The medical van and trail car are in back of that. The runner is always conscious of being part of a procession.

Halfway through the run you could identify the security people by the elastic wraps around their thighs, protecting the muscles they pulled while hopping on and off the vans.

The motor homes and other support vehicles are strung out on the highway like Hannibal's elephants crossing the Alps. If they manage to stay in some kind of visual contact, this imposing supply line may wind along the road for half a mile. The convoy attracts almost as much attention as the AT&T runner with the torch, in a thin white uniform with the American-colored trim and an AT&T logo across the front. The track suits were so sheer that the last barriers of modesty were threatened whenever they became rain-soaked.

By far the most popular bus on the caravan was the mobile medical lab, known as the EMS (for Emergency Medical Systems). "It was the only vehicle in the pod," said Kate Washburn, "that had a bathroom. You didn't realize how important that was until. . . . And, you could bring your meals there. It wasn't easy eating lobster with a plastic spoon, but it was a sanity area. You could come in and talk and actually walk around. People didn't realize they were going to have to sit for hours in their cars or vans.

The EMS was literally a small hospital on wheels. "We have everything from Band-Aids to advance cardiac life-support systems," said Dr. Joseph Cillo. The relay was remarkably free of major injury. The most common problems were runners scorching their

■ 115 ■

Like the vanguard of an invading army, the motor pool pushed ahead. Many a casual motorist was startled to see the long column snaking its way through mountain roads and over city streets.

arms from the flame, sore joints, pulled muscles, and colds. Kate suffered stress fractures of both legs from the constant running she did and from hopping off the buses. "That sounds crazy," said Lou Putnam, "but you get carried away with the moment. And sometimes you had to get out quick to help the security people."

If not done right, distance running inflicts considerable physical damage. The cell walls of muscles rupture. Tendons become inflamed. Joints wear away at cartilage. Blood blisters form. One recalls what Albert Schweitzer referred to as "the brotherhood of pain."

The medical staff changed weekly— a physician, nurse, and exercise phys-

iologist. Local physicians in a given area might ride with them a day or two at a time. "Our main concern," said Dr. Cillo, "was with the excitement level among people who may have signals that they should slow down or be checked out. But because of the intensity and excitement, they just say, well, it's a bellyache or just a sore knee and they will continue doing whatever they are doing. That includes everyone in the entourage. I was concerned about the Pioneers and the people from other companies working with us. The excitement just makes you fly at a level that you are not accustomed to flying at."

While the medical bus was rolling across America, AT&T was establish-

ing for this summer festival in Los Angeles, at the Olympic Village, the most sophisticated communications system ever employed. The initials were the same, EMS, but these stood for Electronic Messaging System. Powered by a dozen computers located in downtown L.A., and linked by special fiber-optic cables, the system was available to nearly 100,000 athletes, coaches, reporters, and officials.

The EMS would provide virtually instant, detailed results from the events, spread out over 28 playing sites and 4,500 square miles. Anyone accredited by the Olympic organizers could communicate with anyone else

The EMS was a traveling hospital. Equipped with such features as a whirlpool bath and an EKG machine, it was ready for the worst. If necessary, surgery could have been performed aboard the $150,000 bus. None was necessary. Complaints ran largely to colds, pulled muscles, and blisters.

Ailing runners are checked aboard the EMS vehicle by a team of medical professionals. The doctors, nurses, and medical specialists would stay on the relay from a day to a week.

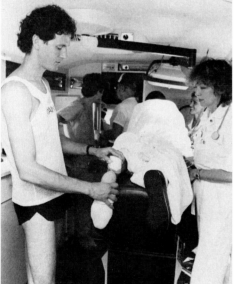

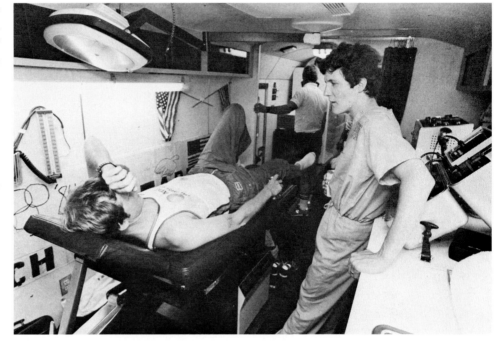

with credentials via "electronic mail." The system even would allow the sender to check and see if the receiver had read the message.

Users could even call up profiles on individual athletes to their computer screens. The system was designed so that even an approximate spelling of someone's name was good enough.

The man in charge of the operation was an electrical engineer from Short Hills, New Jersey, named Al Corwin, who spent eighteen months designing the system. Sophisticated though the EMS was, and skilled as the AT&T communications team is known to be,

Corwin would wind up with a name tag that read: CERWIN.

With a grin he explained: "We didn't get around to computerizing that."

Back on the torch caravan, the human condition was still the major one. The number of people involved, including the cadre runners and the support teams, all worked in one-week shifts, remained fixed at 100, give or take a body or two. The shifts changed every Saturday. It did not always go like clockwork.

"A typical day," said Ruth Berry, a trip director on McGuire's advance team, "starts between seven and eight in the morning and goes until almost midnight, often beyond. All of the

days get typical, but all of them are different. You know, it depends on whether you're running in the heat, running in the Rockies, you've got events to do, they all adjust to the peculiarities of a given day. We're dealing with runners who have different strengths.

"Some days the rhythm is really easy. But then we had a runner who had knee surgery two months earlier. One runner coming off back surgery. We had women runners who had not adjusted to the stress of carrying the torch. One of them was particularly afraid of the torch."

The daily ritual was clearly established, and the runners defined it as ranging from "boredom to stardom."

AT&T called on its resources for experienced technicians to operate both the radio network and its computer programs. On the radio, Ron Moorefield passes word down the line on the relay's progress while two Pioneers look on.

When they were not on the pavement, they were spending eight to ten hours in the shuttle vans.

The days began and ended with calls to the National Storms Forecast Center, in Kansas City, placed by one of Bill Mattman's security force. The morning call was to discover if tornadoes, floods, heat, or hurricanes threatened the caravan. Hail had forced them off the road in New Jersey for a half hour. During the simulation run in March, they had encountered a blizzard in West Virginia that sent them to shelter for most of an afternoon. When your day is already running eighteen hours, any delay is not treated as good news. The late calls determined if the runner would wear sweats or shorts the next morning.

□ □ □

The only way to make this passage work, to keep the runners composed and the support crew busy but not mutinous, was to take the trip a day at a time—just as it was intended. Otherwise, if you take it from the top in New York, knowing that the torch must travel 9,000 miles, weaving across America and enter the Coliseum at 3:43 P.M. on July 28, it would be a little like throwing a dart at the moon.

"The first three weeks were the worst," said Boehner. "We took so much screaming and yelling from the runners and support crew. I mean, you just had to stand it. There was nothing you could say, so you were either going to smile and grit your teeth and take it, or you'd explode. I know I'd hemorrhage emotionally every night."

The changing of the guard was a double-edged sword, as Lou Putnam saw it. "In terms of the people who came on each week, they were trained by the time they got to Saturday, so you hated to lose them and get a new group. On the other hand, a week was about all most of these people could take. And the ones who were trouble,

On a starry night, the flame fluttered in the wind as a security man steadied the YLK runner. The lighting of the torch was always a more dramatic moment after dark.

*Four men bunking on a motor home was a little like living on a submarine. In spite of close quarters, grinning and bearing it were: Paul Kerns, (*LEFT*), and Paul Knoll (*UPPER BERTHS*); Earl Owens, (*LEFT*), and Dan Lyndgaard (*LOWER BERTHS*).*

at least you knew you were going to get rid of them."

"It was like the famous movie scene about the Marine drill camps," added Boehner. "It's like six weeks at a time, and you see the group come in and what a bunch of misfits they are. And then, at the end of the term, they're all spit and polish and precision drilling, and they're marching off to get killed or whatever. So here came the next misfits off the bus. We had that constant turnover, people being worked into the system."

Each Saturday they assembled in gymnasiums or cafeterias or armories, for the briefings that would let the next shift know what to expect. By the third week the relay leaders had their speeches down pat. These were a mix of straight talk and pep rally but with a visible pride in what they were getting done. There was an echo of Patton's classic speech to the Third Army in World War Two.

The implication was this: When people talk about the great Torch Relay in years to come, those who were there wouldn't have to say that they stayed home and watched it on the evening news.

Putnam made it clear that the managers would be flexible, up to a point. "We've already changed the driving assignments for ten people," he said at one of the briefings. "If it really bothers you, just come and see me or Dick Boehner and you're welcome to go home. And I'm serious about that. If during this week you get real frustrated, just let us know, because basically we don't have time to deal with a bunch of little problems."

Boehner passed the word that the run would be dry. "As of right now," he said, "everybody who's involved in this project for the next week is an absolute teetotaler. If you have any problem with that rule at all, you can see me or Lou Putnam after this meeting. We'll make arrangements for your hotel tonight and your transportation home tomorrow. If you have a bottle with you, don't take it on board the vehicle at all. Leave it behind, please.

Parked side by side, the GMC motor homes provide a sense of their dimensions. In addition to the ten sleepers, the medical bus, and the security cars, there were two mini-homes and two magna-vans, two press vans, two tractor-trailers that served as a chuck-wagon, and one van used entirely to carry extra torches and spare parts for the rest of the convoy.

The man responsible in the field for the care and maintenance of the relay's rolling stock was Tom Smith, a master mechanic hired by General Motors. An uncomplaining professional, Smith was known around the caravan as Dr. Golden Tool. He even made night calls to fix their microwaves.

If there were to be an accident out on the highway, somebody runs into you and your driver swerved to miss an animal and hits a pothole and runs off into the ditch, not only would the police be there but the press as well. The media would swarm around it. And all it would take would be for some local cop to walk into that vehicle, look around the inside, and find a bottle. And the next day the headlines would read, OLYMPIC TORCH RELAY DRIVER INVOLVED IN ACCIDENT; ALCOHOL FOUND ON BOARD."

Then Bill Mattman got their attention by covering the security procedures. He told them they would be able to recognize the security van by the running boards on the side. "You see people standing on that," he said. "It's for security personnel only and key AT&T people. I'll ask you right now, whether you're a runner or anybody else, stay off. We have had extensive training in jumping on and off vehicles. It may look easy to you, but believe me, there are cadre runners out there who can attest to the fact that it's pretty damned hard to do and it's easy to get hurt.

"In the security car we carry from three to five people. It depends on where we are and what the risk factor is. Now the most important rule, and I ask you not to forget it: Just because you are driving a vehicle that has Olympic decals on it, an Olympic Torch decal or an amber light bar, does not exempt you from obeying all traffic laws. You are just like any other driver out there. And in the interest of safety I have asked the state police to ticket any driver who does something illegal. And I'll tell you why. We were in the Smokies and the cadre shuttle car [the car carrying a runner to his next dropoff] passed the motorcade on the double yellow line in a blind curve. We missed a head-on by about half a second. Now you can't imagine what an accident of that severity would do to the Olympic Torch Relay.

That's news. And the whole relay would be blemished.

"Just this morning, and without naming names, the caravan went from the overnight site to the staging area, and the person that was leading us for some reason thought he had the right to run red lights. He didn't even have a flashing light on his car. It was just his private automobile. So one more time: Unless you are inside the core, behind the police lead car, or in front of a police tail car, you may not run red lights. You may not run stop signs. You may not cross double yellow lines."

Part of the job of the cadre runners was to accompany, coach, and protect the sponsored runners. They were instructed to keep on the traffic side of them. If the road was one-way or divided, they were to take the curb side and act as a shield in the event of large crowds. "When you're running," Mattman advised, "please do not shake hands with the people. And believe me, the first day you're out there, they'll come running up to you.

They want to shake your hand, they want to touch you, they want to touch the torch. There are some very moving scenes out there, but even the people who have no intention of harming you can make things scary. You're moving at eight or nine miles an hour. If somebody grabs your hand, he can really throw you off-stride, especially since you're already a little off-balance with the torch. So if they come on, actually move away and put your hand out if necessary. Do not go toward the crowd. Stay on your path. It's very

From lobster thermidor to chicken cordon bleu, those in the caravan dined on gourmet food. But for the runners the ARA chefs had to pile on the carbohydrates.

tempting when the crowd is out there, with big signs and flags. And gifts. You will get gifts ranging from flowers to strawberry pies. This is true. In Connecticut somebody tried to hand a runner a strawberry pie.

"There's enough to eat on this caravan, believe me. We'll take it, and if you come around at the end of the day, we'll give it back to you. Also, do not accept water or oranges. I'm from Los Angeles. Some of you may be from the big cities and you've heard about razor blades in oranges and LSD in water or juice."

There was another subject that needed to be aired, and it was never very far from anyone's mind: vandalism, demonstrations, even terror. "If you see something that worries you," Mattman said, "smart-ass kids trying to steal the torch or something like that, just come on back to the security

car and we'll react to it. We don't ask you to fight those people. You may have a demonstration where someone will lie down in front of the lead car, or you may have some kids trying to throw something off an overpass. And I tell you, a watermelon hurts. Let us know. Don't be embarrassed if you hear that a bunch of kids are trying to put out the torch with a garden hose. It would be very, very embarrassing if it happened and they got away with it."

There was little about the relay that could be described as uncomplicated. Food, without which no army, big or small, travels far, was prepared and served cafeteria-style in three tractor-trailers. One, a forty-five-foot-long

monster, was used for freezing and refrigeration. A second featured a stainless-steel kitchen and the third, forty-eight feet long and nearly fourteen high, was the dining room, where thirty people could be fed at a time and some two hundred meals were served daily.

A short, 29-year-old brunette named Branka McNally, born in Yugoslavia, was one of two representatives in charge for ARA Services. She turned out to be fluent in Russian, French, Bulgarian, and Serbo-Croatian. Her English was also flawless, a credit to her schooling at Mankato State University in Minnesota.

When you think about it, the achievement was a major one, serving

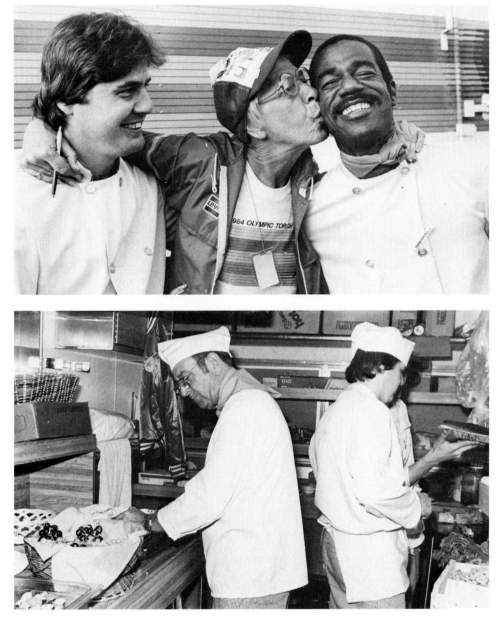

three meals a day, never twice in the same town, for eighty-two days. The food selection was staggering, eighty different items on a given day. Nearly twelve tons of food had to be prepared to keep the torchbearers running to their goal. The menus offered enough variety so that each could get the amount of proteins, fats, carbohydrates, and calcium or potassium he or she wanted.

A typical dinner menu offered choices of chicken gumbo; spinach salad with hot bacon dressing; boneless breast of chicken with Bordelaise sauce; baked lobster tail with drawn butter; wild rice, vegetable lasagna, asparagus spears; Harvard beets; Amaretto cheesecake, chocolate truffle.

In addition to the regular menus, each motorbus was equipped with a microwave oven, sandwiches, and snacks—popcorn and Snickers bars topped the list—that were available on a twenty-four-hour basis for those who had the munchies.

Then there were the cars especially engineered and designed for this extended cross-country run. Nothing like it had been attempted before; there are not many 9,000-mile parades held each year. So Buick had to provide cars that could maintain an average speed of six miles an hour, for up to twenty hours a day, for nearly three months. The company came up with heavy-duty cooling on the engine and transmission. The engines were calibrated for high-altitude emissions to get them through the mountains. They carried special radio equipment

The Torch Relay touched something deep in the American consciousness, something mothers didn't want their sons and daughters to miss. They waited in front of familiar offices—here Everts Electric and Owosso Plumbing—and waved their arms to signal the arriving runner.

and power accessories with separate modes, so that they could be shut off separately to relieve the drain on the engine.

The driver's side of the car contained a hand throttle control, allowing the driver to regulate his speed without having to constantly shift his foot on the gas. Two of the cars were always in the pod, and twice each day they would be rotated with two backup cars, so the engines could be cooled out at fifty to fifty-five miles an hour.

One of the Buick representatives was Terry Booker, out of Flint, Michigan, who felt the same sense of bonding as nearly everyone else involved in the relay. "It's amazing," she said, "how you get so close to your drivers or whomever you may be working with. It becomes like a family. Every-

body looks out for each other. You don't have to worry about someone saying, 'Well, that's not my job, I'm not going to do it.' Everybody just pitches right in and helps.

"The thing that really touched me is when we would go through these smaller cities. It could be a city of two hundred and there would be nine hundred people waiting when we came through. They just came from

"Without the ham radio operators," said one AT&T spokesman, "the relay wouldn't have worked. They held it together."

everywhere. They invited you into their homes to take a bath or just to have dinner with them."

If at any point the relay fell behind schedule, a computer in a small office in White Plains, New York, could kick out the names of faster runners, suggest a shorter route or a flatter terrain, to speed the flame along.

Doug Jeffcoat ran the office out of Torch One, the communications bus, when he was with the caravan. "To make the caravan move properly," said Jeffcoat, "it takes a whole series of things that are in the computer. If we're behind, we ask the computer who are the runners who can run

some five-minute miles, and we just change runners."

Jeffcoat was one of the people working twelve hours a day: eight for his company, AT&T, and four for his club, the Telephone Pioneers of America. Pioneers had driven over every inch of the torch route, checking to see if bridges were wide enough and tunnels high enough for the motor homes.

Most of the vehicles were equipped with ham radios, operated by Pioneers who had mastered the technique of economic speech. With a minimum of words, they located a missing runner or a lost car, passed on a weather traffic alert, and the latest schedule change. The radio operators reported to Jim Metzger, who ran what was

called "Network Control" with a calm and mellow assurance. Jeffcoat, an owlish character with a southern twang, paid the ham operators his highest tribute: "Without them, the torch stops."

Other Pioneers drove the mobile homes and vans for a week at a time. Some of them spent their entire summers on the road. Henry Wesley, a Pioneer from Burlington, North Carolina, who organized the route through his state, celebrated his sixty-second birthday on the relay, July 21. "One day I saw a little, eighty-year-old lady sitting out in a chair on her lawn, waving a flag as we passed," he said. "And, brother, if that doesn't get to you, nothing will."

Each time the caravan rolled into

In the midst of scenic Pine Mountain Park in Pineville, Kentucky, Jack Rice hands a torch from the backup supply to his brother Jim. Propane gas fuels the flame (note the no-smoking sign).

a campsite, scores of weary men and women stepped down from their trailers and fell to work. Like circus roustabouts, they moved almost automatically, making arrangements for the next day. Before turning in, someone peered into each of the miner's lanterns to be sure they were still glowing. Then they fell into their bunks for a brief night's sleep.

The lanterns were housed separately. Two were mounted on a wooden platform at the rear of a Buick convertible, which rolled directly in front of the torchbearers during the relay. The position of the lanterns allowed for almost instantaneous recovery of the flame if it blew out during a run.

Another pair of lanterns rested in the torch truck, casting a dim light over the hundreds of bronze-coated torches stacked there, waiting to be used down the line. The lamps stood about ten inches high and were made of glass and gold-plated panes. The flames they cradled were no taller than three-eighths of an inch.

To light the runners' torches a supervisor had to unscrew the top, dip a sparkler into the flame, then lift the burning stick to the torch. Fueled in pairs, the lanterns usually went out the same way, two at a time. A volunteer designated for the task quickly refilled them, then re-ignited them from another lantern. What spectators saw as a rare and fleeting glimpse of a century past became a job of long hours and unusual rewards for the custodians of the flame.

In truth, there were as many ways to carry the torch as there were torch carriers. There were left-handers and right-handers and those who kept switching to ease the weight. Some choked up for a better grip, and others held it at the end, boldly, like a drum major setting his troupe in motion.

All of them, the 200 AT&T cadre runners and the 4,000 YLK runners, had one technique in common. They carried it proudly.

Wes Bartlett said he preferred the one-hand carry, first the right, then the left, when his right arm got tired. Occasionally he would carry it in two hands across his body—the lacrosse carry, he called that one.

"Some people like to hold it down

Spectators snap pictures, raise their own torch replicas as a salute, and a reflection, of the passing runner. Legs weary, throats dry, they often found that the reaction of the crowd revived them—and up went the torch.

Gordon McKinnie of St. Louis wipes the sweat from his eyes during his four-mile leg just east of Jefferson, Missouri.

by the end and high over their head," he said. "That's hot-dogging it."

Among the celebrity runners it was noted that O. J. Simpson resisted the temptation to tuck it under his arm, and former Dallas Cowboy Bob Hayes didn't try to spike the torch when he reached his goal.

All of the runners were quick to absorb one particular instruction: Keep the torch high and far enough away so that a sudden gust of wind would not blow the flame back in your face and set your hair on fire.

Meanwhile, every day, the relay team was putting out other fires, to keep little logistical problems from becoming big ones. The relay would suc-

ceed beyond his wildest dreams. "Not only has it worked logistically," said McGuire, "but the turnout of the American people was overwhelming. I mean, they're out there at one-thirty A.M. in the rain, at six in the morning, waiting on the road to see us flit by a couple hours later. There was something out there in America waiting for this to happen. Some spirit. Some say patriotism. I think it's more than that. They thank you for coming. There was something that needed to be unleashed. People were crying . . . out of joy.

"I think I can safely say what a lot of people have felt and witnessed. This has been probably the highlight

of my life. I mean, it's going to be very tough to top—to be even a small part of something that makes so many people happy and proud."

One year earlier, Dick Boehner and Lou Putnam had prepared an operations plan that was four inches thick. It started there, on paper, and ended 9,000 miles later, on pavement. Boehner was on the road every blessed mile of it, and his mind kept racing when the other engines had been cut off. "A lot of thoughts went through my head," he said. "Some of them were spiritual things, like the fact that I was running with the Olympic Torch and the symbolism it implied. Other things were more basic, like, God, I hope I can make it through these final two miles because this is a *bitch* of a hill."

■ 127 ■

Travel and enterprise have been always at the center of city life in St. Louis; the Torch Relay typified both. The Gateway Arch provides the runner's backdrop.

If Missouri is the Show-Me State, the people went out of their way to be shown. In Lee's Summit, Nita Tripp closed down her garage sale to wait for the flame. Mrs. Tripp was one of 700 who lined Highway 50 for more than a mile.

It would be begging the obvious to point out that you cannot journey 9,000 miles across America and avoid the villages and towns and hamlets that make up so much of the landscape. But at every bend in the road the runners seemed to find new reasons to be impressed. It was like Chinese theater. The crowds were part of the show as well as the runners.

The appearance of the torch revived an almost forgotten piece of sporting lore. The third of the modern Summer Olympiads was staged in St. Louis in July of 1904. The Games were moved from Chicago at the request of President Theodore Roosevelt, to coincide with the World's Fair, held in St. Louis on the centennial of the Louisiana Purchase.

Travel conditions in 1904 were such that by taking the Games to the American interior, few countries were able to send teams. In the unofficial point standings, the first three finishers were the New York, Chicago, and Milwaukee Athletic clubs.

In front of the Gateway Arch, in St. Louis, former Olympic runner Wilma Rudolph handed off to Ozzie Smith, who sped down Market Street while a lunchtime turnout of 5,000 surged and clapped and chanted, "Oz-zie!" In another of those ear-digging declarations by a professional athlete, caught up in a moment of passion, Smith said, "This is probably the greatest moment of my life." Less than twelve months later he would sign a new Cardinal contract reported to be worth nearly $2 million a year.

Ozzie Smith passed the torch to 9-year-old Charmin Smith, no relation, whose mother, a secretary, had won the run in a drawing. Nervous at first, Charmin managed a grin as her father trotted alongside and shouted, "You got it."

Days and miles blended one into the other, and then came a story of the kind told by Mark Sevier. "Most of the kids along the course," he said, "they

*For many the run was a 9,000-mile travelogue. But always there was a reminder—*GO FOR THE GOLD, *the sign reads—that at the other end of the journey an Olympic deadline had to be met.*

St. Louis Cardinal baseball fans call him The Wizard of Oz for his artistry as a shortstop. Ozzie Smith holds the torch for son O. J. and wife Denise to admire.

want to touch you to touch the torch. But then I met Kyle, just a little boy. He was afraid of the torch, I guess because of the fire. He wouldn't touch it, even when we begged him to. Well, we worked on him and eventually he gave in. And he was so happy. Then he stuck out his hand, like he wanted to shake mine. But, instead, he pulled me down and kissed my cheek.''

If you are looking for a fresh example of our national talent for improvising, we refer you to tiny St. Mary's, MO. There two cadre runners from Indiana, Carol Hayden and John Olszewski, left the bus they were riding in to mingle with the crowd. Some of

the locals, standing in front of a bank, wanted a photograph to capture the occasion, but no one had a camera. So an executive of the bank took everyone inside, hit a button in the security system, and the pictures were taken by a camera whose normal function is to identify bank robbers.

The runners were struck again and again by the patience and good humor of the people who waited for them, often for hours, to watch the two minutes it usually took to exchange the torch. It must have been a little like watching the Kentucky Derby. But in those two minutes, all the politics and hype of the Olympics were forgotten,

and perhaps a few personal problems as well.

The caravan left Missouri with an unusual added cargo. At the intersection of U.S. 50 and Toelke Lane, Joe Robinson had been waiting to take the flame from another runner. ''I saw a couple of little girls with a bear coming toward me,'' he recalled, ''and one of them said, 'Will you take my bear to the Olympics?' ''

If that sounds like an opening line for Fairy Tale Theater, you can imagine Robinson's reaction. Yet a kind of enduring relationship developed. The bear was not real, we ought to make clear. But he had a name: Albert the

Running Bear, and he became famous in Beaufort, Missouri, as the mascot of the Olympic Torch Relay.

The two girls were 11-year-old Aimee Perakes and her 9-year-old sister, Elizabeth. Albert was dressed in running clothes when Robinson accepted delivery and promised to take him to Los Angeles. Each week, when a new team moved into the motor home occupied by Robinson and his mates, the runners agreed to watch over Albert and pass the bear on to the next group.

The father of the girls, Dan Perakes, had doubted that they could get through the security around the runner and close enough for the sisters to try to arrange a trip for Albert to the Olympics. But they did, and curious as the sight may have been, when the caravan rolled into Kansas, a teddy bear was perched on a front seat in one of the buses.

In Kansas, Dorothy's point of departure for Oz, as well as the home turf of American milers named Glenn Cunningham, Wes Santee, and Jim Ryun, the torch found a natural constituency. Here the sky is big, the air is cleaner, and the prairie seems endless, open, and flat, and all nature calls to them: "Let's run."

Among the YLK runners were Larry Brown, the University of Kansas basketball coach; Royals' pitcher Larry Gura; and TV news anchorperson Anne Peterson. In St. Louis the list included Ozzie Smith, the Cardinals' millionaire shortstop.

In Topeka, the torch was passed on the steps of the Capitol as Governor John Carlin stood by. Topeka mayor Doug Wright left the ceremony early to run his leg of the relay in another part of the city.

Casey Converse—now that would make a fine name for a runner—also spoke to the gathering. Converse, now a swimming coach, was eighteen when he swam in the 400-meter freestyle at the Montreal Games in 1976. He remembered what a boost he got from spotting a fan waving a huge American flag in the stands, a re-

Ringed by onlookers, two jubilant runners, a blonde and a brunette, appear to be doing a well-timed dance step as they start their kilometer. They seem oblivious to the security men around them (in white shirts, black shorts) and the motorcycle police forming a file to their left.

minder of support from his countrymen. "We send our strength and spirit with the torch," he said.

Just south of Topeka, Joe Kearney, a Pioneer who had volunteered as a driver, dropped off a runner around 11 P.M. There was nothing but farms and woods as far as the eye could see. Nature called, but not to run. Joe got out of his truck and took a little walk into the foliage. He had started back to the road when a small boy appeared out of nowhere and asked, "What's up, mister?" When his heart started beating again, Joe explained that the Olympic Torch Relay was heading their way. Without a word the boy disappeared back into the woods. A short time later he emerged with the rest of

his family—mother, grandmother, sisters, and brothers. They watched the torch go by and then vanished back into the woods, still without a word.

It was hard to miss the truck that Joe Kearney drove during his week on the relay. He hung a sign on the tailgate, the message a play on the year's favorite hamburger slogan. In large block letters: FORGET THE BEEF. WHERE'S THE GOLD?

The night before, on the campus at Lawrence, Larry Brown carried the fire. Brown had played on the 1964 Olympic basketball team and coached the 1980 squad that did not go to Moscow.

The Lawrence celebration was cut

short by hard rains and bolts of lightning. "We'll run in spite of heat, cold, rain, dust, dogs, and snakes," said Boehner, "but we get 'em off the road when we see lightning. With the torch the runner becomes a lightning rod."

At Loose Creek, Missouri, as the new runner's torch flared to life, someone in the back of the crowd began to hum. Within seconds, as if a signal had flashed through the people, the words became audible: "Oh, beautiful, for spacious skies . . ." The hats came off and right hands sprang to so many hearts. It was a scene that repeated itself on other days in other towns.

It is in the countryside, out beyond the range and interest of the big-city

It was a sight that caused a ripple of electricity as the caravan entered a town: a torch-bearer in running silks, looking Olympian, amid a formation of protective cars and vans and motor buses.

The beginning of the run was when their faces seemed to show everything they were feeling: the pride, the pleasure, the adrenaline rush that lifting the torch seemed to give them. Topeka, Kansas, provided this example.

television states, that the runners found themselves most touched by the efforts of the citizenry to get involved. The crowds of a thousand in a town of 500. The little communities that lined their sidewalks with scores of candles, their own glowing echoes of the traveling torch. The lone bugler who serenaded the runner one day at dusk.

"Hold it high, laddie," one man told the torchbearer. Later, another man ran alongside the flame, holding a baby up to see and be seen. The infant clutched a slim wad of aluminum foil crumpled in the shape of a torch.

Police escorts discovered that one boy riding his bike behind the caravan was actually fifteen miles from home,

having decided to go to California too. Some threw roses, offered cold beers, or sprinted up to touch someone, anyone, connected with the torch. "They are making heroes," marveled Dick Boehner, "out of everyday people."

The spirit generated by the torch even got to supposedly hardened newspaper reporters. It got to *everybody*. A feeling had been created that was magic to the eye. A feeling? Yes, there are sights the mind may sense but the eye itself cannot see.

To begin with, the runners were attractive as people, part of the Body Proud generation. Yet they shined a

light on our nine-to-five lives for the simple reason that we could identify with them as men and women who worked for a living, at normal jobs. They were our neighbors. They were us.

In *The New York Times*, writer Andrew Malcolm marveled at the crowds "gathered in this front yard or at that rural intersection to watch the wordless roadside exchange of the flame. . . ." One of the runners, Don Sherrod, assured him: "If you ever need a cure for cynicism, all you need is to be here with us for a week."

Chris Talbott, an AT&T media-

MOUNT STERLING, MO

Sharon Miller and 71-year-old Oscar Hagemeyer lived on adjoining farms for eight years but had never met each another. Then they both drove to the windy corner of Highways 50 and K to see the Olympic Torch caravan. And they both shed a tear at the sight. "You see what the torch did?" said Mrs. Miller. "It brought us together."

Michael Pauls ran the torch through the streets of Jefferson City, Missouri, up the steps of the Capitol, and passed the flame to Governor Christopher Bond, in front of the statue of Thomas Jefferson.

relations manager, had another point to make: "Some of the media reported the relay in terms of a 'renewal of patriotism.' People believing in the country again. But it was something more than that. It was a reaffirmation of faith in human nature. I hate to say it in these terms, but it was a transcendental kind of thing that rose above our normal awareness and consciousness. We find it hard to explain such things in words."

In Kansas City, a self-described cynical newsman described the scene: "The applause rolled like a slow wave along the street. The flatbed went by. Finally the torchbearer could be seen. Two other runners steadied him at the sides. His face streamed perspiration as, by repeated acts of will, the disabled young man put one foot ahead of the next in a shuffling run—his eyes fixed on the course ahead and the distance yet to go.

" 'C'mon, Brian,' the people on the flatbed called down encouragement.

All around him, as he passed, the cheering swelled. 'That's for you,' one of the runners at his elbow was heard to cry. 'Listen to it. That's for you!'

"And, sure, it was just another American spectacle. But where, in such a sudden moment, did all my cynicism go?"

Running through Kansas, a cadre runner learned that a boy sitting in the window of a roadside house had cancer. The runner flustered the security people by veering off the road, through the crowd, and onto the sidewalk, so the boy could get a closer look.

When the torch reached Oklahoma, the symbolism was carried to a peak on the steps of the Capitol. Michelle Dickinson, 16, of Blanchard, who won her kilometer in a supermarket drawing, delivered the torch to Governor

■ 134 ■

Running and sometimes shuffling, by repeated acts of will, Special Olympians finished their race, eyes fixed on the course ahead and the distance yet to go.

Ansel Stubbs, 99, the oldest of the nation's 4,000 sponsored runners, helped carry the torch through Kansas. Before he ran in the Torch Relay, his proudest achievement was a book he wrote about mushrooms, when he was 90. He passed the flame to Katie Johnston, 4, the youngest of the relay's torchbearers.

Some of the runners, such as this one in Kansas City, made attractive stand-ins for Miss Liberty.

George Nigh, who was standing with Richard Thorpe, one of the sons of Olympic immortal and Oklahoma native Jim Thorpe. The crowd closed in around them as Michelle lit the torch held by Ken Hardwick, who had to walk 200 yards to get clear enough of the masses to begin his run.

"When you think of the Olympics," the governor said, "and you think of Oklahoma, then you naturally think of Jim Thorpe. We use his name again and again to tell young Oklahomans, 'you can do it.' "

If it is possible to analyze the character of a crowd, you would have to say that the kind the torch attracted differed sharply from the typical sports crowd.

There was little of any rowdiness (at least, none until they reached California); no scary release of pent-up energy, no turning over of police cars and setting them on fire in an expression of joy. What you saw was an exercise in good manners and small kindnesses. When Olympic committee staffer Bill Schulz left behind his work folder at a market in Pauls Valley, the manager drove sixty miles to catch up with the caravan and returned the folder.

The torch had entered Oklahoma at 1 P.M. on a Sunday and moved south to Tulsa on famed U.S. Route 66. For not the first time, they ran into muggy weather that resulted in some mild cases of heat exhaustion. But they kept the pace. Each runner was expected to cover four miles, twice a day for a week. They had to average a mile in seven minutes to meet the schedule that would bring the torch on time to Los Angeles.

At Chandler, a farmer named M. A. Ozment aimed his camera at the highway and said, "This is Main Street, America. We get all sorts of things that go by here. We once saw a dude on stilts, advertising something. It's because of what this road is—it's history."

From Chandler to Edmond and on to Oklahoma City, motorists pulled over in their cars, farmers stopped by their tractors, groups gathered at intersections, outside country stores, in their front yards.

In Tulsa, tens of thousands took part in a square dance to celebrate the

*At sunset in Dallas, Texas, the torch exchange featured two former Olympic gold med-
alists: Rafer Johnson (LEFT), won the 1960 decathlon. Sprinter Bob Hayes took two golds
in 1964 and later starred for Cowboys. They flank an AT&T cadre runner.*

passage of the torch. In Sapulpa, scores of Little League baseball players in uniform waved flags. In Paoli, a line of giggling girls held up a row of placards that spelled out: MOM. APPLE PIE. CHEVROLET. USA. Reflecting the unselfish spirit of the sponsors, Buick didn't sue anybody over the reference to a competitor.

The runners no longer recall which town they had gone through or the name of a certain motel, but they won't soon forget what they saw there. As the relay drew nearer, guests swimming and sunbathing at the pool crowded against a chain-link fence to smile and wave. When the runners smiled back, three pretty young things dropped the tops of their swimsuits. It was as if they wanted to

do something for the team, and a smile and a wave were just not enough. This was not one of the scenes that replayed itself over and over.

Dick Boehner brought the torch into Texas as the convoy rolled across the bridge that spanned the Red River and into Whiteboro, a town of 3,100. That was six times larger than Tioga, twenty miles to the south, where nearly half the people turned out. The town's two red fire engines were parked on U.S. 377 as a sign of welcome.

"People in big cities are too busy

It was 9:16 P.M. by the clock when this runner, in fine form, entered Tulsa, Oklahoma; the low beam of the van behind him provided a kind of footlight for him to run in.

sometimes," said Mary Scott, "to care about this. But small towns are different. This is just too special for words." Mary described herself as the town's main daytime fireman (not fireperson).

Nancy Clark, who owns a barbecue restaurant near the town's only traffic light, decided that the Torch Relay coming through Tioga ranked second in importance only to the birth there, in the early 1900s, of the singing cowboy, Gene Autry.

Autry left Tioga as a schoolboy to work for the Frisco railroad line as a telegrapher, in the town of Chelsea. It was into this office one night that Will Rogers appeared to file a newspaper column back to New York. Rogers overheard Autry singing to himself and helped launch an enduring show business career—and a splendid story of how talent gets discovered.

On further reflection, Nancy Clark added that the torch was an even bigger event than when baseball star Mickey Mantle came to Tioga and stopped for some of her barbecue.

At the end of a gravel road north of the town of Pilot Point, Betty Heitzman, camera in hand, stood across the way from her house and waited for the torchbearer to appear shortly before noon. "I'm just trying to get a picture of him with my house in the background," she said. "It amazes me

that in this big ol' U.S.A., they're coming right in front of my home."

In Aubrey, population 900, a housewife named Pat Strange ignored the ninety-degree heat to watch for the torch. "Just standing here by the road is all I can do," she said. "But I want to do it. This is to show we don't need the Russians and those others who pulled out."

Dallas was the scene of a sunset ceremony that revived the weary runners. It featured the passing of the torch from two former Olympic champions: Rafer Johnson and ex-Dallas Cowboy Bob Hayes. The cheers were deafening as Johnson's flame ignited the torch of Hayes, the winner of the

With the Dallas skyline silhouetted against the darkening sky, two runners—in the lyrics of the country-and-western song—"are movin' on down the line." One city official had said: "Dallas residents don't come downtown at night, but we hope people join us. If the Coca-Cola runs out, we know we have a success." Thousands turned out.

The dead end sign definitely seems out of place. While Dallas youngsters wait for action to start, this runner seems tuned in to her Sony Walkman.

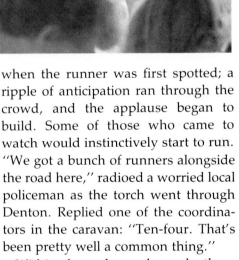

100-meter dash in 1960 at Rome. He trotted out of City Hall Plaza to run his kilometer, heading west toward Grand Prairie. The fans spilled out onto the plaza behind him.

If there was an element of the publicity stunt in much of this, it was the most inspired one since the circus parade. The route was brilliantly plotted, not along dreary interstates, nor just through distracted, urban cities, but through the real heartland of America.

Running through Texas, in the clammy heat of early summer, left Kate Washburn with an unexpected memory. "I will never forget the sound of the cars going over snakes in Texas," she said. "Rattlesnakes. They would come up to the pavement because it was warm at night. The security people actually perfected a technique for getting rid of them. They had tried to shoot them, literally, but they were worried about the ricochets. So they ended up driving over them and backing up, and it would make a pop, pop, pop sound. The first time it happened, I said, 'What was that?' and somebody said, 'We just ran over a snake.' And I said, 'Don't give me this!' "

The noise was like popping the air pockets on the plastic insulation you find in boxes. It was a sound not quite as consistent as the ones Kate swore she heard in her sleep: "The sound of 'U.S.A.! U.S.A.!' constantly and the sirens going off for six or seven straight hours. You get all that during your run and you still hear it while you sleep. The chant and the sirens."

There was always a special moment when the runner was first spotted; a ripple of anticipation ran through the crowd, and the applause began to build. Some of those who came to watch would instinctively start to run. "We got a bunch of runners alongside the road here," radioed a worried local policeman as the torch went through Denton. Replied one of the coordinators in the caravan: "Ten-four. That's been pretty well a common thing."

Within the cadre each week, there were new and different accounts of sacrifice and grit. Jeannie Dixon, of Theodore, Alabama, had trained since January with a replica of the torch designed by her husband and welded by a friend. She had filled the hollow interior with dirt to approximate the five-pound heft of the torch she would later carry from the plains of Texas to

This is what many Americans saw: a solitary runner, a security van trailing behind, running on an open road through the flat and endless Texas prairie, running across America. But this was the essence of the Torch Relay: "Promises to keep, miles to go before we sleep."

the mountains of Colorado.

Dixon, 34, became a serious runner in the 1960s, after the birth of her second child. The idea was to shed weight, but she found herself hooked. In 1983, she competed on AT&T's running team, which won the National Corporate Cup in Palo Alto, California.

Ray Tinnin, a 54-year-old resident of Houston, flew into Fort Worth to run his kilometer, aided by a walking stick. Tinnin had suffered leg injuries and lost an eye in an auto accident eleven months earlier.

At least one young Texan earned his kilometer by producing, literally, a work of art. David Neal, 17, entered a project in a contest sponsored by his father's employer, the Sun Exploration Company. With an idea he remembered from a third-grade crafts project, he collected about a hundred old nuts, bolts, and screws and fashioned them into a twelve-inch sculpture of an Olympic torchbearer. He was one of the two contest winners—Lance Cowart was the other—chosen to represent the company as YLK runners.

In Arlington, hundreds of residents poured into the middle of Abram Street to welcome a hometown favorite, 20-year-old Kevin Procaccino, a cancer survivor, who brought the torch up the steps of the City Hall.

It must have seemed to those on the relay that it took forever to get out of Texas. Boehner was puzzled by the fact that they would pass by miles of nothing but sagebrush and an occasional steer, and then at intervals of fifty miles a small town would rise out of the prairie. Finally a native explained it to him. When Texas was a republic, the laws required that one county seat be located not more than one day's ride on horseback from the next. Fifty miles. In some vague way, this was probably seen as a long-term solution to the traffic problem.

ROCKY MOUNTAIN HIGH

And suddenly the scene changes; majestic snowcapped mountains rise in the distance, and the runner struggles on, lonelier than ever.

The AT&T runners knew, when they reached New Mexico, that they had completed twenty-five states but still had as many miles ahead of them as they had covered. Looming just ahead was a stretch that, in their idiom, would be known as "gut-check time."

Colorado. The Rocky Mountains. Altitudes a mile high and inclines so steep it was like running up a wall.

And so the modern-day wagon train of mobile homes crossed the tracks into New Mexico on the sixteenth day of June. Patty Byrd was the cadre runner bearing the torch, and she was greeted with the cheering words, "Welcome to New Mexico . . . you've made it halfway."

New Mexico was the land of the painted desert. Again the runners were struck by the diversity of the landscape and the sound of the many voices of America. G. Lyle Sparks is 62, and he was suffering from laryngitis because "I talked and talked about this for a solid week." He missed his thirty-seventh wedding anniversary because he wanted to carry the torch, and so he left his home in Peoria, Illinois, and helped carry the flame across New Mexico.

In Clovis the spectators sat on the hoods of their cars or in lawn chairs. They squatted by the side of a state highway and leaned against fenceposts. In the sky above Clovis a small airplane, the kind used for crop dusting, circled the caravan, trailing a banner that read, CLOVIS GREETS THE OLYMPIC TORCH.

Under a solitary sky the runners held the torch aloft, past blooming yucca trees and cholla plants, sometimes with only an occasional cow or sheep for an audience. They ran through rain, heat, and cold. They ran past the remains of skunks killed by cars and snakes still very much alive. Mostly, they just ran.

In Albuquerque, people lined both sides of the main street, thousands of them, from construction workers to Indian dancers. Here Jay Mason, a 34-year-old lawyer from Dallas, was part of the relay team. For him the event was a chance to fill in a blank from the past. As a University of Kansas track-

In Clovis, New Mexico, every eye seemed riveted on the runner and the flame that almost teased his hair. People had squatted alongside Highway 60, leaned against fence posts, sat on the hoods of cars, or settled deeper into their lawn chairs. All of Clovis met the torch.

man, Mason had failed in a bid to make the Olympics in 1972.

Among the spectators that day was Steve Shoup, 23, who lived in Albuquerque and had taken part in the Torch Relay for the 1980 Winter Games, from Virginia to Lake Placid. Shoup kept the torch he carried four years ago and held it in a salute as the 1984 procession passed by.

Stephen Drogin, of San Diego, carried the flame to the end of the historic Santa Fe Trail. As the crowd applauded and cheered he touched the tip of his torch to one carried by 74-year-old Bess James, the last of four YLK runners that day. Mrs. James, who said she started running at the age of 69, returned the flame to the cadre.

The torch passed through Tres Piedras, the only village in a stretch of nearly sixty miles between Ojo Caliente and the Colorado line.

A cadre runner named Frank Jones was startled when a police-escorted Lincoln Continental pulled up beside him and Governor Toney Anaya jumped out. With his three-piece suit flapping in the breeze, Anaya ran more than a quarter mile with the caravan before getting back into his car and leaving.

The running boom in America had kicked into high gear by the 1980s. We had been bombarded with books and theories about the mystique of running, the discovery of the inner self. There was an ongoing debate about the cardiovascular benefits of running and jogging, as opposed to the risks. In a troubling irony, James Fixx, the

Besse James, 75, walks the torch through the streets of Santa Fe while the largest peacetime crowd in the city's history watched the procession. Mrs. James, who took up running at 69, was the last of a relay of four YLK runners.

author of *The Complete Book of Running*, died of a heart attack while jogging. So had a congressman, Goodlow Byron, and a popular CBS sportscaster, Frank Glieber, along with a growing list of persons less visible. The wry and portly coach of the Utah Jazz basketball team, Frank Layden, said what many non-runners felt when he explained why he didn't jog: "I want to be sick when I die."

But the AT&T cadre runners were advertisements in motion for the health-promoting side of the argument. Men and women, old and young, from different backgrounds and different corners of the country, they may have had just one thing in common. None were overweight. Whatever else this form of exercise does, the evidence is clear that it leads to introspection. Perhaps it has something to do with the constant slap of the soles of one's shoes against the ground, jarring loose random thoughts.

Robin Paine, whose home is in San Diego, joined the relay in Texas and helped carry the torch across New Mexico and Colorado, through the high plains and mountains. Later she said, "I'm going to be showing that torch all over town, you better believe it. It's kinda like, if you've ever run a marathon, you've shared something with everybody that ran in it. Well, we've shared something with everybody in this country. . . . The love is out there and it's just great. Just gives me goose bumps.

"We women don't have that upper body strength—and they're not making it any lighter for us. We carried the

A security man runs alongside and sprays water on an exhausted Robin Paine battling the midday New Mexico heat. The torch seems to grow heavier with every stride, and by the end of her run, she grips it near the neck.

same weight as the men, so that's a real challenge. I'm glad to say that we all met the challenge. We conquered the torch."

Paine, 34, an employee of Pacific Bell, had trained with a torch that weighed two pounds and four ounces. When she joined the relay team, she discovered they were using one— with the new flame enhancer—that raised the weight closer to five pounds. "In Clovis," she said, "it was so heavy I had to cradle it. Later in the week, when I went through a small town and had gotten used to it, I held the torch high over my head to do penance for Clovis. By the end of the

week we were all holding the torch high."

At one point she ran up a steep mountain road at night, with wind gusts up to fifty miles an hour driving the rain into her face and lightning bolts darting across the sky. "That storm didn't stop the people from coming out to stand by the road and watch," she said. "I probably was not as patriotic as the people that we saw along the way. I mean, they had driven hundreds of miles to come and see us. Being from a big city, I don't understand it completely. I live in a rush, rush world. I don't know that I would have been able to say, 'I'm

going out a hundred miles away to watch the torch today.' But you can believe that I'd do it now. I'm going to be cheering them on when they come through San Diego. All of them, the cooks, everybody. The people that dropped us off, they really took care of us. They protected us, watched out for us, made sure we had juice and that we were eating right. I'm going to be so spoiled when I get home, they won't know how to live with me."

Robin thought the Torch Relay was about sharing. It was less personal than running a marathon and less

A triumphant Albuquerque man has his arms full, the torch held high in one hand, a baby in the other. Thousands of New Mexicans, from hard hats to Indian dancers, lined both sides of the city's main street—once a part of Route 66.

Veterans of Foreign Wars Post 3280 turn out in force in Clovis, New Mexico, as a glowing runner adjusts her two-handed grip and prepares to start her run from the Sears parking lot. Some who came to watch would spontaneously start to run too.

sheltered than actually competing in the Olympic Games. "This could be very personal," she said, "in the sense that you get up every day and you say, 'I'm going to do it. I'm going to be running proud. The people who are cheering you on are sharing your feelings with you. And the pain. I mean, I'm sure I had some pretty painful expressions on my face going up those hills, and the people could see, and they just cheered me all the way, with 'Stay with it, honey.' It was great. They weren't criticizing anybody for going slow or holding the torch down low or because they looked tired. They were just with us all the way."

For Linda and David Thurston the relay became a family affair. They were textbook cases, tennis players until a tennis elbow forced David to give up the game. They took up jogging and, by 1979, were distance running.

Linda won the second marathon she ever ran. In 1982, she finished the New York Marathon in 2:56, then the eleventh fastest marathon ever run by an American woman. She had been running just three years.

David did not resent and, in fact, was quick to acknowledge that Linda was the better runner. The first time they ran in New York, she left him behind on First Avenue. "I'm not the first guy," he told friends, "to get left by a woman on First Avenue."

Linda, 37, had returned to school to pursue a master's degree in exercise physiology. She interned under Kate Washburn at the AT&T Communications fitness center and replaced her as

Many of the runners caught the eye: their faces had the same complex light. What was it? More than healthy good looks, it was a mix of patriotism, confidence, and some reawakened, inner warmth. Lost in thought, this runner holds her torch tightly.

director when Kate was assigned to the Torch Relay.

But it was David, 38, who made it through the selection process to be chosen as one of the AT&T cadre runners. His turn to run came on Week 7, from Littlefield, Texas, through New Mexico and on to Golden, Colorado. He was taking oxygen in the medical bus one day and noticed that the torchbearer had company. A spectator, caught up in the moment, was running alongside for a few yards.

David thought about Linda, at home in New Jersey, working and taking care of their two little girls. His week was running out. He learned that there was no rule against his wife running part of the way with him on one of his shifts. He hadn't thought to ask.

He wanted Linda to share what he was seeing and feeling. On Thursday he found a pay phone at a Laundromat and called her at work. He told her to drop everything and meet him as soon as she was able, in Colorado.

She couldn't get away until the end of the business day. Her mother agreed to look after the girls. She caught a 5 P.M. flight Friday out of Newark, connecting in Denver with a commuter flight to Colorado Springs. Most of the caravan soon knew about the plan. A Buick rep volunteered to meet Linda at the airport while David was running his last four miles that day.

The flight left Newark two hours

late, and Linda missed her connection in Denver. David had finished his run when the lady from Buick rejoined the caravan—without Linda. He had no idea what had happened, and there was no way for either of them to contact the other. He persuaded the lady from Buick to take him back to the airport in case she had caught a later flight.

In Denver, Linda stationed herself in front of a ticket agent and stood by for every shuttle flight to Colorado Springs. The next two were full. The planes held only sixteen passengers.

New Mexicans called the torch the faralito. *The mixed cultures of Albuquerque are much in evidence as the elated runner brandishes his torch; the shops offer Indian jewelry and desert treasures.*

When the last flight of the night was called, she watched them board and counted . . . eleven, twelve, thirteen, fourteen. There was no one left in line. She grabbed her bag and raced through the jetway, the fifteenth person on the plane.

Meanwhile, in Colorado Springs, the Buick lady was growing uneasy about being away from the convoy so long. David pleaded with her to stay. It was nearing midnight. There was only one more flight.

As the passengers emerged from the last shuttle, David scanned each face, his hopes sinking. Then, at the same instant, his eyes met Linda's. They ran toward each other with tears streaming down their cheeks. The Buick lady must have felt like a *yentl* (in Yiddish, a person who arranges marriages).

Back at the caravan, room was made for Linda in one of the buses housing the women runners. She felt like a stowaway that night. The next morning, in a sweatsuit borrowed from David and worn over her clothes, she went to the dropoff point with her husband for his final run. Beaming, David turned to Linda and said, "Now I'll show you how to work the crowd." He walked over to the people lining the streets and began to chat and sign autographs. A few minutes later he turned around to say something to Linda and discovered she was gone. When he found her again, she was being interviewed by a television crew.

David Thurston's experiences ranged from the miniature to the nearly metaphysical. Dropped off on a lonely stretch of road, he glanced around and saw a post office, a general store, and a few houses. A young woman stood a few feet away, cradling a baby. He asked her where he was.

"You're in Yeso, New Mexico," she

The onlookers would be legion . . .   *Or just a mother and child.*

said. He asked her what the population was. "Five," she said.

Thurston could not conceal his amazement. "Five," he repeated. "Well, I can see two," he commented after a moment.

"My husband is at a neighbor's house," she offered, "helping him repair his fence."

"How far is your neighbor's house?"

"Oh, about a hundred miles down the road," she said.

Just then the woman's mother and mother-in-law appeared on their way to visit the family matriarch, Great-Grandma Mae, 86, in frail health, and living in a house over yonder. Thurston could not resist going with them. When the group entered the house,

the old woman got an eyeful of David in his white togs and drew the logical conclusion that the angel of death had come to fetch her. One of the women helped Grandma Mae put on her hearing aid, and as best they could, they explained what this intruder was doing in Yeso. Half an hour later, with the aid of a walker, she went outside and watched as David Thurston's torch was lighted. He carried the torch past her yard and through the town of Yeso, New Mexico.

In another New Mexico town, David finished his run in torrents of rain, sending the townsfolk into even greater spasms of joy. It had not rained in the area since October, nine months earlier. The more superstitious among them thought the torch

somehow had brought an end to the drought.

Unknown to Linda and David, a friend in Denver had borrowed a video camera and taped them as they ran up a hill, narrating it as they ran. He presented them with the tape as a keepsake. Not that anything would be required to stir their memories. "It might be the only thing that I will be remembered for," said David. "Maybe my descendants will say, 'Great-Granddad Thurston ran in the 1984 Olympic Torch Relay.'"

It was in New Mexico that Kate Washburn's leg gave out, and she had to resort to a bicycle to keep up with the action. One day, when the tem-

ANTONITO, CO

As the relay neared Antonito, a city about 10 miles north of the New Mexico border, an engineer in a waiting Cumbres & Toltec Railroad locomotive blew the whistle of welcome. Townspeople, some weeping with joy, cheered and applauded from sidewalks and store windows.

Few objects speak so eloquently of time and distance as a rural mailbox, resting on a frame in front of a plowed field. There were days when the hours were long and the weather unkind, and it might have been tempting to mail the torch in.

perature on the pavement was 120 degrees, a runner named Jim Smiley remembers Kate riding up to him on her bike and squirting his face with water, just as he thought he might collapse.

Smiley was the Rocky Mountain coordinator for the relay. After the simulation runs, the managers were aware that they might have problems with the torch staying lit in the higher altitudes. They shipped a torch to Jim and asked him to go to the highest point in Colorado and give it a test. Jim piled his wife and children into the family car and took off for Loveland,

which has an elevation of 12,000 feet. It was winter and the snow on the ground was deep and consistent.

The skiers were out in force when Jim Smiley got out of his car and lit the torch. It caught but wouldn't stay lit. Meanwhile, the sight of a man in the dead of winter lighting a torch on a mountaintop attracted a crowd. It was after this test that an extra burner and a richer fuel was added to the torch, to keep it burning in the thinner air.

As the torch crossed into Colorado, truckers sounded their horns, and an

impromptu caravan of about twenty cars joined the procession. Five miles north of the border, in the town of Antonito, a railroad engineer blew his locomotive whistle in welcome.

The route took the flame and its entourage along U.S. Highway 40, west of Golden, through Idaho Springs, Empire, and over Berthoud Pass, which lies on the Continental Divide and rises to a peak at 11,314 feet. The thin air made breathing difficult. Trying to reach the top of the pass was almost more than Tom Quinn bar-

Walt Whitman once wrote, "Afoot and light-hearted, I take to the open road. Healthy, free, the world before me."

gained for. Minutes into his run, Quinn thought about quitting. But one sight spurred him on, a third of the way up the mountain. "I don't know how she got there," he said, "but I passed an elderly lady with tears streaming out of her eyes as she waved her flag. I just took off after that. The adrenaline was flowing. You got your strength from the people."

As the runners came through Golden on a Sunday morning, hundreds of onlookers lined the streets, and about forty people held a dawn cookout in a tent on Lookout Mountain as they kept their vigil for the flame. The going was hard. The

cadre runners never cut their mileage to accommodate themselves to the rugged, if scenic, terrain. They normally ran in four-mile relays, but on that Sunday they ran two miles at a stretch.

As the torch neared Colorado Springs there was a growing apprehension among the relay managers, a feeling that the spell of national support might be broken in, of all places, the city that housed the permanent U.S. Olympic Training Center.

In places like Manitou Springs the atmosphere had been electric. So many people, so much excitement, some surprising themselves by reacting so openly to the symbolism of the torch. Then on through Old Colorado

City, the upbeat emotions continued. From there the numbers slowly thinned as they entered Colorado Springs, across the bridge just west of downtown. Through the main part of the central business district, the small knots of spectators were not what the contingent had been accustomed to seeing.

Obviously, though, the Torch Relay crew had been psyched up for Colorado Springs. But where was everybody? Not at the Olympic complex, where about 500 congregated. That left a final stop for the torch to be appreciated in what might be considered its home base. And that was at Berry

The sponsored runners celebrated the completion of their kilometers in a variety of ways. Not every contestant was greeted by a young lady with a Smurf clutching a large torch (and wearing a shirt with a red heart and initials, the meaning of which is unclear).

Stadium, where the day's event had been in progress for an hour, with a musical Olympic salute by the Colorado Springs Symphony. A ham radio report to the convoy indicated that the crowd was good. The adjective turned out to be a little weak.

Nearly fifteen thousand were waiting for the torch, more than the throng that had attended the National Sports Festival's opening ceremonies in 1979.

The most often repeated phrase in the eighty-two days of the relay was the bare sentence, "Here it comes!" The cry was heard again at the city limits of Poncha Springs, where a crowd of 3,000 turned out—more than the listed population of the town. A

few minutes before 10 P.M. the runner appeared, his hair soaking wet and sweat pouring down his back. He was clearly struggling to hold the torch high. The torch may have weighed five pounds, but from the grimace on his face, it might as well have been fifty.

In hundreds of small Colorado towns, like Breeze Mountain, Snake John Reef, Rabbit Ears Pass, and Plug Hat Rock, news of the relay spread by word of mouth. In those parts the torch rekindled a patriotic spark that Americans hadn't felt in decades.

The length of the relay in time and distance, the rotation of the runners, the rigid nature of the schedule, and

the collective effort involved did not lend itself to the star system. But the American instinct demands stars, as Andy Warhol so deftly reflected, when he predicted that each of us would be famous for fifteen minutes.

There were AT&T cadre runners who, by their intensity or grace or openness, drew the interest of the reporters and the eye of the cameras. One was Mary Verdugo, who became a kind of heroine of the Colorado run.

The lilt in her voice and her fine, high cheekbones indicated her Spanish and Indian heritage. She was 37 at the time of the relay and looked younger. People were stunned to discover that Mary was a grandmother.

Her week was spent running from

If there had been a contest for the largest American flag along the route, this one at Golden, Colorado, would surely have been a contender. When the torch left Golden, hundreds of onlookers jammed the streets, and about forty people held a dawn cookout in a tent on Lookout Mountain.

Golden to Mountain Home, Idaho, and there was no question which memory was her most lasting. "In Colorado," she said, "I ran with a young man by the name of Joey. He had been afflicted with cerebral palsy, and I accompanied him while he was pushed in his wheelchair for his kilometer. A friend of his pushed, and I ran alongside. To see the excitement in Joey's face was just unbelievable. My adrenaline was flowing. My emotions were so high. I cried. I laughed. I cried again. And the crowds were beautiful. They were chanting, 'Go Joey. We love you.' And he was giving everybody the high sign, and they were all saying, 'Yeah, Joey.' And I would touch him and I'd say, 'Joey, this is for you. I mean, these people are here to see you.' "

Her voice caught and her eyes glistened. "As you can see," she said, "it's still with me."

It is still with everybody, those who ran and those who watched. It stirred them in a way you would not have imagined, this advancing of a flame from hand to hand, from day to day, across a continent. It was a curious, quintessentially American drama, and even the audience went to curious lengths to be there.

A woman named Mary Peacock, wearing a gaucho hat and a jacket with leather fringes, said she and her husband had a "small mishap" when they drove to a point where they thought they would see the torch. "The caravan took a different route out of Golden than was expected," she said. "And we were there at seven-thirty in the morning to see

The caravan followed U.S. 40 west of Golden and over the 11,000-foot Berthoud Pass, which lies on the Continental Divide. Lou Putnam doesn't seem to mind that the run is uphill. He smiles broadly to spectators along the mountainside as the convoy fans out behind him.

them, so we waited two hours before anyone told us they went another way. So we went back home, pulled down the windows in case of a shower, packed a picnic lunch, and took off again. For one hundred miles or so, we've been chasing them, but we got here and we saw it, and no one will ever take that away."

Somewhere in Colorado the runners realized that they had been followed by a woman on a bicycle through town after town. She turned out to be a third-grade school teacher named Anne Brown. She started out following the torch in a car festooned with flags. Then she removed a bicycle she kept in the trunk and began to pedal along behind them. She stayed with them through the state of Washington, sometimes riding more than 100 miles a day. Either a friend would follow in her car, or she would hitch a ride back to wherever she had parked

it. The cadre runners nicknamed her "Bicycle Annie," and it was clearly a term of endearment.

The power of the torch was found not so much in the spectacle that surrounded it. It was more to be seen as a collection of individuals whose lives were touched, even changed, by the passing of the flame.

There was Stacey Luft, who kept seeing the same two faces wherever she ran. They were her parents, Mr.

For eighty-two consecutive mornings the flame was lit from the miners' lamps by touching a sparkler to the propane-filled, four-and-a-half-pound torch.

and Mrs. Leon Mark, who kept leap-frogging ahead of the relay just to see their daughter go by. Said Mrs. Mark, "We always participated in everything she's done, ever since she was a little girl, and it's fun to be allowed to share this, and fun for us that she wanted to share it.

"Our son was a graduate of the Air Force Academy. He was killed six years ago in Germany in an F-15 accident. We aren't maudlin about it, he isn't an obsession with us, but we all still love him very much, and if you noticed, Stacey is wearing a little silver falcon on the waistband of her run-

ning shorts. That is in memory of Mike. He kind of runs along on her shoulder, keeps her going, keeps her from getting tired."

There may be no sadness harder to bear than that of a mother who has lost a son in the military. But here was Mrs. Mark, and her daughter, Stacey Luft, and with dignity and a gentle touch, they gave more meaning to the living flame.

By now you would have thought the runners were in danger of getting jaded. There are just so many wonder-

fully cornball scenes a mind can absorb, this side of a Norman Rockwell museum. But just when the runners thought they had enjoyed all the reaching out a normal person can handle, here came something else.

In the town of Craig, Colorado, Jim Smiley finished his last leg around 7:30 P.M., to be greeted by what appeared to be the entire population of 10,750. In a scene that has been repeated countless times across small-town America, people are grouped in families, several generations together, infants on Grandpa's shoulder, lining the streets three deep in front of the Westward Ho Motel, the Moffat County State Bank, and the Centennial Mall. As torchbearer Duffy Swan, 39, a native of Denver, nears the main

people. And, perhaps, to all who were so moved by it, it stood for all that is positive.

intersection, a tight formation of jets from the Colorado Air National Guard screams overhead.

Larry Schultz, 39, another Coloradan running behind Swan, said, "To have those jets buzzing us blows me away. It made my heart swell up so I couldn't swallow."

At roughly the same time, hot-air balloons were released, and the members of a skydiving club parachuted to a point near the caravan. From that point on, the group of cadre runners who came through Craig were known as "The Fly Boys."

Swan saw the experience as part of "a bonding the torch seems to create in people. Everyone seems to feel of a common mind, a common spirit." The response was just as gratifying to Jim

Suennen, one of the trip directors, who grappled with the daily logistical headaches. "This cuts through all the ideology and all the cynicism that politics so often evokes," he said. "This is something everyone can feel proud about without having to defend anything."

The message in the outpouring of emotion seemed both simple and profound: Americans feel good about America.

At Muddy Pass, 83-year-old Pete Lepponen showed what a little impro-

Carrying the flag, wearing a Peaceful Valley t-shirt and ever alert, a young Boy Scout follows his scout leader across the road, seeking a better vantage point from which to observe the passing of the flame.

visation could do. "We were short of flags," he said, "so I brought my red-white-and-blue long underwear." As the runner passed, Lepponen frantically flapped his underwear.

The torch moved through mean city streets, across sagebrush-covered flats, over snow-streaked mountain passes. Yet no matter how desolate the area, there was nearly always a smattering of people every few hundred yards to take snapshots, wave a miniature flag, or sing out their pep rally chants.

At Steamboat Springs, one of the playgrounds for winter sports, thou-

Colorado's majestic Mount Princeton over-looks Kevin Leonard as he carries a torch designed to burn at high altitudes. Even the runners had difficulty with the thinness of the mountain air, which forced them to shorten their runs.

The relay heads toward the Utah state capital in Salt Lake City. The original route had the relay passing through all fifty state capitals.

sands of people braved a cold drizzle to cheer as Carol Schuller, a 19-year-old California girl, carried the flame into town, running on an artificial leg.

The sight brought a puddle to the eyes of Fred Rausch, a hardened 60-year-old veteran of World War II and the Korean War. "For an old soldier this is really something," he said. "It makes you tingle from head to toe, makes you glad to be an American. I'm ready to re-enlist right now."

Short of surviving an amphibious landing, nothing could have relieved the relay members more than leaving the mountains of Colorado behind them.

It was in Utah that Dick Boehner, Colorado-born and the workhorse of the relay, nearly had a bite taken out of his running time. A Salt Lake City

dentist who performed root canal work faster than McDonald's can fry a hamburger was the unlikely hero of one of the relay's more offbeat moments.

Boehner had been living with a dental problem the entire transcontinental run. He broke a molar four days out of New York, ignored it for weeks, until it abscessed as they were making their exit from Colorado. Boehner's jaw was swollen, and the handful of aspirin he kept tossing down no longer provided any relief. AT&T arranged for him to be seen on June 28 by Dr. Jay Soren-

son, at Holy Cross Hospital in Salt Lake City.

Boehner arrived—on the run—at 11:45 A.M. and told the dentist: "You've got to fix this fast because I have to take the torch at one P.M." Dentists usually allow two hours, and up to three visits, for a root canal and reconstruction.

Sorenson gave him an injection of novocaine, did the root canal work, gave him a shot of penicillin, and had him out the door at 12:35 P.M. Boehner ran to the Capitol and was in time to take the torch from Mayor Ted Wilson.

Lee Miller, 36, a burly Vietnam veteran, rode a bicycle to the top of a steep Rocky Mountain pass to watch the torch go by: "This means a lot to me, especially after what I've been through. This is what it stands for. I wanna see this baby!"

The air in Utah was filled with a feeling of wholesomeness. As a choir readies to sing "God Bless America" a young man savors the moment.

The mayor had taken the torch from Danny Searle, a 19-year-old Special Olympian from Payson, Utah. Danny's mother had watched her son practice for a month, jogging around the high school track at home. She said her son suffered from retarded bone growth and had the mental capacity of a 10-year-old.

Mayor Wilson had warmed up the crowd, announcing over a public address system, "When we see him, we want to start a chant that says, 'Go, Danny, Go.' "

When Danny Searle finished his kilometer and ran to the arms of his mother, the mayor observed, softly, "There's more than propane in that torch."

In Salt Lake City, a choir sang "God Bless America" as the torch passed. The mood, the spirit, the unity, all seemed contagious. On a farm road in Utah, Mary Verdugo noticed a group of migrant workers gathered off to one side.

"At first they were maybe a little puzzled," she said, so she walked over and talked to them in Spanish, explaining what was happening, telling them about the Olympic torch and the people carrying it across America. "Their faces lit up," she added. "I just wanted them to know they were as much a part of the relay as I was."

Later, Mary was asked if there was a correct or preferred way to hold the torch. There was nothing self-conscious in her reply: "I hold the torch high because it symbolizes so many things. Freedom, patriotism. You just hold it up there because you're proud. You want everyone that

Five Utah children (ABOVE) wait two hours on the tailgate of a pickup truck to hold up a body-size flag and wave as the torch passes. Kelly McGill (BELOW) stumbles and falls at the beginning of his run in Ogden, Utah. A slight muscle defect makes it difficult for him to run. Nonetheless, he recovers and finishes his run.

comes out to see you to feel as proud as you feel when you're carrying that torch."

□ □ □

If one sometimes had the impression that the route had been drawn through Main Street, U.S.A., the impression was often right on target. In Centerville, Utah, on a glaring hot afternoon, Todd Randall jogged slowly up Main Street, toward home. He called out, "Hi, Dad!" as he went by the gas station his father has owned for thirty-seven years, and kept going, over the same two-lane road he walked along from school as a boy.

But on this day, running down Main Street, 24-year-old Todd Randall carried the Olympic flame. For nine months he had worked two jobs at school and had spent his weekends home from college going door to door to raise the $3,000 he needed to buy his kilometer. The local steel company chipped in $500; his sister-in-law chipped in $100 in baby-sitting money; a stranger named Carol Smedley rounded up donations and pressed a plastic sandwich bag, filled with $60 in

Most of the relay was on the wide-open road where the runners were kept company by the personality of the country's landscape—and, occasionally, a herd of cows.

quarters and dimes, into his hand.

As the neighborhood kids pedaled their bikes across shady front lawns, straining to keep up, he trotted steadily on, between the thronged sidewalks of cheering and whistling neighbors and friends. Now, in the town his ancestors had helped to found, the onetime Eagle Scout was a hero. A few days before he had asked his mother if she thought anyone would be there. Nearly the whole town was. And when it was over, said Todd Randall, "I had to be by myself.

So I walked over and sat down under a tree and cried."

And westward the torch moved, into Idaho, where just across the border thunder and lightning stopped the relay. Crowds waited in the storm, huddled in their cars or in doorways or under umbrellas that threatened to blow away. Even lined up on the side of the road, doing nothing, the convoy was an impressive sight. "A lot of people," noted Steve Cross, "when they think about the Torch Relay, think, it was just a runner and a Winnebago."

The magic of the relay was not only that it marked America's Olympics—and, for a time, America's flame—but that in town after town it provided five minutes that would last a lifetime. In Mesa, Washington, population 260, Gene Russell, a local grocery owner, said the townspeople were inspired to repaint the post office, remove weeds and sagebrush, and spruce up the area. "Someday," said Russell, pointing to the repaved parking lot, "We'll say, 'That's where we had the dance when the torch came in.'"

CALIFORNIA, HERE WE COME

Steve Cross (CENTER, RIGHT), *a relay spokesman, came from behind the scenes to run a kilometer in Wenatchee, Washington, on an old-fashioned fourth of July.*

In California the stars came out, as expected. Movie and television stars. Sports stars. Political stars. People who were famous for knowing people who were famous. But some of the lasting impressions of this grand trail drive occurred on the last lap heading west.

The trail the runners blazed, almost literally, led them on the Fourth of July into rural eastern Washington. People waited for them in the small towns and at the crossroads, amid the amber hills and the smell of fertile farmland.

There was one emotional spin after another. They did the next best thing to parting the waters of Moses Lake. They parted the population, as the Olympic flame came through the streets of a cheering, flag-waving throng. A brass band on a flatbed truck struck up the "Bugler's Dream," a theme ABC made famous.

To appreciate the eagerness of the people to bask in the glow of the flame, it helps to get a sense of the isolation of Moses Lake. The town is 179 miles from Seattle, 107 miles from Spokane, and 25 miles from Soap Lake.

Moses Lake has two new traffic lights and the second longest airport runway in the U.S. (after Edwards Air Force Base in California). The runway is part of an old, now inactive base for the Strategic Air Command. The runway is so long that it serves as a backup landing site for the space shuttle, and also as an alternate strip in the event the supersonic Concorde has to make an emergency landing. Until that happens, the arrival of the Olympic Torch is the biggest thing ever to hit town.

Given the purity of the air and the vastness of the skies, it is no trick to see the snow-capped summit of Mount Rainier, 175 miles away. The only trick is getting there. But the torch did, and 62-year-old Ken Hen-

In the high desert country of the Pacific Northwest, the runners went in one day from 400 feet above sea level to 4,000. From Moses Lake, Washington, you could see the summit of Mount Rainier.

drix, a retired telephone installer, ran with it. Then he embraced his joyful 82-year-old mother. It was Hendrix who produced one of the more poetic lines of the entire journey: "If you figure the torch is a needle and the runners are a thread, the run is something to sew up the country."

In Ephrata, Wayne Collett, a silver medalist in the 400-meter dash in the 1972 Olympics, flew in from Los Angeles to run through the town. He brought his three children with him and said, "Small towns and kids are what it's all about."

A couple from New Mexico, Ralph and Mary Smith, may have set the record for waiting on the torch. They parked their camper near the railroad tracks, a block from downtown Ephrata, and waited three days to see the caravan pass by.

In Wenatchee, Steve Cross, after helping plan publicity for the relay for the previous six months, finally had a chance to carry the torch. He ran it into Wenatchee's Apple Bowl before a roaring crowd of 20,000. As he reached the top of a platform and passed the flame to the next runner, a ground display of fireworks lit the sky. It featured a red torch spitting white fire, bordered by an American flag and the Olympic rings.

Cross, a bearded and unfailingly good-humored fellow, savored the moment. "I knew those people weren't cheering Steve Cross," he said. "They were cheering the torch runner. I've seen this thing twenty times and I still get emotional. I don't think New Yorkers are necessarily cynical"—Steve is

In Ephrata and Moses Lake the crowds found the shade to wait for the torch and wave the flag. The word would spread for miles down the road.

from Staten Island—"but the Olympic relay is just another parade for them. In small towns this is an international event."

From that star-spangled peak, four days later, the mood changed briefly but sharply. Word had arrived ahead of them, in Eugene, Oregon, that a bizarre attempt would be made to put out the flame—by a woman dressed in a clown suit. There was a moment of confusion when the woman did appear, clown suit and all, standing on the side of the road, before the security people swooped and hustled her away.

Lou Putnam saw the scene, the gar-

ish costume, the idea of fun perverted, and felt something turn cold inside him. For the first time, he said, he was ready for the Torch Relay to end. At a moment when their spirits should have been soaring, with California almost in their sights, this mean and unsettling scene had cast a cloud over the road. If you can't send in the clowns, who do we ask to be sent in when we are sad, a waiter?

□ □ □

Out of that pall, Putnam and the other, less sensitive runners tried to regain their buoyancy. They may or may not have been cheered by romantic Nevada legends. Twice in four days the torch crossed into the state, first at

the northern tip, into Reno, and over the Virginia Street bridge. From that same bridge, in another time, disaffected wives would toss their wedding rings into the Truckee River, south of the courthouse, after obtaining their speedy divorces.

The torch left Nevada at the southeast shore of Lake Tahoe. Bruce Jenner, the 1976 decathlon champion, carried the torch across the California line for the second and last time, as part of a promotion staged by the Caesar's Tahoe Hotel. Caesar's had purchased fifty kilometers and given away one a day over a seven-week period.

Jenner took the torch from Mike

KLAMATH FALLS, OR

A hometown hero, Ralph Hill, peers upon a crowd gathered for a ceremony honoring both him and the Torch Relay's passage. The sight takes him back to a scene earlier in his life.

"When I came back from the 1932 Olympics," he remembered, "there were about 2,500 people at the train depot. When I looked out at the people today, that's what I thought of first,"

Fifty-two years later, the town still respects its Olympic hero. The silver medalist in the 5,000-meter event in the 1932 Games, in Los Angeles, Hill is presented with one of the torches used to carry the flame.

The caravan reached Bothwell, Washington, at dusk. At wide spots in the scorching roads, entire towns turned out for hours ahead of the torch.

Mecca, the manager of the hotel, and passed it to Tracy Gluck, daughter of Caesar's chairman of the board. Even at 7:30 A.M., an hour when the action in the Nevada casinos is usually at a minimum, the streets were packed with 5,000 people waiting to get a glimpse of the torch.

"It was just wall-to-wall people," said Jenner. "The torch came right down Main Street. They even had the fire trucks out there. The crowd was so thick we couldn't move them back. We ended up doing our kilometer in a

kind of fast walk. A cadre runner lighted the flame and went with me. He just shook his head and said, 'Here I draw Bruce Jenner and it winds up being the slowest kilometer of the run.' "

For Jenner, the moment offered a redemption of sorts. He was coming off a broken leg, suffered two months earlier when he fell off a motorcycle—in his own driveway. Proving that super-athletes are human too.

As his leg mended, Jenner followed the progress of the torch across Amer-

ica. "The Olympic Games have a special place in my heart," he said. "I can remember the first time I saw the torch, the flame, in Munich, Germany. It was sheer excitement. It's nice to be out of sports for some years and then to have an involvement even briefly. There is a lot of magic there. I didn't expect all the yelling and screaming. My family couldn't get through the crowd to see me run . . . or walk."

It was Jenner who wore a running outfit under his suit and acted as an alternate if Rafer Johnson had been unable to climb the Coliseum steps and light the torch. Johnson was bothered by leg problems in the week or two before the opening ceremony.

A runner pauses to admire the mountain scenery before starting his stretch. The sun beat down on them through the thin, clean air; they were alone with the heat of their torches and the dryness of their throats.

Jenner was one of a handful of people who knew that Rafer would be the "mystery" runner selected to perform this timeless ritual. "We practiced together for a few days," recalled Bruce. "We ran the steps together. I kept telling Rafer not to trip. After all, I was the one whose leg had been broken."

Earlier, the torch had crossed the Oregon border carried by 11-year-old Ethan Halpern, who passed it to Betty Bickhart, 49. On either side of the border, Oregon and California state police stopped traffic while the exchange was made. Police lights flashed, and more than two dozen reporters, photographers, and television camera operators waited as young Halpern

jogged up to them at the WELCOME TO CALIFORNIA sign. Minutes before he arrived, a freight train thundered through the rural Northern California crossing, its engineer blowing the horn and waving to onlookers. Overhead a helicopter equipped with pesticide-spraying pipes hovered briefly to observe the scene, then swooped off.

The crowds lined the roadway leading into Tulelake, the site of a detention camp in World War II, where

thousands of American citizens of Japanese descent were interned.

Many in the crowd waved small flags. Some snapped away with their Kodak Instamatics. A 70-year-old woman named Jan Fish had driven 400 miles from Jackson, in Amador County, to be there. In a railcar just off Highway 139, two track inspectors for Southern Pacific waited for the torch, and the Klamath Falls freight, to come through. "How many times in your lifetime," asked one of them, Mark

The torchbearer trots down the circular driveway of the capitol building in Olympia, Washington. Another link in the chain. . . .

Feelings flared with the fuel each time the flame was passed. In Salem, Oregon, the runners clasp hands and raise their torches.

Holst, "are you going to see something like this? This is history."

And still the runners tried to analyze what was happening around them, reaching for words to describe what they had seen and heard and felt. "We feel like a living Statue of Liberty, the torch and I," said Betty Bickhart, whose home is in San Jose. And always there was the interplay between the actors and the audience. "One of the cadre team," she went on, "climbed atop the fire engine to get a better view. Just then a fire alarm sounded. The engine raced off, our Olympian still aboard. It was nice. The firemen put out the fire and then gave us our man back."

Along the road, Bickhart passed the

John O'Neill potato shed, where a burly farmer in jeans solemnly held his Caterpillar hat over his heart.

An answer as good as any was offered by 31-year-old Leonard Marsh, an out-of-work trucker who lived with his parents in one of a row of nine faded green "cabins" aligned behind the equally faded sign proclaiming the establishment to be the Stateline Motel. For once, the Marshes had a ringside seat for something a little more pleasant than the wrecks that they said were the only other excitement that usually came to this intersection. They were out early to watch it all.

Marsh stared down at a pair of well-worn cowboy boots and pondered the

question of why the torch had seemingly turned on the entire country. "I think the people are patriotic," he said, "and they want the United States to win a lot of medals. But more than anything, I think they want to show the whole world we still have things to be proud of like this in our country."

The relay was now in the seventieth day of a journey that had taken it more than 8,000 miles from New York, across the back roads, and into the hearts of America. Steve Cross described the runners and their support team as "exhausted and exhilarated. I don't mind admitting that when we crossed that state line, it was really special. We all sang 'California, Here I Come.' "

Cross had seen the journey brighten

The runners were not prepared for being received as celebrities. Spectators (ABOVE) waited on a roof of a building in Corvallis, Oregon, with a sign of welcome. (BELOW) Two teenagers have a curbside view in Corvallis. Every time a shuttle van dropped off a runner, people seemed to pop up out of the earth.

and become more celebrated as the flame moved closer to its Los Angeles goal. He recalled increasingly warm and energetic receptions, strange but friendly voices giving traffic information over the ham radio. And, most vivid of all, the camaraderie that developed among the volunteers on the road. There was always time to exchange stories over a meal or a cup of coffee, even though the days grew longer and busier in California, where more runners were sponsored than in any other state.

Their verdict was already in: The Olympic relay had served to unite Americans, whose ways are often as different from each other as they are from people in foreign lands. Traveling with a Pioneer from North Caro-

lina, Henry Wesley, Cross was introduced for the first time to a southern delicacy called grits. "They're great," he said. "You can eat 'em with anything."

Of all the towns and crossroads and fly specks on a map that the convoy rolled through, none may have been more suitably named than Hallelujah Junction, an uninhabited patch of sagebrush where Highways 70 and

395 meet, eight miles north of Reno, near the Nevada border. About 200 people waited there to catch a glimpse of the torch.

"Not since World War II," said Harry Usher, the general manager of LAOOC, and Ueberroth's right arm, "has there been such an outpouring of patriotism as we have seen with the torch. I think the mood has followed the flame across the country." Usher

EPHRATA, WA

Vacationers Ralph and Mary Smith may have outdone all others who waited for the torch. Parked near the railroad tracks a block from downtown Ephrata, they sat waiting for the torch that would arrive five hours later. The Albuquerque, NM, couple had been camped there for three days. "We were headed for Spokane, and when we heard about the torch coming through here, we backtracked and have waited here since," Mr. Smith said. "We were thrilled," said Mrs. Smith. "We knew we had to get somewhere where we could see it. Now we'll have a ringside seat."

The cadre runner adjusted his pace to that of the sponsored runner, who savored the moment, responding to the crowds and air horns and honkings in Salem, Oregon.

could only regret, later, that the mood did not follow him to his next job as the commissioner of the ill-starred United States Football League.

And so it went. Nancy Dietz of Menlo Park, who had won the San Francisco and Oakland marathons, carried the flame onto the Golden Gate Bridge. The orange glow of the torch was barely visible in the morning fog. With beach chairs, baby strollers, American flags, and cameras at the ready, San Franciscans swarmed by the thousands onto the city streets to cheer the passing of the fire from Mount Olympus. It was a morning of shameless, elated, patriotic delight.

Wendy Nelder, 43, president of the San Francisco Board of Supervisors, picked up the final leg over the southern end of the span. She was welcomed with a hug and a kiss by Mayor Diane Feinstein as a brass band played "When the Saints Go Marching In."

Standing near City Hall were two visitors from Fresno, Virginia Miller and Rosalind Gray, winding up what had turned out to be a rather colorful vacation. "We found everything in the world here," exclaimed Miller. "The Democrats, a labor march, a gay rights' march, and now the Olympic Torch."

Across the bay, Mayor Lionel Wilson carried the torch to Oakland's City Hall. His honor had taken his Olympic responsibility seriously, even to the point of running through his neighborhood early in the morning brandishing an ax over his head (to condition himself to the weight and distraction of the torch). That unusual posture was one of his warm-up routines, until his wife questioned it.

A different set of emotions took over when the crowds were left behind. It was peaceful and satisfying to run alone, or with a teammate, beside a lake with the mountains in the distance.

"People will see you running around with this ax at six-thirty in the morning," Dorothy Wilson said, "and they might get the wrong impression." He later switched to a hammer, holding it upside down so just the handle cut the early-morning air.

Mayor Wilson was met by a cheering throng, and when he merged his torch with that of Chikako Naka-shima, a runner from Oakland's sister city of Fukloka, Japan, the whoops rose even louder.

Don Barksdale, a member of the gold-medal winning U.S. basketball team in the London Olympics in 1948, acted as master of ceremonies as the

crowd awaited the arrival of the mayor. Nearly fifty former Olympians sat on the reviewing stand, musicians and dancers entertained, and bright-colored balloons were released as the torch appeared.

"The great beauty of this moment," said Dr. George Rhoden, who won the 400-meters gold medal at Helsinki in 1952, "is that irrespective of one's position in life, he or she can say, 'This is history. I have been a part of this great Olympic movement.' "

In the kind of encounter that seemed right out of "We Are the World," Bill Montgomery, a Pioneer from Fremont, was riding on the torch

truck when the crew stopped for supplies at a shopping mall in the Bay area. Quickly they were encircled by shoppers and store clerks, drawn by the uniforms and the markings of the truck.

The Pioneers proudly opened the rear of the truck to display the torches and allow those with cameras to take snapshots. In the crowd, Montgomery singled out a small, neatly dressed black boy, his face somber, shrinking from the excitement. He approached the boy's parents and offered to let their son pose for a picture with the torch.

As they chatted, Montgomery

At Lake Tahoe, Nevada, former Olympian Bruce Jenner posed with a spectator's baby. Jenner had just recovered from a broken leg.

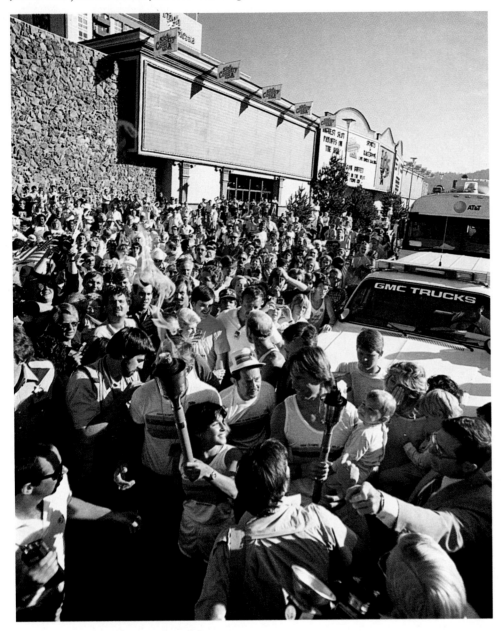

thought he detected a very distinct accent. He asked where the family was from, and the father answered, "Nigeria."

Montgomery had been involved fourteen years earlier with a student exchange program called "Youth for Understanding." He recalled placing a Nigerian student, whom he remembered only as "Henry," with a family in Fremont, where he attended a local college. The boy's father handed him a business card and pointed to the name. "I'm Henry," he said. Tears welled up in the Nigerian's eyes, and

he and Bill Montgomery, who had helped bring him to America, embraced in the parking lot on a sun-dazzled day in California.

A flame had brought them together, halfway around the world.

In North Beach, as the torch passed the world-famous topless nightclub, The Condor, two scantily clad dancers peeked through red velvet curtains and waved. A block away, an iconoclastic observer "mooned" the passing runner.

At Fisherman's Wharf, a character who called himself "The Automatic

Human Jukebox," and who dressed the part, was touched by the torch. Although he does not normally perform for less than a quarter, he was moved to play a free rendition of "When the Saints Go Marching In."

Then there was a Vietnamese immigrant, his small son riding on his shoulders, who dodged photographers and police motorcycles to cheer on a 19-year-old black man pushing an 88-year-old white woman in a wheelchair, holding the torch. The woman was Edna Karatsis, a retired department store salesclerk from San Francisco, and as she rolled through the streets, her thin white hair was flying and her face was a great crinkle of smiles. She was pushed by a jogging Greg Compton, a college student. "It was wonderful," she said, "the big-

Crowds were so thick that Jenner was unable to work up a gallop. Some runners joked that their retinas were "whited-out" from flashbulbs popping.

gest thrill of my life. After eighty-eight years I had to do this for myself."

The money that enabled Mrs. Karatsis to take part in the relay was raised by the forty-two branches of the convalescent hospital where she lived. She was selected by the other residents to represent them. At the end of her kilometer she was handed a bouquet of roses from her friends.

A bearded disc jockey, a 5-year-old girl, and a 26-year-old engineer helped carry the torch to City Hall, where people scrambled up park trees to get a better view.

One spectator described the relay, and its fringe commotion, as "all-American hokum at its best." Only a real live nephew of his Uncle Sam could have put it that way and know that it would be taken as a compliment.

If there was a repetition to many of these scenes all over the U.S.A.—peo-

ple in wheelchairs, the blind, the elderly, the terminally ill—few seemed to regard it as a kind of overkill, or even as exploitation. Time and again different runners, in different weeks, in different parts of the country, described vignettes similar, and sometimes identical, to those others had reported before them.

Certainly no one had imagined that the relay—this powerfully physical demonstration—would attract so many who were handicapped or disadvantaged. It was almost an invitation to a certain kind of nightclub humor. But something else was at work, another dynamic, a celebration of hope. No one planned it that way. It just happened.

On July 24, a little piece of Olympic

nostalgia was reenacted. Two Pioneers, Carol Stalcup and Vern Holbrook, were assigned as marshals to assist the YLK runners whose routes included the Black Mountain Road in San Diego County.

The runners were Horst Rick, his daughter, Erika, and his son, Roland. As each member of the family finished a kilometer, they continued to run alongside the other until all three laps had been completed. Waiting for them at the end of their run was Horst Rick's father, who had been a torchbearer in the 1936 Olympics in Berlin. Herr Rick stood proudly with tears streaming down his cheeks, holding the torch he had carried in 1936 as he watched his son and grandchildren carry the 1984 Olympic flame.

■ 171 ■

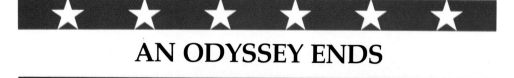

AN ODYSSEY ENDS

All roads, literally, led to the Coliseum in Los Angeles. An injured Rafer Johnson carried the torch to the top of the steps to ignite the final flame.

The torch would spend ten days moving across and around California, north to south, the runner at times silhouetted against the Pacific Coast Highway, the blue waters shimmering in the background.

For many runners the relay meant a second chance, a way to extend or recapture a dream or a piece of one. Charles Jamison first became enamored with the Olympics, when as a runner from a small town in rural Idaho, he qualified for a spot on the 1920 decathlon team but didn't compete. Some sixty-four years later, his dream of taking part in the Games became a reality, as the retired, 79-year-old lawyer loped down State Street in Santa Barbara, proudly bearing the

Olympic Torch past a boisterous, flag-waving crowd of thousands. Jamison lifted the torch high in a toast to the cheering throng, which urged him on with shouts of "Go for it, Charlie!" and "Aw right!"

From Ventura to Oxnard to Malibu, the torch was trusted to such a variety of runners that once again we were provided a panorama of American society—from a college president, Robert Hutteback, the chancellor of the University of California at Santa Barbara, to a member of the famed bikers' club, the Hell's Angels, George (Gus) Christie.

There could hardly have been a more richly theatrical run than the one made by Christie, who heads the Ven-

tura Chapter of the Angels. His is another story of "only in America." There was a collective gasp around the offices of the Olympic committee when it was revealed that one of the Youth Legacy Kilometers had been purchased by a member of what many refer to as a "renegade" motorcycle club. A gang. Bikers. Road warriors. Immediately the picture came to mind of a menacing fellow in the dignified Olympic running outfit, embellished with touches like a silver skull neck chain and lurid tattoos. It was rumored that the application had been submitted under the name of H. Angel.

But Christie turned out to be an ex-Marine, a man who had several busi-

With American flags lining the road as far as the eye can see (ABOVE), *Hell's Angel George Christie prepares to carry the flame in Ventura, California. The run proved to be a PR coup for the biker club.* (BELOW) *Back in more familiar garb, George Christie shows off his torch to friends and onlookers and says a few words for ABC. His run took him past an honor guard of 300 Hell's Angels on motorcycles.*

ness interests and a conventional background, whose motives were not very complicated. Nor was it meant to be a joke or a blow struck against wimpiness.

Months before the Olympics, various law enforcement agencies began checking out what they thought might be potential pockets of trouble. "Like the police," said Christie, "we have a network of information that keeps us informed. We got word that some of our people had been approached as to what our stand would be, what our feelings were about the Olympics. Some remarks were dropped that we might want to possibly support certain terrorist groups.

"We wanted to set the record straight. We're not terrorists. We support the American government and the American way of life. We thought the Olympics were a positive thing for the country and around the world. It's true that we have hassles with law enforcement agencies at the local level, and everybody in our club is used to it. So we met and discussed this as an organization, how we should conduct ourselves—if we should get involved and let people know how we felt about the country.

"We're a motorcycle club and that's it. We're an international group. We have charters throughout the world. We know what people think we are. But this organization was founded by the Hell's Angels bomber wing, mostly pilots who had flown missions over Europe during the war, and the

Billy Mills, the Sweet Sioux, a true native son, was an unknown, 26-year-old Marine lieutenant in 1964, when he became the first American to win the Olympic 10,000-meter run. He started his kilometer in the shadow of the state capitol at Sacramento, California.

The bonding process took several forms. In Sacramento, two runners exchange kisses after exchanging the flame.

San Francisco Mayor Diane Feinstein greets the runners under a statue in Golden Gate Park. Here the runners began to feel Olympic fever: this was where the Gold Rush began.

103rd paratroopers. A lot of them stayed together after the war and formed this club.

"We thought about supporting a particular athlete, financing somebody, if that option was available. Then we heard about this Torch Relay and that the money went to finance children's activities. So we decided to take a kilometer and make our statement that way. We voted to send our donation to the Special Olympics.

"We just passed the hat and came up with the money. It didn't take long. Members all over the country contrib- uted. I was picked because I run daily."

Christie ran his kilometer on Los Passos Road in Camerillo, thirty minutes from Ventura. It is a picturesque spot, with farmland on both sides of the road and the Pacific Ocean dead ahead. He took the torch at sunset, and as he neared the end of his run, he was received by an honor guard of 300 Hell's Angels on motorcycles, most of them holding an American flag. "It was like running into a tunnel of American flags," he said. "It literally raised goose bumps on the back of my head. I'm grateful that the Olympic committee didn't take this opportunity away from us.

"We had considered that there might be some sort of negative reaction, that people would be suspicious of us. We seem to have this image, created over the years, some of it warranted, some of it not, that if you treat us good, we treat you better; if you treat us bad, we treat you worse. There are people out there who really detest us. But most of them know nothing about us."

Christie, 37, is on the stubby side at

Through the streets of San Francisco, with the Trans-America Building looming behind them, runners toe the line. (You can never find a cable car when you need one.)

5'8" and 150 pounds. He has dark hair, a goatee, and a mustache. He could pass for a martial arts instructor, which he is, or a rock music promoter, which he also is. The son of a Ventura restaurant owner, he combines his hobby and his business instincts by working in his own shop as a motorcycle mechanic.

He considers the relay to have been a positive experience for the Angels. "If the law enforcement people had left us alone," he says, "we might not have entered. So it sort of backfired on them. But as a result of the relay, I got involved in a slight way with the Special Olympics. We asked that our donation be sent to a group in Pottstown, Pennsylvania, and they started corresponding with me. Letters and pictures. We had jackets made up for them.

"After the relay we went back to the clubhouse and had a party open to anyone who wanted to come. We don't do that often. There were doctors, lawyers, tourists, drifters, bikers . . . all walks of life. I kept the torch. Have it in a case in my front room, definitely on display. Definitely. I'm proud of it, and I'm proud of the relationship we have with the kids in Pottstown.

"I once saw a documentary on television showing mentally retarded people competing in sports, and I was overwhelmed. I felt that retarded children is an area that people don't want to deal with. It's like us, like the Hell's Angels. They know we're there. But they don't understand and they don't want to deal with us.

"So we took up another collection and raised the money to buy windbreakers for the kids, blue-and-white,

(BELOW) *Young America turned out with props in place. At Pacific Grove, California, the relay ran past a* GO FOR THE GOLD *sign.* (TOP, RIGHT) *There was nothing inscrutable about the reaction of these children in San Francisco's famed Chinatown. They pointed, giggled, and had fun.* (BOTTOM, RIGHT) *Remember kids with noses pressed against candy store windows . . . when there were candy stores? Playground fence achieves the same effect as the torch nears.*

with the Special Olympics logo. See, I look at it this way. When the torch went out, the relationship didn't."

There is one last mystery to be cleared up. The name on the original entry was H. Amcus. "When we picked up a cashier's check at the bank," says Christie, "we gave the teller our official name: Hell's Angels Motorcycle Club, United States. The teller abbreviated the name. I guess that's how the other story got started.

We weren't trying to fool anybody."

There is no need to torture the point of this episode. America is not only churches and charities and choral groups, and when it was over, no one could argue that the Hell's Angels had not added a certain texture to the run across America.

In Santa Barbara the major news was the fact that 50,000 onlookers—the largest crowd in the city's history, a police spoksman said—were drawn

to the torch. On upper State Street, the crowd began lining the sidewalks early, and the noise erupted at the first sight of Jessica Arnold, a tiny 9-year-old girl in pigtails, carrying the heavy brass-and-leather torch with the help of a cadre runner. After her kilometer Jessica touched her flame to the unlighted torch of 17-year-old Steve Bailey, disabled by spina bifida. Bailey carried the torch in a specially built wheelchair, beribboned in red, white

Burson-Marsteller's Bill Morrison, with walkie-talkie, faces photographers and TV cameramen from the back of the press truck.

SACRAMENTO, CA

As Billy Mills stood poised to receive the Olympic torch, his thoughts flashed back to Tokyo and the 1960 Games. He was 26, a virtual unknown, competing in the 10,000-meter run. Up to then no American had won a race at a distance longer than 3,000 meters in fifty years. But Mills outdueled Australia's Ron Clarke to win the gold medal.

Once again attired in a track suit, Mills told the crowd how proud he was when his daughter, then 7, asked one day if she could take his medal to school for show-and-tell. His daughter had dreams of becoming a figure skater. That night he hurried home from his office to get a report on how impressed her classmates were. Sure enough, she had held up her father's cherished possession and announced to the class, "This is the kind of gold medal Dorothy Hamill won in figure skating."

and blue. He gave the thumbs-up sign as he rolled himself along his assigned route.

The path of Steve Cohen, a 29-year-old employee of Anheuser-Busch, took him past the historic Santa Barbara mission. The mission bells rang as he turned the corner, giving him "a sense of what an athlete must feel. A burst of exhilaration." But a former jock said it was even better than that. Nick Carter, 81, who ran in the 1,500 meters at the 1928 Olympics, said, "It was more than just an athletic thing. It was just like the Fourth of July."

Carter took the torch from Mary Armstrong, 22, who earned her kilometer by writing the winning essay in a contest, on "What the Olympics Mean to Me." It meant peace and friendship, she said.

The persistence of one would-be runner paid off with not one, but two, trips on the torch caravan. Ann Lee Brown, of Princeton, NJ, was visibly disappointed when her husband objected to her plan to run one of the legacy kilometers. She had even

trained for it, running laps around her neighborhood.

Mrs. Brown was able to ride as a passenger on the Torch Relay, riding in the core vehicles. She joined them first in Oregon, then in California, the second time insisting that her husband join her as an anniversary trip. The choice of a destination was usually a surprise, left up to Mr. Brown. This time Ann Lee made the decision, and it was an anniversary on wheels, at about six miles an hour.

She turned out to be a careful observer, with a nice touch for turning a phrase. "We are a great people," she

All in the family: Ballard Smith, president of the San Diego Padres baseball team, passes torch to his all-star first baseman, Steve Garvey.

Pro football Hall of Famer O. J. Simpson took a fast lap, then ran another to keep company with 7-year-old Michael Bailey. Luckily O. J. is used to big crowds.

said, "and we like to identify with doing our best. That's what I think this torch and this flame coming through the country has been saying." She was rhapsodic over the landscape she saw through her window, moving through Oregon. "You came through fields where there were wildflowers, wonderful crops growing, where people who had ridden up on horses and had come on their tractors waited by the side of the road. We saw mothers with little children. There was a tiny little baby and I asked how old she was, and the lady said five days old. Well,

I think for that lady to have gotten out there after having a baby five days ago was pretty incredible."

What impressed her the most about riding inside the caravan, at times directly behind the runner, was the sense of kinship among those who made the torch move and the people responding on the roadside. "This is something spontaneous," she said. "It's something in people's hearts, and that is one of the loveliest things about it. Nobody's putting on a show, nobody's orchestrating this whole thing. It just comes from people want-

ing to be a part of something very lovely, very wonderful."

Happily, her husband agreed. Ann Lee's husband, it might be noted, is Charles L. Brown, AT&T's Chairman of the Board.

Traffic on the busy coastal highway, U.S. 101, slowed to a crawl as motorists, including some California highway patrolmen, pulled out their cameras and bikini-clad beach goers shouted encouragement. What traffic the torch didn't stop, the beach bunnies did.

As the relay passed the country club

■ 179 ■

Gritty Pete Strudwick, (RIGHT), of Buena Park, carries the torch along the beach in San Diego County. A birth defect inhibited the full development of his hands and feet. Yet he runs to win.

Wheels of fortune: First, a few bicycles and motorcyles fell in behind the torch, then more, and soon a full-fledged caravan had formed in San Diego, California.

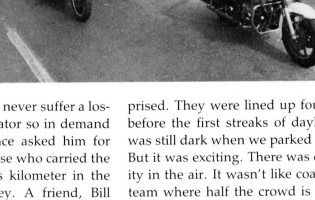

at Pebble Beach, members sat on lawn chairs, sipped champagne, and waved. Clearly, there were no rules or guidelines as to how the spectators should respond—or the runners, either. "If you don't get a chill or two every day and a tear every night," said one of the cadre runners, Jerry Neel, "you're not human."

You could understand the emotional highs of people unaccustomed to the center of the stage. But it was surprising how deeply their role in the relay affected people who have heard the roar of the crowd, have been to town and seen the lights.

George Allen, the only man to coach more than ten years in the National Football League and never suffer a losing season, a motivator so in demand that Lee Iaccoca once asked him for help, was one of those who carried the torch. Allen ran his kilometer in the San Fernando Valley. A friend, Bill Hightower, an executive with AT&T, picked him up at three in the morning and drove him to his starting position somewhere on Ventura Boulevard.

"I remember thinking how nutty it was to go out that early," said Allen, who normally rises at 5 A.M., even when he has nothing to do. "I was the day's first runner, but I thought, there won't be anyone over there. I was sur-

prised. They were lined up four deep before the first streaks of daylight. It was still dark when we parked the car. But it was exciting. There was electricity in the air. It wasn't like coaching a team where half the crowd is for you and half are against you. You had everybody cheering for you. I enjoyed that."

Allen, who could have picked the colors of any of several teams he coached, including the Rams, wore his Washington Redskins coaching shorts and an Olympic tank top. He had prepared himself by running at the beach with a two-pound rock in his hand,

over a period of several months. "I ran two or three miles a day," he said, "and I used a different rock every day. I wanted to be able to run at a pretty good clip so I wouldn't slow anyone down."

Given the vulnerability of the runner, security was always a concern. But nothing that could be described as a threat occurred until those tumultuous days in California, when the very size of the crowds became a problem.

The turnouts were so large that they spilled into the street and sometimes brought the procession to a complete stop. The relay managers worried about meeting the schedule and about runners waiting for the torch and those needing to be retrieved.

Such a delay caused them to be hours late reaching the campus at Santa Clara. It was nearly three in the morning, and by then, most of the

convoy had peeled off to head for the campsite. Only one security car was left to follow the torchbearer, and he was no longer in sight.

The lengthy wait had given the crowd, many of them jocks, time to load up on beer and other spirits. They had grown rowdy and playful. Someone reached through the window of the security car and grabbed the eyeglasses off the driver's face. He jumped out and gave chase. Dick Boehner slipped behind the wheel. When one student climbed onto the roof of the car, Kate Washburn leapt out and threw him off. "We were pan-

icked," she said. "All we could think of was catching up with the torch. It was getting crazy."

But as had been the case virtually from the start, the rich, the famous, and the recently athletic were upstaged by those who did not have widely known names or faces.

When a man named Dallas Bixler carried the torch in Buena Park, his memory windmilled back to 1932, the last time the Olympic Games were held in Los Angeles. He was there, as a gymnast. "I took the gold medal there in '32," he said, "and I never thought I'd see it come back to Califor-

California police and security guards team up to hold back exuberant crowds; the sheer numbers brought the relay to a stop in Santa Barbara.

nia this way. I only made the team five days before the Games opened in 1932. And it was one of those times that they had picked the team in New York and then picked the two individual champions in California. They picked a number-three man, and I was it for the high bar. That's how I happened to make the team.

"I don't think we had a torch relay in 1932. They just brought everyone into the Coliseum and lighted the torch right there."

Bixler tried out for the U.S. team again in 1936 for the Games at Berlin, but a shoulder injury spoiled his chances. Instead he turned to judging, and has judged national gymnastics

for years. At 74, he still runs a mile and a half four or five times a week, and swims about as often. He was the last American to win the gold medal on the horizontal bar, until the 1984 Games.

Possibly the most interesting crowd reaction of the day came in what is known as the Little Tokyo section of the city, where Toshihiko Tahara ran his kilometer. A singer, described as the Bruce Springsteen of Japan, Tahara was mobbed at the end of his run by his teenage admirers. No one on the caravan was aware of Tahara's celebrity, and they looked on with some detachment until the security people realized that he might get hurt. They

dived into the crowd, rescued Tahara, and whisked him aboard the flatbed truck, where he concealed himself behind the press and cameramen.

There were a few sponsored runners from around the world, but Tahara was one of over a hundred who had flown in from Japan to take part.

The performing arts provided their share of runners in the Los Angeles area, and by and large they responded pretty much as did the ones with faces less known. Dennis Weaver was so excited that he left a motor home dressing room with his trunks on backward. The adrenaline of Hal Linden, of *Barney Miller* fame, was also flowing. After his kilometer, he handed his torch to a lady he thought

Although the pace may have been slow, some runners would not let any obstacles break their strides—nor keep them from holding their torches high.

On its winding route the torch crossed the path of many famous landmarks. Here the runners salute the Queen Mary, *docked at Long Beach.*

There are times when a moment is so right and true, the air crisp, the road straight, and the cause just that a barefoot runner can't resist kicking up his heels.

was his secretary. When he asked her for it, his dismay was genuine at discovering that she didn't have it. Luckily, the startled lady who was handed the torch returned it to his wife.

Henry Winkler (The Fonz), sponsored a boy and produced a videotape of the run as a gift. Later, Winkler went around collecting autographs from the AT&T torchbearers. Jamaal Wilkes, of the Lakers, ran a kilometer, and O. J. Simpson ran his own, and another with a handicapped child who had trouble holding the torch O. J. handed him.

Before his record-setting pro football career with the Buffalo Bills, O. J. was a world-class sprinter at Southern Cal.

He showed a flash of his old speed when he ran his kilometer along the California incline. They were raving about it on the caravan the rest of the day.

One of those who observed Simpson's effort was another benefit runner, Tom Hayden, now a California assemblyman, the husband of actress Jane Fonda, and well remembered as a 1960s radical. Hayden put some of his Torch Relay thoughts into a letter. Describing Simpson's gentleness with seven-year-old Michael Bailey, a cerebral palsy victim, harnessed into a carriage, Hayden wrote "All the Olympic slogans . . . took on a new meaning for me as I watched this valiant little boy begin his kilometer." On his own run, down Wilshire Boulevard, he

added, "In all my running, I have never felt my emotions lifting and pulling my body forward."

In the end, Hayden, the onetime campus revolutionary, sounded little different from the crewcut ex-Marine who blinked back tears in Oklahoma.

□ □ □

Of all the 4,000 special runners, none seemed to enjoy his outing more than a man with the alliterative name of Maurice Merle Matthews, a senior window cleaner, who won a Los Angeles city lottery to select a runner for the Torch Relay. His name was drawn by Mayor Tom Bradley in the cafeteria on the tenth floor of City Hall—a building where Maurice on occasion

In the town that invented fantasy, where Cecil B. DeMille boasted of his cast of thousands, and where Disney built a better mousetrap, the L.A. Coliseum welcomed the world to the 1984 Olympics.

was responsible for seeing that the windows were kept clean.

After his run he was asked to describe his feelings. "Well, I tell you," he said. "It was like you had hit the home run, you know, and won a World Series, or run with the football for the winning touchdown. Seemed like you had no enemies that day. Everybody was excited with you. It was a great feeling. It was a great emotional high."

In some respects, the actual lighting of the flame to open the 23rd Olympiad was an anticlimax for those who had carried and protected the torch for eighty-two days in a remarkable cross-country voyage.

As noted before, the mystery runner whose identity had been so carefully guarded by Peter Ueberroth and his staff was to be Rafer Johnson, the most awesome athlete in the world twenty-four years earlier and still a champion of amateur sports. Rafer carried the flame up ninety-nine steps and ignited a fuse just above him, at the peristyle end of the Coliseum. Moments later, the flame was funneled to the top of the torch, and the receptacle ignited with a *whoosh*, fueling the cheers of about 100,000 spectators and athletes.

The 48-year-old Johnson, his face stoic, his chest heaving with exhaustion, turned and faced the crowd as the setting sun's rays illuminated the scene beneath a soft blue evening sky. Johnson had received the torch from Gina Hemphill, the grandchild of Olympic legend Jesse Owens. Gina, who had run the symbolic first kilometer on May 8 with Bill Thorpe, Jr.,

brought the flame onto the Coliseum floor. Her torch was modified to enhance the size and brillance of the flame, which shone brighter than it had at any time in its American pilgrimage.

They exchanged smiles as Johnson took the torch from her, but he appeared deadpan as he worked his way up toward the large Coliseum cauldron, first up a permanent set of steps and then, as the crowd watched in amazement, onto portable stairs that were hydraulically projected before him so he could reach the fuse in the shape of the five-ring Olympic logo.

There was no guard rail along the steps, and several times Johnson had to put his hands out for balance as he worked his way to the top, more than 100 feet above the Coliseum floor. Until the last minute there was a question that Johnson would be able to

The Olympic flame—an ancient symbol indeed, as ancient as Prometheus and the other fire stealers, fire givers, and messengers of the gods.

Cameras clicked as Rafer Johnson, hero of the 1960 decathlon, already moving, takes the torch from Gina Hemphill and starts the last lap of the relay. Until this moment the identity of the runner who would light the final flame had been kept secret.

carry out his assignment. He had been plagued by ankle and foot problems.

But he went on and completed a full circle that had begun on May 8, in New York, when Rafer ignited a sparkler from a small flame that had been flown across the Atlantic from Olympia, Greece. Johnson used the sparkler to ignite a small cauldron from which the first torch of the relay was lighted.

Half the world—at least half of the world that watches television—watched this celebrated runner carry the Olympic Torch to its last stop. Meanwhile, Dick Boehner was just a face in the crowd. The one yawning.

Rafer Johnson had to negotiate only

the difficult final hundrd yards. Boehner had escorted the torch the previous 9,000 miles. Few would recognize his name, but he acompanied the flame every step of the way and ran it himself an estimated one thousand miles. When he reached Los Angeles, his feet were blistered. His lips were chapped and cracked. He had sores on the inside of his mouth and over his scalp. He was underweight and dehydrated. He might have seen a doctor, if he hadn't felt so terrific.

Boehner averaged two hours of sleep a night during his eighty-two days on the road. Exhaustion sank in

even as the opening ceremonies enthralled the crowd and the television audience that reached around the globe. While the pigeons fluttered and the trombones blared and the teams paraded, Dick Boehner fell asleep in the stands with his head on Kate Washburn's shoulder. Lou Putnam dozed off while watching the activities through a pair of binoculars, his head slowly tilting forward until the binoculars rested on the back of the spectator in front of him.

Kate had to nudge them awake. When they opened their eyes, above the vestibule of the Los Angeles Coliseum, they could see the Olympic flame burning.

■ 185 ■

EPILOGUE: COSMIC DANCE

On Broadway a huge crowd salutes the U.S. Olympics and the AT&T torchbearers at a ticker-tape parade in their honor.

"So may a thousand actions, once afoot,
End in one purpose, and be all well borne
Without defeat."
                                        —Shakespeare
                                        King Henry V
                                        Act I, Scene ii

At dusk on the night of July 27, those watching on television heard Jim McKay, on ABC, describe a scene that might have made a Greek statue blink.

"The picture is live, the moment is now, six P.M. on a summer Friday evening in Los Angeles, but a Friday like none other in the history of Southern California, because the picture is of the Olympic Torch being carried through streets on West Pico Boulevard by Dr. Matt Ellenhorn. He just took the torch from another runner. He's a retired physician from Beverly Hills. What a moment for him! The moment, of course, the eve of the 1984 Summer Olympics.

"Tomorrow a runner, yet to be named, will climb the final steps in the Memorial Coliseum and touch off the flame that will burn throughout the Games. But right now, this moment, this is a chance for many thousands who won't be at the opening ceremony to see the torch outshining the rays of the early evening sun. . . . It started in controversy . . . but the relay will end tomorrow as a moving, dramatic story, one that has involved great athletes and handicapped peo-ple, the strong, fleet, and handsome, the lame and the blind. In the story of the flame, there is a story of America in the year 1984."

□ □ □

Up to the very moment that Rafer Johnson touched the torch to the cauldron, some critics still thought of the 1984 Olympics as a kind of athletic flea market.

Finally, though, it was time for the politicians, the peddlers, the promoters, and the protesters to get out of the way. In the town that invented the word fantasy, where Disney built

Rafer Johnson, who feared that a heel injury might keep him from taking part, bounds up the steps on his way to lighting the flame that would burn throughout the 1984 Olympics. As an athlete, Rafer had stood on the top step of the victory platform before.

The interlocking rings on the Olympic flag, being raised in the opening ceremonies at Los Angeles, symbolize peace among the five great continents of the world.

a better mousetrap by using a fictional mouse, the athletes of the world paraded to open the 23rd Olympiad. Ivan didn't know what he was missing.

Not even the absence of the Russians and fourteen of their stablemates could diminish a day so long and troubled in the making. For all the crises that arose along the way, some major and some merely strange, the opening ceremony was a world-class spectacle. A drill team composed of 1,200 handpicked college musicians played the songs of George Gershwin, Marvin Hamlisch, and Aaron Copland. The

band included ninety-six trombones, breaking by twenty the record once imagined by Meredith Willson.

□ □ □

With the lighting of the Olympic rings, the flame swirling up the peristyle of the Coliseum, the athletes of the world paraded around the track, team after team, nation after nation. In the stands, Charles L. Brown, the chairman of what had been the largest corporation in the world, AT&T, the sponsor of the Olympic Torch Relay, looked on and tears filled his eyes. Kate Washburn, a low-level manager in the AT&T hierarchy, left her seat

and walked over and gave him a hug.

And not for those on the inside alone was the picture of the solitary runner, the flame held high, the lasting image of the 1984 Olympics. The people who write words for the President of the United States were so impressed, they worked it into his acceptance speech in August, at the Republican National Convention.

"All through the spring and summer," he said, "we marveled at the journey of the Olympic torch as it made its passage east to west. Over nine thousand miles by some four thousand runners that flame crossed a

For all torchbearers, regardless of their individual style or preference, there was only one basic way to carry the torch. Very carefully.

For preschooler Katie Johnston, the youngest torch runner, whether or not to hold the torch was a decision that required some serious thumb-chewing.

portrait of our nation. . . . All along the way that torch became a celebration of America. And we all became participants in the celebration. Each new story was typical of this land of ours. There was Ansel Stubbs, a youngster of 99, who passed the torch in Kansas to four-year-old Katie Johnson. At Tupelo, Mississippi, at seven A.M. on a Sunday morning, a robed church choir sang 'God Bless America' as the torch went by.

"The torch went through the Cumberland Gap, past the Martin Luther King, Jr. Memorial, down the Santa Fe Trail, and alongside Billy the Kid's grave. In West Virginia, the runner came across a line of deaf children and let each one pass the torch for a few feet, and at the end, those youngsters' hands talked excitedly in their sign language. Crowds spontaneously began singing 'The Battle Hymn of the Republic.'

"And then in San Francisco, a Vietnamese immigrant—his little son held on his shoulders—dodged photographers and police motorcycles to cheer a 19-year-old black man pushing an 88-year-old white woman in a wheelchair as she carried the torch.

"My friends, that's America."

It isn't likely that a President of the United States had given ever before a more descriptive travelogue in the middle of what was basically an address on foreign policy. But a spirit indeed had been rekindled, a faith restored in the oldest American virtues: the melting pot. Something about the torch, the people who carried it, the way they carried it, sang out to us.

In mid-August, a crowd estimated at two million packed the sidewalks of New York to watch a tickertape parade for the Olympic team, accompanied by forty-seven of the AT&T cadre runners. For the runners, this

It was rare that many of the cadre runners would be together at one time, in one place, for very long. The camera caught most of them in New York, for a post-Olympic parade, ticker tape and all.

After the journey of Albert the Running Bear received national coverage, the stuffed animal mascot was returned to the Perakes family in Beaufort, Missouri.

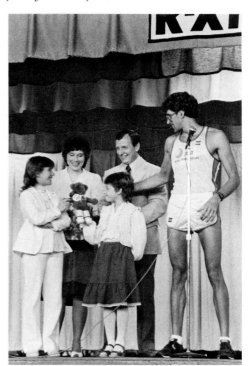

parade was much shorter than the last one.

Months later, the emotions had not really subsided for the people who had, one way or another, passed the torch. Steve Cross, AT&T's spokesman on the relay, still had flashbacks. "Mostly when I'm doing mindless things," he said, "like mowing the lawn or trimming the hedge. I remember a house where we walked in and used the phone. And in Santa Fe, Henry Wesley and I went in the dining room, and two people asked us to join them for dinner. That doesn't happen when you're a tourist on va-cation. But we had T-shirts that read OLYMPIC TORCH RELAY, and it hap-pened to us."

And fans of Albert the Running Bear will be pleased to know that story had a happy ending. Cross had custody of Albert for two weeks in a Long Beach, California hotel room, and brought him along when he flew home. He de-cided it was time for Albert to do the same. He wrote a note to the Perakes family and enclosed it in a box con-taining the bear.

□ □ □

What *did* happen here, all across America, between May 8 and July 28,

in the days before and during the 23rd Olympiad? It might have been some-thing as simple as this: the sight of the torch held high, burning day and night, had returned us to a period when America was the land of unlim-ited promise—and hope. Essayists might call it a catharsis of the Ameri-can soul, a reaffirmation of core Amer-ican values. Undeniably, it reminded us all of Miss Liberty and the torch that lighted the way for millions of new Americans. Time and the immi-gration laws have placed certain limits on the Lady in the Harbor. But dreams, like butterflies, are still free.

Isn't that what the Olympics are all about? If you were scoring the Games, on a scale of one to ten, what grade would you have given it? Would you give or take points for the woman marathoner who traveled the last lap on legs that were not obligated to her body? How much would you deduct for the spill that left Mary Decker in tears on the track and made an also-ran of shoeless Zola Budd?

And which Carl Lewis did you discover, the good Carl, who equaled Jesse Owens's historic four gold med-

als, or the imperfect Carl, who poured salt on our candy by passing up a chance to go for the world mark in the broad jump? The crowd booed. We tried to tell him that winning isn't everything; we expect a few world records too.

Did your heart melt watching Mary Lou Retton flying down the mat and landing on the side horse with a flair and a confidence that would have made Gene Autry or Roy Rogers weep?

For two weeks we saw the self-

renewing spirit of America at work, and it seemed an acceptable time to go crazy. When the man with the net came for us, he was carrying a volley-ball and a basketball. There was truly something for everybody. You could get down with the Greco-Roman wrestlers or row, row, row your boat with the canoeing team.

It was not the solid goldness of the American performance—eighty-five first-place medals—that surprised us, so much as the reaction of the millions who could not stop watching, down

Was America's fascination with the 1984 Olympic Torch Relay somehow related to the Lady in the Harbor and all that she represents?

to the final minute of the closing ceremony. There is something almost senior-promlike about that moment. People have come together as much by accident as by design. They have profited or not, gone their way vowing to stay in touch, meaning it, and then find themselves waving across a room a few years later. But a bond is there, a connection. It always will be. A bridge four years long.

One might argue that feeling good,

while not a bad thing to have happen to you, is not generally a permanent condition.

What contribution, if any, did the Torch Relay make? It was a question that Bill Higgins, among others, found himself turning to time and again.

He knew what the event had done for AT&T. It helped keep hundreds of thousands of AT&T employees together in spirit, providing a focus for the company as it sought a new iden-

tity. From that standpoint alone, it had been worth every cent of the $10 million the relay cost.

There may not have been a tangible, lasting benefit. One may not have been needed. "We didn't do what Jonas Salk did," said Higgins, "but we did something. Philosophers talk about life as a cosmic dance. A tiny atom vibrates and the cosmos vibrates, and we're part of that. The dance is really all that we have. There may be no tangible social benefit, but to me it

"The success of this torch run has exceeded our fondest dreams. Millions and millions of our fellow Americans stood by along the roadsides, cheering the runners and thereby becoming part of the Olympic movement. These Americans have two messages to give to the world. The first is an enormous rekindling of pride in our country, the United States of America. And, more importantly, these millions and millions of people turned out along the way to express a friendship and a love and a caring for all nations of the world. It was an outpouring of pride and love that was demonstrated by a people toward an idea that through sports we can take an important step toward world peace and understanding."

—Peter Ueberroth at the opening ceremony of
the 1984 Los Angeles Summer Olympics

They carried a flame, and no one had to curse the darkness. . . .

was one of the sweetest parts of the dance."

Within the Torch Relay itself there was an apparent contradiction. If you developed a profile of the typical runner and compared it to the media coverage, you would find a clear inconsistency. The coverage focused on the elderly, the very young, the crippled and infirm. The Olympics are not about 80-year-olds and four-year-olds or blind people. But the relay was more than a marathon. It was about life, about chariots of fire.

□ □ □

The movie of that title touched on this theme: young heroes, runners, who burned brightly but only for a

time. We saw them as old men and realized that no one cheats the clock. And so we responded to the passing of the torch because we saw it in the context of our own humanity. If you talk about pro basketball, you talk about Larry Bird and Julius Erving. But it is in the limitations of life—with the old man and the baby and the invalid in the wheelchair—where the celebration is the most meaningful.

One of the AT&T cadre runners recalled his return flight on United, from Oregon, a last celebrity fling. Heading home to New Jersey, he had his torch with him, and the crew and other passengers dropped by his seat for a glimpse of it. Then a stewardess asked

him to take it back through the cockpit for the other passengers to see. The runner was Lou O'Leary, who three years earlier had listened to a proposal that became the Olympic Torch Relay. He watched the opening ceremonies on television with a few friends, and he wrote down his thoughts; "I cried when Rafer lit the Coliseum torch, holding on to my own scorched and singed veteran. I'll bet I had a lot of company, all around the country— just one link in the long chain of runners. But, oh, my friends, and oh, my foes, we carried a lovely flame."

THE TORCH RUNNERS

AT&T CADRE RUNNERS

A

ABBOTT, R. GREGORY Birmingham, AL
ALAGGIO, PATRICK Greenbrook, NJ
ALDRICH, LYNN Birmingham, AL
ALLEN, RON Lake Oswego, OR
ALPHONSO, SANDY O. Ponte Vedra Beach, FL
AMMON, SALLY L. Bernardsville, NJ

B

BAKER, PHIL Rome, GA
BALABAN, JOHN F. Piscataway, NJ
BANAS, JOSEPH P. Norwich, CT
BANKES, KYLE ANN West Reading, PA
BARBIN, RONALD P. Pittsburgh, PA
BARNES, JOHN Glen Allen, VA
BARRETT, GARY R. Bolingbrook, IL
BARTLETT, F. WESTON Montville, NJ
BEATTIE, JACK Boulder, CO
BECKLEY, EDWIN J. JR. Reston, VA
BECKMANN, GORDON Elmhurst, IL
BEHRENS, MARTIE R. Antioch, CA
BLETTE, KERRY J. Valley Stream, NY
BOEHNER, DICK Chester, NJ
BONET, ANGEL South Plainfield, NJ
BOYLE, EILEEN Bayonne, NJ
BRAIG, JAMES W. Dubuque, IA
BRANDON, LYNN Birmingham, AL
BRASELL, JOHN A. JR. Marietta, GA

BRENNAN, THOMAS M. Berkeley Heights, NJ
BUNN, JULIA L. Mechanicsville, VA
BYRD, PATRICIA J. Kansas City, MO

C

CALEFATI, PAUL J. Jersey City, NJ
CANNON, JOHN A. Prospect, CT
CANNON, THOMAS C. Atlanta, GA
CASE, JOHN W. Independence, MO
CATT, GEORGE Cincinnati, OH
CHRISTIAN, DALE F. Naperville, IL
CONDON, PATRICK Riverside, RI
CONDON, SUSAN Chico, CA
COOK, DANIEL H. Reynoldsburg, OH
COOK, SANDRA F. Atkinson, NH
COTTER, AMIE H. Hermitage, TN
CRAMER, MARGARET K. Portland, OR
CROWE, ROBERT M. Lakewood, CO

D

D'ANDREA, ANTHONY Bayonne, NJ
DAHM, JOSEPH M. Atlanta, GA
DANIELS, JERRY WARD Anaheim, CA
DANIELS, ROGER K. Novato, CA
DENONCOURT, MARG Holmdel, NJ
DIXON, JEANNIE Theodore, AL
DONAHUE, THOMAS F. Denville, NJ
DOYLE, KATHLEEN Mill Valley, CA

DUNN, JOHN P. Stanton, CA

E

EDENS, PAUL Silverton, OR
ELSON, JERRY Bridgewater, NJ
ETZEL, BOB Lenexa, KS

F

FAHERTY, F. DAVE Pompton Plains, NJ
FARLEY, DOROTHY T. Bridgewater, NJ
FELDER, DONALD Phoenix, AZ
FITE, MARK F. Warminster, PA
FRANKLIN, CAROL S. Spokane, WA
FULLER, RICHARD C. Fair Haven, NJ
FULMER, FREDERICK F. Lyndhurst, OH

G

GALUPPO, FRANK R. Long Valley, NJ
GILES, GUY Smyrna, TN
GREEN, ELSY A. Miami, FL
GRIFFITHS, PAT Derry, NH

H

HALLINAN, CHRIS Bernardsville, NJ
HARPER, DONNA JEAN Norfolk, VA
HARRIS, BRIAN Royal Oak, MI
HARRIS, STANLEY Lithonia, GA
HASLINGER, GREGORY C. Milford, CT

HATCHER, JAMES Helena, MT
HAYDEN, CAROL ANN Indianapolis, IN
HERMANN, RICHARD C.
    Morristown, NJ
HIEBERT-DODD, KATHIE
    Albuquerque, NM
HIGHTOWER, W.A. Warren, NJ
HOGG, WILLIAM E. Blythewood, SC
HONEYCUTT, KENT W. Conyers, GA
HOOPES, E. JANE Hammonton, NJ
HOTHAM, LEONARD E.
    Warminster, PA
HYER, BOB Matawan, NJ

J

JONES, JOHN FRANK Jacksonville, FL

K

KADEN, RALPH H. Stratford, CT
KASTEN, ALEXANDER Bridgewater, NJ
KAYE, WILLIAM F. New York, NY
KAYSER, CLIFF J. New York, NY
KEOGH, GEORGE Kearny, NJ
KERNS, PAUL L. Switzerland, FL
KIMBALL, LAWRENCE Williston, VT
KINSELLAGH, JAMES Brookline, MA
KITA, RON Granville, OH
KNOLL, PAUL A. Fargo, ND
KOSCIELSKI, RONALD J. Matteson, IL
KOSHICK-SELESTOW, SUE
    Wauwatosa, WI

L

LANCE, MAUREEN Shingle Springs, CA
LANZARIN, EDDIE San Francisco, CA
LEAHY, JANE E. Camp Hill, PA
LEARNED, GIRARD A. Bow, NH
LEGERE, JAY Basking Ridge, NJ
LEITZ, ERIC Dunellen, NJ
LEONARD, KEVIN G. White Plains, NY
LUFT, STACEY Aurora, CO
LYNDGAARD, DANIEL P. Roswell, GA

M

MADONIA, TERRY Pompton Lakes, NJ
MAHER, ROBERT E. Hingham, MA
MAYTE, MARSHALL E. Sylmar, CA
MCALISTER, JAMES V. Plainfield, NJ
MCABEE, NORMAN K. JR. La Jolla, CA
MCKINNIE, GORDON L.
    Manchester, MO
MCPHERSON, CLYDE Flanders, NJ
METZ, LINDA J. Flanders, NJ
MILES, WILLIAM F. Santa Clara, CA
MINK, SUSAN Parsippany, NJ
MOFFAT, ROGER S. Atlanta, GA
MOIRAO, DARLENE Walnut Creek, CA
MOYLES, JAMES A. Redwood City, CA
MULVANEY, GERALD P. Marlton, NJ
MURPHY, DONALD E. White Plains, NY
MURRAY, DOERTE San Francisco, CA
MURRAY, JAMES Lee's Summit, MO

N

NEEL, JERRY A. Fisherville, KY
NEIS, JEFF Millburn, NJ
NOONAN, NANCY J. Cleveland, OH
NOVELL, AL Granite Springs, NY
NUGENT, TAMMY G. Corona, CA

O

O'BRIEN, JAMES H. Renton, WA
O'LEARY, LOU Madison, NJ
OLSZEWSKI, JOHN M. Indianapolis, IN
OWENS, EARL L. Charlotte, NC

P

PAAL, RICHARD G. Winston-Salem, NC
PAINE, YVONNE A. San Diego, CA
PASLEY, BETSY San Antonio, TX
PAULS, MICHAEL J. Overland Park, KS
PETERSEN, CATHERINE Haverhill, MA
PETERSON, MARIANNE J. S. Bound
    Brook, NJ
PUTNAM, LOU Short Hills, NJ

Q

QUINN, THOMAS M. Boulder, CO

R

RANDAZZO, DANIEL Troy, MI
RICE, JAMES E. Naperville, IL
RIGG, GARDINER K. Havertown, PA
RIGGLE, JUDY Campbell, CA
ROBINSON, JOE Des Moines, IA
ROY, DENIS A. Exeter, NH

S

SAVOLD, JIM Bloomsbury, NJ
SCHULZ, BRIAN L. Middletown, NJ
SCHWARTZ, BRUCE Portola Valley, CA
SEPSAS, CHRISTY Birmingham, AL
SEVIER, MARK QUINCY Kansas City, KS
SHEELY, JOSEPH S. Denver, CO
SHERROD, DON Franklin, TN
SHULTZ, LARRY E. Alamosa, CO
SISTO, JOANNE New Providence, NJ
SKELLY, RALPH J. Basking Ridge, NJ
SLOAN, JAMES F. JR. Atlanta, GA
SMASAL, LORI ANN Lisle, IL
SMILEY, JIM Englewood, CO
SMITH, ANN D. Little Rock, AR
SMITH, DONALD F. Stewartsville, NJ
SPEIGHT, CHUCK Doraville, GA
SPRAGUE, RANDALL D. Cincinnati, OH
SQUIRES, PAUL Maplewood, NJ
STEPAN, MIKE Vancouver, WA
STOTLAR, RICHARD K. Shrewsbury, PA
STOW, GLEN J. Destrehan, LA
STREETER, GINGER Bossier City, LA
STRIGL, DENNIS F. Burr Ridge, IL
STROUD, DANNY E. Dublin, CA
STROUD, RANDY L. Marietta, GA
SUAREZ, NORMA Miami, FL
SWAN, DUFFY Littleton, CO

T

TAHAN, DAVID G. Willingboro, NJ
THAXTER DAVID C. Wilmington, MA
THOMPSON, BURNETTE Sugarland, TX
THURSTON, DAVID C. Somerville, NJ
TODD, DENNIS, Chicago, IL
TOOLE, JOHN Roswell, GA
TOOLE, PATRICK J. Boulder, CO
TORRES, PHIL R. Bell Gardens, CA
TORTORETE, JAMES Saddle Brook, NJ
TRAMMELL, ERIC B. Buffalo, NY

V

VALLE, JERRY Oklahoma City, OK
VAN DEN BRANDT, JOHN
    Appleton, WI
VAN HENGEL, VIRGINIA New York, NY
VERDUGO, MARY MARTHA
    Phoenix, AZ
VIGIL, DAVID A. San Francisco, CA
VILLARREAL, GENE A. San Antonio, TX

W

WASHBURN, KATE Peapack, NJ
WEAVER, TIMOTHY R. Birmingham, AL
WEEKS, DEBRA L. Spencer, OK
WESCHLER, CHARLES J. Matawan, NJ
WHITE, SAMMY L. East Point, GA
WIEAND, RAYNOLD R. Belmont, CA
WILLIAMS, JONATHAN L. Bronx, NY
WILSON, DONALD P. St. Albans, WV
WILSON, STEPHEN A. Harrison, OH
WINTERS, HARRISON R. Oak Brook, IL

Y

YANNEKIS, GREGORY C.
    Morristown, NJ
YATES, KEVIN F. Chester, NJ

Shinston, WV

The names and hometowns on this list were provided with the cooperation of the Los Angeles Olympic Organizing Committee

A

ABBOTT, PERRY Wichita, KS
ABBOTT, SUE Palmyra, IN
ABE, FUMIHIRO Tokyo, Japan
ACKERMAN, ARI New York, NY
ACKERMAN, JAMES
   Huntington Beach, CA
ACKERMAN, JIM Huntington Beach, CA
ACKERMAN, JIM Santa Cruz, CA
ACKERMAN, KATIE
   Huntington Beach, CA
ACKERMAN, LEE Huntington Beach, CA
ACKERMAN, LORAINE Huntington
   Beach, CA
ACKERMAN, NANCY Huntington
   Beach, CA
ACKERMAN, STEPHEN H.
   Studio City, CA
ACKLEY, EDWARD J. Pittsford, NY
ADAIR, JULIE Monroe, MI
ADAMLE, MIKE Chicago, IL
ADAMS, HOWELL, E., JR. Atlanta, GA
ADAMS, JAMES H. Bellflower, CA
ADAMS, JOSEPH A. Santa Barbara, CA
ADAMS, MARK New Milford, CT
ADAMS, MARK VAN Brentwood, CA
ADAMS, WILLARD P., M.D.
   Whittier, CA
ADDISON, SCHARYL DENISE
   Pueblo, CO
ADELIZZI, JIMMY San Diego, CA
ADER, JACK Ft. Thomas, KY
ADLER, RITA Northridge, CA
AEZO, JACIENTO São Paulo, Brazil
AGOSTINI, RALPH Alta Loma, CA
AGUILAR, TINO Fresno, CA
AGUILERA, AMALIA Santa Barbara, CA
AGUILLON, CLARIZA Fairfield, CA
AGUIRRE, CARLOS E., JR.
   San Diego, CA
AIGELDINGER, MATTHEW Wilkes-
   Barre, PA
AIHARA, DEAN Montebello, CA
AKERS, BOB Seattle, WA
ALATORRE, DARELL J. Walnut, CA
ALBA, RAYMOND Sherman Oaks, CA
ALBANY, LISA TONI
   Marina Del Rey, CA
ALBRIGHT, CONNIE Citrus Heights, CA
ALDERMAN, PHILIP K. St. Louis, MO
ALEXANDER, DAVID L. New York, NY
ALEXANDER, HONEY Knoxville, TN
ALEXANDER, REHA MARIE
   Anaheim, CA
ALI, MUHAMMAD Louisville, KY
ALIAS, FRED Atlanta, GA
ALLEN, GEORGE Bedminster, NJ

ALLEN, JANET G. Santa Barbara, CA
ALLEN, JOHN Miami, FL
ALLEN, RUSSELL Buena Park, CA
ALLEN, YOLANDA Los Angeles, CA
ALLRED, LINDA Rancho Santa Fe, CA
ALONSO, RODOLFE D.
   N. Hollywood, CA
ALSTON, DARIA Pittsburgh, PA
ALSTON, MICHAEL D. San Diego, CA
ALSTON, PATRICIA Waterbury, CT
ALTMAN, CHARLES S.
   North Andover, MA
ALTMAN, DAVE Covina, CA
AMADOR, DE LUNA Bedminster, NJ
AMBLER, DALE Santa Maria, CA
AMMANN, ARTHUR S.
   San Francisco, CA
AMOLSCH, CHRIS Monroe, MI
AMOR, ANTHONY R. San Francisco, CA
AMSTADTER, ROBERT L., M.D.
   Newport Beach, CA
ANAS, PAUL San Diego, CA
ANAYA, LEONARDO Bakersfield, CA
ANDERLE, CHARLES Arlington, TX
ANDERSON, AMANDA Studio City, CA
ANDERSON, CHARLEEN
   Garden Grove, CA
ANDERSON, CHRISTINE, Fresno, CA
ANDERSON, DIANE Cincinnati, OH
ANDERSON, ERIC LEE St. Joseph, MO
ANDERSON, HOWARD Northbrook, IL
ANDERSON, JAMES Grapevine, TX
ANDERSON, JOHN Pacoima, CA
ANDERSON, KATE Studio City, CA
ANDERSON, KEN Sacramento, CA
ANDERSON, MARCIA San Francisco, CA
ANDERSON, NANCY Minneapolis, MN
ANDERSON, NANCY L. Arlington, TX
ANDERSON, NEILL E. Northridge, CA
ANDERSON, PAUL Studio City, CA
ANDERSON, RONALD E. Missoula, MT
ANDRADE, FRANK Pawtucket, RI
ANDREOLI, JEFFERY R. San Ysidro, CA
ANDREWS, ALLAN Fresno, CA
ANDREWS, BECKY Peachtree City, GA
ANDREWS, SERAFINA M. Klamath
   Falls, OR
ANGEL, AIMEE Portland, OR
ANGEL, BACHARIAH Portland, OR
ANGEL, SHANNON Portland, OR
ANGLIN, MICHAEL Z. Kirkland, WA
ANKENY, DAVID Irvine, CA
APONTE, CARLOS Ashtabula, OH
ARANA DIANE S. Stockton, CA
ARCHULETA, ERIC D. Englewood, CO
ARGUE, BETSY Los Angeles, CA
ARGUE, JOHN C. Los Angeles, CA
ARKELL, JOHN G. San Ramon, CA

ARKENBURG, LARRY Toledo, OH
ARMOUR, HENRY OGDEN
   San Diego, CA
ARMOUR, K.C.E. San Diego, CA
ARMSTEAD, KEITH C.
   Laguna Beach, CA
ARMSTRONG, MARY ANGELES Santa
   Barbara, CA
ARMSTRONG, MEGAN Clovis, CA
ARMSTRONG, MICHAEL
   Los Angeles, CA
ARMSTRONG, RON Irvine, CA
ARNOLD, JAMES Beverly Hills, CA
ARNOLD, JEFF Canton, OH
ARNOLD, JESSICA Santa Barbara, CA
ARNOLD, LILA Sacramento, CA
ARONBERG, CHARLES
   Beverly Hills, CA
ARONBERG, CINDI Beverly Hills, CA
ARONBERG, SANDRA Beverly Hills, CA
ARRITT, PAUL El Toro, CA
ASHWORTH, ANN Poway, CA
ATKINS, JAMES Pomona, CA
ATKINSON, DOUG Evanston, IL
AU, JAMES Burbank, CA
AUSHERMAN, DONALD Glendale, CA
AUSMAN, SHELDON I. Encino, CA
AVALOS, PETE Pinole, CA
AVILA, KELLY Oceanside, CA
AXEL, CAROLYN Los Angeles, CA
AYALA, HUMBERTO Los Angeles, CA
AYERS, JOYCE M. Burbank, CA

B

BABCOCK, ANN KELSEY
   San Marino, CA
BABCOCK, JOHN San Marino, CA
BABCOCK, SARAH Richmond, VA
BABCOCK, SUSAN San Marino, CA
BABICH, KATHY South Lake Tahoe, CA
BACH, TROY Salem, OR
BADOVINAC, MARK Sacramento, CA
BAFFICO, R. E. Burlingame, CA
BAILEY, AL Onkville, MO
BAILEY, STEVE Santa Barbara, CA
BAILY, MICHAEL DAVID
   Santa Monica, CA
BAKER, CARL San Francisco, CA
BAKER, DAN Seattle, WA
BAKER, DONALD J., JR. Moorefield, WV
BAKKEN, ELLEN St. Louis, MO
BALCH, NANCY L. Louisville, CO
BALDWIN, JASON Laguna Beach, CA
BALDWIN, SHAWN Laguna Beach, CA
BALLESTEROS, RODOLFO
   San Diego, CA
BALMER, JIMMY Lubbock, TX

BANE, GARY Santa Barbara, CA
BANNISTER, JOHN Alta Loma, CA
BANTON, FELIX New Orleans, LA
BARBER, SUE Redmond, WA
BARBERA, BARBARA Hollywood, CA
BARBIAR, LORRIE San Francisco, CA
BARDSLEY, KATHY Sandy, UT
BARHAM, DAN Solano Beach, CA
BARHAM, DAVID Solano Beach, CA
BARHAM, DIANE Solano Beach, CA
BARHAM, GARY Solano Beach, CA
BARKHOUSE, JOHN
    Long Island City, NY
BARNES, JAMES L. Visalia, CA
BARNHART, DONNA Chatsworth, CA
BARNHART, TAMELA ANN
    Escondido, CA
BARNWELL, NANCY Glendale, CA
BARON, DEBORAH A.
    Pacific Palisades, CA
BARRERAS, JOEY San Diego, CA
BARRETT, BUCKLEY San Bernardino, CA
BARRETT, MARSHALL Chicago, IL
BARRY, JAMES P. Cleveland, OH
BARSKY, BERNARD Los Angeles, CA
BARTELS, BUNNY Stockton, CA
BARTELS, RONNIE Mt. Morris, MI
BARTLETT, ROBERT W. Chicago, IL
BARTOLIC, RICHARD Fullerton, CA
BARTON, BLAINE Peachtree City, GA
BARTON, JAMES H. Anderson, SC
BARWICK, JAMES F. San Diego, CA
BASCIANO, NICHOLAS J.
    Millersville, MD
BASHOR, JAMES T. Rancho Santa Fe, CA
BASSETT, KIMBROUGH S. Palos Verdes
    Estates, CA
BASSETT, MATHEW SHELL
    Bremerton, WA
BATES, MOMAN E., III Hot Springs, AR
BATTERMAN, LAURA GRACE
    Janesville, WI
BAUER, GUNTHER R., M.D. Palos
    Verdes Peninsula, CA
BAUER, JEFFREY ALLEN Stateline, NV
BAUER, TEDDY Glendale, CA
BAUMAN, DAVID THOMAS
    Ventura, CA
BAYLES, GREGORY REX
    Los Angeles, CA
BAYLIS ROBERT M. Darien, CT
BAYNHAM, BARBARA ANN New
    Castle, PA
BEACH, GREGORY Atlanta, GA
BEALL, DONALD R. El Segundo, CA
BEARD, MARTHA JANE Midlothian, VA
BEARDEN, JIMMY Conyers, GA
BEATTY, JIM Charlotte, NC
BEATY, THOMAS E., JR.
    Mt. Clemens, MI
BEAUDOIN, DONNA Cranston, RI
BECKER, HOWARD M. Marquette, MI
BECKER, JOE North Bergen, NJ

BECKERT, ARTHUR W.
    San Francisco, CA
BEDFORD, WILLIAM J.
    South Pasadena, CA
BEDWELL DIANE Los Angeles, CA
BEELI, ANDREW Sylmar, CA
BEESLEY, EDWARD Hawthorne, NJ
BEHREND, MARK San Jose, CA
BEIM, STEVE Encino, CA
BEISELL, JANET
BLUE, JONATHAN S. Louisville, KY
BLUM, ROBERT Florence, NJ
BLUM, ROBERT M., DR. Cypress, CA
BOECKMANN, BEAU Valencia, CA
BOECKMANN, BRAD Northridge, CA
BOEHNLEIN, JOHN Chatsworth, CA
BOESCHE, AMANDA REYNOLDS Los
    Angeles, CA
BOESEN, MICHAEL R. Alexandria, VA
BOGDEN, RAYMOND E. Woodland
    Hills, CA
BOHNER, DENISE Gettysburg, PA
BOHNET, DAVID J. Arabi, LA
BOHR, VERNON J., DR. Pasadena, CA
BOLAND, JENNIFER LYNN Hunting
    Valley, OH
BOLAY, ROGER Willis, TX
BOLDEN, DAVID E. Birmingham, AL
BOLE, JAMES R. Long Beach, CA
BOLIN, DANIEL, M.D. Wichita Falls, TX
BOLKER, JOSEPH R. Los Angeles, CA
BOMER, IMKE M. North Hollywood, CA
BONDS, DELANO Memphis, TN
BONETTI, BERNARD
    Franklin Square, NY
BONILLA, KENNETH S., DR.
    Claremont, CA
BONNER, MICHAEL
    Menomonee Falls, WI
BORISON, CRAIG Oklahoma City, OK
BORISON, MARK Oklahoma City, OK
BORSCHEL, TOM Richmond, CA
BOSCON, JOHN T.
    Huntington Beach, CA
BOSTON, JANICE Santa Ana, CA
BOSWELL, CLAY Spartanburg, SC
BOUCHER, JONATHAN
    Santa Barbara, CA
BOURGEOIS, ARNOLD Kenner, LA
BOURGERIE, MIKE Skokie, IL
BOUTOT, BOB Wolcott, CT
BOW, JUDY Mt. Storm, WV
BOWDEN, DONALD P. Saratoga, CA
BOWEN, LINDA South Lake Tahoe, CA
BOWERS, PAULA Long Beach, CA
BOWEY, TERRY Eagle, WI
BOWIE, BARBARA San Francisco, CA
BOWMAN, LISA La Canada, CA
BOWMAN, RICHARD L., III, MAJ.
    Citrus Heights, CA
BOWN, KENNETH W., DR. Denison, TX
BOYCE, JAMES Escondido, CA
BOYKIN, DON Stone Mountain, GA

BOZZUTO, MICHAEL A.
    Middlebury, CT
BRAADEN, RANDY L. San Diego, CA
BRACHEN, MICHAEL Jamul, CA
BRACKETTE, BRIAN Kansas City, MO
BRADBURN, DAVID., MAJ. GEN.
    Manhattan Beach, CA

Salem, OR

BRADLEY, CHUCK Cotati, CA
BRADLEY, FRED C. San Diego, CA
BRADLEY, SEAN Hermosa Beach, CA
BRADSHAW, JOHN Los Angeles, CA
BRADY, DANIEL G. San Pedro, CA
BRADY, DUANE Phoenix, AZ
BRADY, SANDRA Warner Robins, GA
BRANCH, SAMUEL Memphis, TN
BRANDON, BLAINE, LT. Jamul, CA
BRANDON, LYNN Birmingham, AL
BRANDT, ROBERT D. Green Bay, WI
BRANHAM, DENNIS
    San Luis Obispo, CA
BRANNAN, MATTHEW Gardena, CA
BRANNAN, WALTER Gardena, CA
BRANNEN, JERRY G., JR.
    Shreveport, LA
BRANTT, DENNIS MICHAEL San
    Leandro, CA
BRASS, PHILIP W. North Olmsted, OH
BRATCHER, ROSALYN Conroe, TX
BRATTON, BOB San Francisco, CA
BRATTON, RON Alameda, CA
BRAUNEIS, ROBERT Oak Park, IL
BRAZIER, JOHN M., III Tacoma, WA
BRAZIER, KIMBERLY A. Tacoma, WA
BRAZIER, STEPHAN N. Tacoma, WA
BREELAND, MARK New York, NY
BREEN, JOHN Shaker Heights, OH
BREHM, DARREN Oceanside, CA
BREIMANN, NANCY Trenton, NJ
BREMMER, TABITHA Hollywood, CA
BRENNEN, KELLY Philadelphia, PA
BRICE, BILLY Los Angeles, CA
BRIDGES, CHUCK Anaheim, CA
BRIGGS, KEVIN Los Angeles, CA
BRIGHAM, ROBERT Kailua Oahu, HI
BRIGHT, CLARITA Brookline, MA
BRILBECK, DAVID A. Syracuse, NY
BRINEGAR, CLAUDE S.
    Pacific Palisades, CA
BRINK, RANDY Sacramento, CA

BRINSKO, CINDY Wausau, WI
BRISSETTE, RICHARD E., JR. West
    Brattleboro, VT
BRODERICK, JIM Kirkland, WA
BRODIE, DUNCAN A. Rochester, MI
BROGAN, CAROL Overland Park, KS
BROOKMAN, DANIEL F.
    Los Angeles, CA
BROOKS, BRETT C. San Diego, CA
BROOKS, DENNIS, Ventura, CA
BROOKS, JAMES R. Fresno, CA
BROOKS, LECIA J. Los Angeles, CA
BROOKS, PATRICIA LOUISE
    La Mirada, CA
BROOME, JOHN S. Oxnard, CA
BROSNAN, TIMOTHY M. Belmont, MA
BROW, JO-ANN Vista, CA
BROWN, ARCHIE, JR. Pomona, CA
BROWN, C. TERRY San Diego, CA
BROWN, DAVE Springfield, NJ
BROWN, EDWARD, JR. San Diego, CA
BROWN, JOHN F. Granada Hills, CA
BROWN, LARRY Lawrence, KS
BROWN, MARY L. San Diego, CA
BROWN, REGINA North Brunswick, NJ
BROWN, RICHARD San Jose, CA
BROWN, SHARON Amarillo, TX
BROWN, STEVE D. Irving, TX
BROWN, TERRENCE St. Louis, MO
BROWNING, LANDON La Canada, CA
BROWNING, MICHAEL G.
    Indianapolis, IN
BRUBAKER, LEE Los Angeles, CA
BRUCE, ROBERT T. Schenectady, NY
BRUNNETTE, JOHN C. Rochester, MN
BRUNSELL, GORDON L. Downers
    Grove, IL
BRUSKO, LOIS M. Schaumburg, IL
BRYAN, DALE G. Studio City, CA
BRYANT, ROBERT E. Santa Barbara, CA
BRYANT, WALLACE Birmingham, AL
BUCE, WALTER HOWARD Austell, GA
BUCHANAN, WANDA Concord, CA
BUCKLAND, LESLIE H. New York, NY
BUCKWALTER, JAMES Sherman, TX
BUDDE, SUSAN Columbia Heights, MN
BUEHNER, CHRIS Louisville, KY
BUENING, KARIN Centerville, OH
BUENROSTRO, SAMUEL Santa Ana, CA
BUFFINGTON, JOHN W. Gilroy, CA
BULLOCK, DEFOREST A. Tacoma, WA
BUMPHUS, JOHNNY
    West Paterson, NJ
BUNGER, BOB San Francisco, CA
BUNSMAN, KEN Imperial Beach, CA
BURDETT, JOHN Clifton Park, NY
BURDETTE, ROBERT S., II
    Los Angeles, CA
BURDICK, JERRY Woodland Hills, CA
BUREN, JOHN San Francisco, CA
BURGER, JOHN Davis, CA
BURKE, ALFRED DAVID Los Altos, CA
BURKE, LISA Canyon Country, CA

BURKETTE, DERRICK Worman, OK
BURKHALTER, DON Cupertino, CA
BURNS, STEPHEN R. Torrance, CA
BURR, GEORGE Ontario, NY
BURZETT, MARVIN Topeka, KS
BUSBY, BRENT EDWARD Mobile, AL
BUSBY, JAMES BARTON Mobile, AL
BUTCHER, PHYLLIS M.
    Canoga Park, CA
BUTLER, ARTHUR F., JR. La Mesa, CA
BUTLER, PETER R. Oakland, CA
BYINGTON, JOAN Los Angeles, CA

■■■■■■■■■ C ■■■■■■■■■

CABA, MICHAEL Whittier, CA
CABEBE, BETTIE San Jose, CA
CADWELL, ROBERT P. Annapolis, MD
CAHOON, GEOFF Laguna Niguel, CA
CALAHAN, CONNIE Mercer Island, WA
CALCAGNI, JASON W.
    Clifton Heights, PA
CALDWELL, GEORGE A. Aberdeen, WA
CALDWELL, PAUL Corpus Christi, TX
CALE, JESSIE R. Los Angeles, CA
CALK, DAVE Valencia, CA
CALMA, MANOLITO Y. San Diego, CA
CALOYERAS, BEVERLY Los Angeles, CA
CAMACHO, DON LUIS Encino, CA
CAMARAS, ELENA E.
    Corona Del Mar, CA
CAMBEROS, ROBERTO Southgate, CA
CAMERON, SCOTT Washington, PA
CAMILLETTI, RICHARD J. Warren, OH
CAMMAROTA, JOSEPH P.
    Greenwich, CT
CAMPBELL, BILL Anaheim, CA
CAMPBELL, SCOTT Scottsdale, AZ
CAMPBELL, STEPHANIE Hacienda
    Heights, CA
CANDELARIA, JOHN Albuquerque, NM
CANDELARIO, ANER New York, NY
CANNON, WALT Far Hills, NJ
CAPLETTE, JACQUES Montreal, Quebec,
    Canada
CAPLETTE, PIERRE Montreal, Quebec,
    Canada
CAPUTO, LORENZO New York, NY
CARACO, RALPH South Laguna, CA
CARAPITO, HUMBERTO BATISTA São
    Paulo, Brazil
CARDI, STEPHEN East Greenwich, RI
CARDWELL, KURTIS L. Fairfield, CA
CARLISLE, DAVID R. Fremont, CA
CARLOS, JOHN Los Angeles, CA
CARLOTTI, VALENTINO New York, NY
CARLSBERG, BARBARA
    Los Angeles, CA
CARLSON, LORI San Diego, CA
CARLSON, RICHARD Sparta, NJ
CARMEN, WILLIAM West Newton, MA
CARMONA, FAUSTINO, JR.
    Brentwood, CA

CARNEY, CHESLEY CLAUDE, II San
    Diego, CA
CARON, F. Johnston, RI
CARPE, DANE M. Granada Hills, CA
CARPENTER, ROSEMARY Denver, CO
CARR, CINDY S. Lindenwold, NJ
CARR, RUTH Coronado, CA
CARRAH, JOSEPH R. Waterbury, CT
CARSON, LEV Cerritos, CA
CARSON, TIMOTHY Lowell, MA
CARSTENS, CHERYL Costa Mesa, CA
CARTER, CHARLES Cincinnati, OH
CARTER, CHRISTINA LYNN Coppell, TX
CARTER, DEAN Burbank, CA
CARTER, DENISE Stateline, NV
CARTER, DON Norwalk, CA
CARTER, DONALD J., JR. Dallas, TX
CARTER, DONALD J., SR. Dallas, TX
CARTER, JANET Washington, DC
CARTER, KIM Lubbock, TX
CARTER, LINDA J. Coppell, TX
CARTER, RICHARD W. Cucamonga, CA
CARTER, RONALD LEE Coppell, TX
CARTER, STEVEN T. Indianapolis, IN
CARTER, SUZANNE Santa Monica, CA
CARTWRIGHT, JOE Redondo Beach, CA
CARVALHO, BARRY J. Hacienda
    Heights, CA

Edwardsburg, MI

CASE, CAROL Santa Monica, CA
CASEY, CAROLYN North Highlands, CA
CASEY, MARCI Atlanta, GA
CASOLA, SAL Santa Monica, CA
CASPER, MELBA College Park, MD
CASSEL, GAIL R.N. Jacksonville, FL
CASTELLANO, PHILLIP
    Baldwin Park, CA
CASTILLO, ARTHUR San Ramon, CA

CASTILLO, MARIO Los Angeles, CA
CASTOR, MARIANO Ventura, CA
CASTOR, RONALD L. Tucker, GA
CATES, EDWARD Baldwin Park, CA
CAVALACANTE, PIETRO M.
  Los Angeles, CA
CEASE, LARRY Brentwood, TN
CECH, BRUCE Bellevue, WA
CELORIE, TOM Los Angeles, CA
CHADO, J. ROBERT Englewood, CO
CHALCRAFT, DIANA L. West
  Hollywood, CA
CHAMBERS, JEANETTE
  Falls Church, VA
CHAMBLIN, DALE Oakland, CA
CHAMBLISS, RICHARD Xenia, OH
CHAMPAGNE, JOSEPH A., JR.
  Covington, LA
CHAN, BENNY Woodland Hills, CA
CHANEY, DAVID Troy, MI
CHANEY, KIRA Laguna Niguel, CA
CHAPIN, R. Reno, NV
CHAPMAN, JEFF Burbank, CA
CHASE, BOYCE Princeton, NJ
CHASE, L. ASHTON Los Angeles, CA

Corvallis, OR

CHENEY, CARI Danville, CA
CHENEY, MICHAEL Danville, CA
CHENG, JASON H. Covina, CA
CHERER, GARY Cardiff, CA
CHIEMI, MANJYOH Higashi Hirano-Ku
  Osaka, Japan
CHILCOAT, CAROL Seattle, WA
CHILCOTE, DEANN Simi Valley, CA
CHIN, TIFFANY Toluca Lake, CA
CHLOWITZ, ALLAN D.
  Marina Del Rey, CA
CHOI, SUSAN Glendale, CA

CHRISTIAN, SPENCER Closter, NJ
CHRISTIE, GEORGE Ventura, CA
CHRISTOFF, ROBERT J. Glendale, AZ
CHRISTOPHER, LYDIA Riverside, CA
CHRISTOPHER, TERESA LYNN Rancho
  Palos Verdes, CA
CHRISTOPHERSON, KATE San Jose, CA
CHUMA, MICHAEL L. Moore, OK
CHUMO, MARGARET EVELYN Pacific
  Palisades, CA
CHUMO, MARLENA LYN Pacific
  Palisades, CA
CHUMO, MICHAEL LEE Pacific
  Palisades, CA
CHURCHMAN, N. FREDERICK
  Baltimore, MD
CIANCI, RON Encino, CA
CICCARELLI, ROBERTA Blairsville, GA
CICCHETTI, CARL R. Waterbury, CT
CLABORN, D. L. Atlanta, GA
CLAPPS, KENNETH
  Huntington Beach, CA
CLARK, DEBBIE Beverly Hills, CA
CLARK, DENIKA New Castle, PA
CLARK, DOUGLAS Tulelake, CA
CLARK, ELLERY H., JR. Annapolis, MD
CLARK, JOHN New York, NY
CLARK, MARY Booney Lake, WA
CLARK, RHONDA National City, CA
CLARK, TODD Oklahoma City, OK
CLARKE, BRIAN Evanston, IL
CLARKE, JAMES T. Hillsborough, CA
CLAUSEN, ANDREW I. Marina, CA
CLAYCOMB, ANN Stockton, CA
CLEARY, MICHAEL PATRICK San
  Francisco, CA
CLEARY, PENSE WELSH Mendham, NJ
CLEGG, SCOTT A. Pepperpike, OH
CLEMENTS, DAVID E. San Diego, CA
CLEMONS, RON Kansas City, MO
CLIPPER, JACK La Plata, MD
COBARRUBIAS, FRANK Fremont, CA
COCHRAN, DICK Sacramento, CA
COFFEE, BOB Sewickley, PA
COFFEY, NANCY ANN Modesto, CA
COFFIN, ALEX Charlotte, NC
COGSWELL, ELIZABETH A.
  Dublin, OH
COHEN, DOUGLAS Highland Park, IL
COHEN, JOAN F. Los Angeles, CA
COHEN, LOUIS Encino, CA
COHEN, STEVEN Valencia, CA
COHNHEIM, SHAWN M. Rothell, WA
COILE, RUSSELL C., JR.
  South Pasadena, CA
COKLEY, JACK Boston, MA
COLACHIS, AUGUST R. La Jolla, CA
COLACHIS, JAMES W. La Jolla, CA
COLE, CARTER L. Woodland Hills, CA
COLE, DALLAS Milwaukee, WI
COLE, GERI ANN Lake Odessa, MI
COLEMAN, BRUCE Los Angeles, CA
COLEMAN, DEIRDRE Waterbury, CT

COLEMAN, ZEDELL Irvington, NJ
COLES, GARY Waterbury, CT
COLLETTE, WAYNE Ephrata, WA
COLLIER, CHRIS Denver, CO
COLLIER, EVAN Englewood, CO
COLLING, KENNETH La Costa, CA
COLLINS, DALE Tulsa, OK

Detroit, MI

COLLINS, JOSEPH L., JR. Chicago, IL
COLLINS, LEE Lakewood, CO
COLLISHAW, MIKE Santa Clara, CA
COLSON, MARY ANN Carpinteria, CA
COLTON, JUNE MARIE Pasadena, CA
COLVIN, TIMOTHY D.
  Hermosa Beach, CA
COMAI, ANDREA L. Cleveland, OH
COMBELLICK, MARILYN Whittier, CA
COMBS, SEAN CRAIG Balboa, CA
COMBS WILLIAM H. Millington, NJ
COMYNS, JAMES A. Westlake, OH
CONLAN, S. THOMAS Seattle, WA
CONLON, WILLIAM
  South Lake Tahoe, CA
CONNELL, JOHANNA Torrance, CA
CONNELL, JUSTIN Irvine, CA
CONNELLAN, THOMAS K., Dr. Ann
  Arbor, MI
CONNELLY, JIM Los Angeles, CA
CONNELLY, JOHN Holmdel, NJ
CONNELLY, KAY Philadelphia, PA
CONNER, JACK W. Los Gatos, CA
CONOPEOTIS, GEORGE Arlington
  Heights, IL
CONOVER, ROGER F. Basking Ridge, NJ
CONSTANTINO, GEORGE E., JR.
  Orinda, CA
CONTRERAS, SAL Lemon Grove, CA
CONWAY, MARION MCKNIGHT Los
  Angeles, CA
COOK, ANDREW Detroit, MI
COOK, BENJAMIN H. Marietta, GA
COOK, LAURA Santee, CA
COOLIDGE, MARK Laguna Hills, CA
COONS, KAYLE San Diego, CA
COOPER, CAMERON Ventura, CA
COOPER, CRAIG R.
  Rolling Hills Estates, CA
COOPER, KEN Bencia, CA
COOPER, STACEY R. Pomona, CA

CORDEAU, RONALD Waterbury, CT
CORDELLOS, HARRY Los Angeles, CA
CORNELL, ANN San Gabriel, CA
COSCIO, FELIX ALBERTO
  Sun Valley, CA
COSGROVE, JOHN Playa Del Rey, CA
COSMI, CINDY South Lake Tahoe, CA
COSTELLO, CINDY Venice, CA
COSTELLO, RICHARD, New York, NY
COTTER, CLINTON B. Palos Verdes
  Estates, CA
COTTER, TERRY Mill Valley, CA
COTTLE, TERRI Thousand Oaks, CA
COTTON, BARBARA, J. Seattle, WA.
COULTER, WILLIAM A. Costa Mesa, CA
COUNCIL, DENNIS Clio, MI
COUVILLON, ROLAND
  Salt Lake City, UT
COVENDAL, JOHN Sun Valley, CA
COWART, JERRY Topanga, CA
COWART, LANCE Richardson, TX
COWLIN, JOHN New York, NY
CRADDIC, SHIRLEY Coresham, OR
CRAIN, JENNIFER Franklin, WI
CRAMPTON, ALEXIS V. San Pedro, CA
CRASKA, RONALD Pittsburgh, PA
CRAWFORD, ARTHUR Indianapolis, IN
CRAWFORD, BRIDGET Cleveland
  Heights, OH
CRAWFORD, JAMES W., II
  Sacramento, CA
CRAWFORD, MATT Willoughby, OH
CRAWFORD, ROGER, II Danville, CA
CRAWFORD, TONY Canby, OR
CRETS, BRIAN Woodland, CA
CREWS, JEAN Philadelphia, PA
CRIST, DON Oakridge, OR
CROCKETT, JIM Cupertino, CA
CROMMELIN, KIMBERLEY Stanton, NJ
CRONIN, WILLIAM Cranston, RI
CROSBY, ROBERT F. Los Angeles, CA

Bristol, CT

CROSS, ROBERT G. Orange, CA
CROSS, STEVE Staten Island, NY
CROSSLEY, MICHAEL Hartford, CT
CROUCH, ARLEN B. Anaheim, CA
CROWE, GARY Irvine, CA
CROWELL, TERESA San Diego, CA
CROYTS, RANDY A. Lomita, CA

CRUM, GLORIA E. Downey, CA
CRUTCHER, JAMES P. Seattle, WA
CRUZ, JIM Hollywood, CA
CULLIGAN, KATHRYN Oakland, CA
CULLY, RUSSELL A., JR. Hawthorne, CA
CUMMINGS, JIM Milwaukee, WI
CUMMINGS, JIM, III Santa Ana, CA
CUMMINGS, STEVE Carpinteria, CA
CUNNINGHAM, GLEN Union Lake, MI
CUNNINGHAM, TIM Romney, WV
CUNNINGHAM, WILLIAM J., JR. Long
  Beach, CA
CUNYA, RONALDO Norwalk, CT
CUPARI, JOSEPH Chicago, IL
CUSHMAN, JOHN C. South
  Pasadena, CA
CUSICK, JOSEPH W. Boise, ID

━━━━━━ D ━━━━━━

D'AMICO, JEANNE Los Angeles, CA
DA RODDA, DANILA Los Angeles, CA
DABNEY, NEIL D. Los Angeles, CA
DAGGS, JIM Valencia, CA
DAGGS, WILLIAM Simi Valley, CA
DAHLKE, GRANT Mt. Prospect, IL
DAHLMAN, WILLIAM North
  Hollywood, CA
DAHLQUIST, ERIC Van Nuys, CA
DAILEY, RICHARD G. Greer, SC
DALESSIO, ROBERT L. Philadelphia, PA
DALEY, JOHN S. Redondo Beach, CA
DALTON, EDDIE Manhattan, NY
DALY, ANTHONY F., M.D.
  Inglewood, CA
DALY, ELIZABETH Chicago, IL
DALY, GAIL Bloomington, IN
DALY, PATRICK S. Pompton Plains, NJ
DAME, MICHELLE Oklahoma City, OK
DANIEL, KIMBERLY Pleasanton, CA
DANIELS, JOSEPH Baltimore, MD
DANNEMEYER, WILLIAM Fullerton, CA
DARGA, JOHN M. Burton, MI
DARLING, DENISE Washington, DC
DAVALOS, DOMINIQUE
  San Francisco, CA
DAVALOS, SALVADOR Oxnard, CA
DAVIDE, ROLAND Coventry, RI
DAVIDSON, MICHAEL Atlanta, GA
DAVIES, CAROLYN L. Youngstown, OH
DAVIES, GREGORY Los Gatos, CA
DAVIS, ALEXANDRA Halifax, Nova
  Scotia, Canada
DAVIS, ANDY Newark, CA
DAVIS, CHRISTOPHER Halifax, Nova
  Scotia, Canada
DAVIS, JIM Evanston, IL
DAVIS, PATRICIA Mill Valley, CA
DAVIS, RICHARD Portland, OR
DAVIS, ROBERT N. Antioch, CA
DAVIS, VINCENT New Orleans, LA
DAVISON, RICHARD D.
  Los Angeles, CA

DAWKINS, SEAN Randallstown, MD
DAY, DEANNE Moline, IL
DAY, JOY Mesa, AZ
DAYTON, AARON Portland, OR
DE CASTRO, ADEMAR São Paulo, Brazil
DE LA ROSA, MANUEL
  Los Angeles, CA
DE LA TORRE, MARC Fresno, CA
DE MACIAS, CAROLYN WEBBS
  Alhambra, CA
DE MONET, GAIL Woodside, CA
DE MONET, JOAQUIN Woodside, CA
DE MONET, JOAQUIN, JR.
  Woodside, CA
DE MONET, MONIQUE Woodside, CA
DE MONET, PHILIP Woodside, CA
DE MONET, RICARDO Atherton, CA
DE OLIVERA, JOAN CARLOS
  Guarulhos, Brazil
DE SOUZA, JOSE SEBASTIAO
  Embu, Brazil
DEFRANTZ, ANITA Los Angeles, CA
DEMENNA, STEPHEN L.
  Huntington, NY
DERENZIS, RICK Easton, PA
DEWITT, ANTHONY Indio, CA
DEAN, CARY MARTIN
  New Brighton, PA
DEE THOMAS, CYNTHIA
  Simi Valley, CA
DEEGAN, WAYNE A., JR. Pottstown, PA
DEFOSSE, RONALD Toms River, NJ
DELANEY, MOIRA La Crescenta, CA
DELANEY, NORMA San Diego, CA
DELANEY, VIRGIL Colorado Springs, CO
DELISTRATY, MARY Diablo, CA
DELLINGER, JOE Springfield, OR
DEMARS, KAREN C. Oxnard, CA
DENNING, KATHRYN D. Horsham, PA
DENSTAEDT, RUTH A. Yorba Linda, CA
DEPOLO, GARY L. Orinda, CA
DEPUY, WARNER K. Stamford, CT
DERRICK, DOUG Celina, OH
DESSENT, BRYN ELIZABETH
  La Jolla, CA
DETELICH, THOMAS M.
  North Wales, PA
DETERS, ANN SCHULTZ St. Louis, MO
DETWILER, JUDITH A. Davie, FL
DEUSTO, CARLOS LOPEZ
  Chula Vista, CA
DEVORE, JOE Los Angeles, CA
DEWEY, CHIP Glendale, CA
DEWHITT, KAY Beverly Hills, CA
DEYNE, RAYMOND San Diego, CA
DIAL, SCOTT B. Lafayette, CA
DIAZ, ART Gardena, CA
DICKEY, JOHN Rocky Hill, MO
DICKINSON, MICHELLE K.
  Blanchard, OK
DICKSON, BRUCE Glendale, CA
DICKSON, DERON Glendale, CA
DICKSON, STAN Louisville, KY

DIEHR-SU, JACKIE San Diego, CA
DIETRICH, MARK E. Playa Del Rey, CA
DIETSCH, ALFRED J. Denver, CO
DIETZ, NOEL San Jose, CA
DILLARD, HARRISON Chagrin Falls, OH
DILLMAN, W.M. Pittsburgh, PA
DIMMICK, STAN Arlington, TX
DION, MITCH Palos Verdes Estates, CA
DIRGINS, TIMOTHY Riverside, CT
DITZ, NANCY Menlo Park, CA
DIXON, MAUREEN Alameda, CA
DOBSON, ANDY Burbank, CA
DOBSON, MARY Burbank, CA
DOCHELLI, HARRY Boise, ID
DOCKERY, DEBBIE Los Angeles, CA
DOCKSON, ROBERT R. Los Angeles, CA
DOJO, YOZO Hollywood, CA
DOLEN, DARRELL Auburn, WA
DOMINGUEZ, JULIA A. Antioch, CA
DOMREIS, RON Longview, WA
DONALDSON, MICHAEL C. North
   Hollywood, CA
DONCHIN, ANDREW Fair Lawn, NJ
DONIGAN, DANIEL Flint, MI
DONOVAN, COLLEEN Lodi, CA
DONOVAN, DANIEL Boston, MA
DORAN, GREG Austin, TX
DORMAN, ALBERT A. Los Angeles, CA
DORN, TORIN Southfield, MI
DORR, BARBARA Jackson, MS
DOSS, ROBERT Oliverhain, CA
DOUBLEDAY, SAM Los Angeles, CA
DOYLE, EVIE Chicago, IL
DOZIER, JOHN, DR. Houston, TX
DRAPER, GARY D. Indianapolis, IN
DRAPER, MARY Overland Park, KS
DREYFUS, TROY Raleigh, NC
DRIER, DAVID, CONGRESSMAN
   Covina, CA
DRINKARD, JANICE L. Covington, LA
DRINKWATER, ARTHUR Hayward, CA
DRODZ, FRAN CONDO Las Vegas, NV
DROGIN, STEVE San Diego, CA
DROMGOOLE, MARK Los Angeles, CA
DROMGOOLE, SYD Los Angeles, CA
DUARTE, MARIO Los Angeles, CA
DUDLEY, JANET Walnut Creek, CA
DUFF, CINDY Oceanside, CA
DUFFIN, MORGAN Salinas, CA
DUFFY, ALBERT G. West Covina, CA
DUGAN, LARRY Cincinnati, OH
DUKES, DARRELL E. Saratoga, CA
DUKKONY, STEPHEN J. Annapolis, MD
DULAC, DONNA Randolph, NJ
DULIN, RONALD H. Long Beach, CA
DUMONT, STEVEN Canton, MI
DUNHILL, TOM, JR. Englewood, CO
DUNLAP, APRIL Santee, CA
DUNLAP, GEORGE H.
   Oklahoma City, OK
DUNN, A. R., JR. Slidell, LA
DUNN, BRIAN Ojai, CA
DUNN, JAMES Westlake Village, CA

DUNN, KEVIN Ojai, CA
DUNN, RICHARD Sherman Oaks, CA
DURBIN, JIM Oklahoma City, OK
DURDEN, GREG Atlanta, GA
DURFEES, BRYCE Louisville, KY
DURKIN, MARY Santa Monica, CA
DVORAK, DONALD D. Santa Clara, CA
DWIGHT, ROGER Lake Oswego, OR
DWYER, EDWARD M. Los Angeles, CA
DYKEMA, DALE L. Irvine, CA
DYSON, BRIAN Atlanta, GA

E

EARHART, ALAN El Cajon, CA
EARL, BENJAMIN ROUSE Irvine, CA
EARL, J. B. Arcadia, CA
EASLEY, JOHN ED Dallas, TX
EASTMAN, J. B. Long Beach, CA
EASTO, RICHARD A. Crown Point, IN
EASTON, GREG Los Angeles, CA
EATON, GARRET Irvine, CA
EATON, SHERRY K. New Brighton, PA
ECHEVARRIA, MICHAEL A.
   Sun Valley, CA
ECKE, LIZBETH Encinitas, CA
ECKE, PAUL, JR. Encinitas, CA
ECKEL, JONATHAN Los Angeles, CA
ECKEL, NATALIE M. Tarzana, CA
ECKEL, SUZI Santa Monica, CA
ECKER, KENNETH San Diego, CA
ECKERT, ELIZABETH MARYANN
   Vista, CA
EDGMON, RONI HATHAWAY
   Modesto, CA
EDNEY, BRUCE H. Seattle, WA
EDWARDS, BRUCE Los Gatos, CA
EGANS, STEPHANIE R. Los Angeles, CA
EGGEN, GIB Des Moines, IA
EGGER, DANIEL San Diego, CA
EGGERT, CHARLES Portland, OR
EGGERT, CHRISTOPHER Portland, OR
EIDE, DEBBIE Salem, OR
EIGHMEY, MARK R. Monroe, MI
EITELJORG, JAMES Indianapolis, IN
EITELJORG, SONJA, DR.
   Indianapolis, IN
ELDRED, GLORIA Long Beach, CA
ELIS, PAUL B. Calabasas, CA
ELKINS, TONYA Pacifica, CA
ELLENBERGER, JOHN L. Paonia, CO
ELLENHORN, MATT, M.D.
   Los Angeles, CA
ELLINGSON, PETER G. Baker, OR
ELLIOTT, JAMES Hacienda Heights, CA
ELLIOTT, JOE DALE Ojai, CA
ELLIOTT, JULIUS Anaheim, CA
ELLIS, CALVIN L. Reston, VA
ELLIS, JAMES K., DR. Cincinnati, OH
ELLIS, RUSSELL E., III
   Redwood City, CA
ELLISON, ANN Inglewood, CA
ELLISON, BOB Boerne, TX
ELROD, DAVID J. Beverly Hills, CA

EMERSON, MARY HOLYOKE
   Denver, CO
ENGLAND, MARSHA J. St. Louis, MO
ENGLANDER, WILLIAM San Diego, CA
ENGLE, HAL Albuquerque, NM
ENGLISH, J. WALTER
   Franklin Square, NY
ENSSLIN, DAVID Portville, CA
EPSTEIN, MICHAEL San Diego, CA
EPSTEIN, STUART Great Neck, NY
ERBECK, JOHN R., DR. Ventura, CA
ERDELJAC, JOSEPH J., JR.
   Columbus, OH
ERICKSEN, BRUCE L. Salt Lake City, UT
ERICKSON, DOUGLAS
   Salt Lake City, UT
ERICKSON, LISA St. Paul, MN
ERICSON, CHERYL Oklahoma City, OK
ERSKINE, JOHN P.
   Huntington Beach, CA
ESTES, EDWIN W., JR. Vista, CA
EUN, KIM Los Angeles, CA
EVANGELISTA, STEVE Johnston, RI
EVANS, KATHLEEN Costa Mesa, CA
EVANS, PATTY Pasadena, CA
EVANS, PAUL Corona Del Mar, CA

Seattle, WA

EVEN, RANDOLPH Woodland Hills, CA
EVERHART, CARL Beverly Hills, CA
EVERSON, RACHEL Edmond, OK
EVERTON, MAX Virginia Beach, VA
EXELER, HUBERTUS Ft. Worth, TX
EYERICK, CARL, DR. Burbank, CA
EYRAUD, ALBERT J. Beverly Hills, CA

FAAS, ERIC Gardena, CA
FACTOR, TITO Los Angeles, CA
FULCO, FRANK Southbury, CT
FAMILIAN, GREG Los Angeles, CA
FANASCI, ANTHONY Santa Clara
   Valley, CA
FANCHER, SPENCER Wichita, KS
FANNING, BILL San Francisco, CA
FARFAN, JOSEPHINE Richmond, CA
FARLEY, DAVID J. Providence, RI
FARLEY, TIMOTHY Vermillion, OH
FARRELL, KATHY South Lake Tahoe, CA
FARRELL, TREVOR K. Caldwyne, PA
FASON, PATRICIA Sunland, CA
FAUS, BEN Salinas, CA
FAVA, TOM Waterbury, CT
FAZ, ANITA Simi Valley, CA
FEATHERMAN, DAVID San Diego, CA
FEDORCHUK, MARY ANNE Hermosa
   Beach, CA
FEE, ANGELA Redmond, WA
FEFLEY, JOHN WILLIAM, JR.
   Alamo, CA
FEHLAND, MIKE Wausau, WI
FEINBERG, BARRY Orange, CT
FEINBERG, MURRAY Orange, CT
FEINSTEIN, SHARON Moraga, CA
FELDER, LINDA Cleveland, OH
FELDKAMP, SUE E. Berea, KY
FELTMAN, DOUGLAS J. New York, NY
FENNER, BEVERLY J. Belleville, IL
FENO, CRUZ Wenatchee, WA
FERER, SHIRLEY Hillsborough, CA
FERGUSON, DAVID M. Chula Vista, CA
FERNANDEZ, JESUS San Diego, CA
FERRARIS, AL Norfolk, MA
FERRIS, JIM P. Baytown, TX
FERRY, JAMES L. Sacramento, CA
FEUERLICHT, SAMMY Los Angeles, CA
FIELDS, DAVID Auburn, MA
FILDES, PETE Newport Beach, CA
FILIZETTI, GARY J. Santa Clara, CA
FIMBRES, CHARLES M., JR.
   San Diego, CA
FIMBRES, RENE El Monte, CA
FINCH, FREDERICK D. Los Angeles, CA
FINDER, MARLT J. Westmont, PA
FINE, SANDY Diamond Bar, CA
FINELLI, JIM Bridgewater, NJ
FIRESTONE, CATHERINE
   Los Olivos, CA
FISCHER, ROBERT M., M.D.
   Northridge, CA
FISHBURNE, EDITH E. Washington, DC
FISHER, DEBRA S. Washington, DC
FISHER, TOM Elyria, OH
FISHMAN, JOEL Los Angeles, CA
FITZGERALD, MICHAEL St. Louis, MO
FLEISCHER, RANDI New York, NY
FLEMING, BEN Encino, CA
FLEMING, JAMES B. Downey, CA

FLEMING, JOHN Wauwatosa, WI
FLESNER, JAYSON Rapid City, SD
FLICK, ALEX Cockeysville, MO
FLINKARD, SHANNON Alturas, CA
FLORENCE, ARTIE Los Angeles, CA
FLORES, JERRY La Habra, CA
FLORES, RAUL GUADALUPE San
   Francisco, CA

Sandusky, OH

FLORIA, JON E. Inverness, IL
FLUG, ROBERT New York, NY
FLYNN, A. THOMAS Danville, CA
FLYNN, ED Ottawa, IL
FLYNN, EDDIE West Roxbury, MA
FLYNN, JOHN Cambridge, MA
FLYNN, RAYMOND, MAYOR
   Boston, MA
FOGERTY, JOHN Berkeley, CA
FOLEY, BENSON L. Rancho Santa Fe, CA
FOLEY, HUGH M. Columbia Falls, MT
FOLGER, LEE A. Charlotte, NC
FONDA, SHIRLEE Santa Monica, CA
FORBES, PATRICK Fountain Valley, CA
FORD, DAVID B. Rosemont, PA
FORD, ROBERT L. Shawnee, OK
FORD, WILLIAM L. Shawnee, OK
FORLETTA, TOM Panorama, CA
FORREST, OTIS Colorado Springs, CO
FORSTOT, JORDAN Denver, CO
FORSTOT, MICHELLE Denver, CO
FORSYTH, JYL Birmingham, MI
FORSYTHE, ANDRE Bradenton, FL
FORSYTHE, HOLLY Santa Monica, CA
FORTSON, TOM Sunnyvale, CA
FORTUNE, STEVEN Philadelphia, PA
FOSTER, BEAU Oakland, CA
FOSTER, BETTY JEAN Mentor, OH
FOSTER, ERIC SCOTT Studio City, CA
FOSTER, GARY New York, NY
FOSTER, GREGORY Washington, DC
FOSTER, JAMES KENT
   Pacific Palisades, CA
FOSTER, JENNIFER Pafific Palisades, CA
FOSTER, TIMOTHY Beverly Hills, CA
FOWLER, MARVIN E. Los Angeles, CA

FOWLER, PHILIP Villa Park, CA
FOX, BRIAN D. Malibu, CA
FOX, JOHN H. Irving, NY
FOX, MICHAEL E. Saratoga, CA
FRALICK, DELMAR El Dorado Hills, CA
FRAMBACK, JOHN Sawyer, MI
FRANCHI, LOUIS Boston, MA
FRANKS, ROBIN Los Angeles, CA
FRATTINI, JOSEPH Sherman Oaks, CA
FRAZEE, LESLIE San Diego, CA
FRAZIER, G. REX Portland, OR
FRAZIER, JOHN, JR. Salt Lake City, UT
FREDERICK, JERRY Upton, WY
FREDERICKS, BOB Glendale, CA
FREEBURG, JOHN Federal Way, WA
FREEMAN, RON North Plainfield, NJ
FRENCH, FRANK Flossmoor, IL
FREUND, DORIE MAUREEN Beverly
   Hills, CA
FREY, BARRY Long Beach, CA
FREY, DALE Walled Lake, MI
FRICKS, JOHN Torrance, CA
FRIEDMAN, LARRY
   South Lake Tahoe, CA
FRIEDMAN, MENDEL Baltimore, MD
FRISCH, ANNETTE Bayshore, NY
FRITZINGER, GRACE Los Angeles, CA
FROEHLICH, ELIAS Ft. Worth, TX
FROST, BOBBIE Westminster, CA
FROST, CLYDE Napa, CA
FRY, RICHARD, DR. Fullerton, CA
FRYE, FREDERICK A., M.D.
   San Diego, CA
FUERST, MARC Covina, CA
FULKERSON, JOHN Costa Mesa, CA
FULLER, EDWARD B. Grand Rapids, MI
FULLER, MICHAEL D.
   Walnut Creek, CA
FULLER, ROBY Macon, GA
FULTON, JERRY Lake Arrowhead, CA
FUNCHES, TYRON Oakland, CA
FUNK, KAREN E. Warren, MI
FURUKAWA, SHOJI Kitakyoishu City,
   Japan

GABBERT, CHARLES C. Santa Ana, CA
GABRIEL, RICHARD Chagrin Falls, OH
GAFFIGAN, JAMES Chesterton, IN
GAFFNEY, JOHN R. Birmingham, MI
GAGE, JIMMY Costa Mesa, CA
GAHL, SARA San Ramon, CA
GALLAGHER, ERIN RYAN
   Olympia, WA
GAMBLE, STEPHEN Alhambra, CA
GAMES, STEPHEN C. Escondido, CA
GARCIA, BOBBY Irvine, CA
GARCIA, CAROLE San Jose, CA
GARCIA, JOSE DE JESUS Huntington
   Beach, CA
GARCIA, JUAN La Habra, CA
GARCIA, RICARDO Bonita, CA
GARCIA, ROSEMARY Glendora, CA

GARCIA, ROBERT, JR.
Monterey Park, CA
GARCIA, THELMA Los Angeles, CA
GARDNER, JIM South Lake Tahoe, CA
GARDNER, WILLIAM Dalton, MA
GARFINKLE, PAUL Broomall, PA
GARLINGHOUSE, THOMAS S.
Capistrano Beach, CA
GARRETT, JIM Topeka, KS
GARRETT, PATRICIA
Thousand Oaks, CA
GARRETT, SUZANNA LEIGH Thousand
Oaks, CA
GARRINGER, DUANE San Francisco, CA
GARRIQUES, JOHN Casper, WY
GARRISON, LETICIA P. Buena Park, CA
GARRISON, TRACY Klamath Falls, OR
GARVEY, STEVE La Jolla, CA
GARY, DANIEL Solon, OH
GARZA, LAURA M. Cupertino, CA
GATES, PHIL Chattanooga, TN
GATTI, ED San Anselmo, CA

GERHARDT, JOHN Morgan Hills, CA
GERICHS, JIM Petoskey, MI
GERNES, DAVID Running Springs, CA
GETZ, EDWIN Los Angeles, CA
GETZ, THOMAS Annapolis, MD
GEWECKE, KATHY R. La Grande, OR
GHEE, STEPHEN B. Torrance, CA
GIBAN, LORI REY Kansas City, MO
GIBBONS, DAVID Morristown, NJ
GIBBONS, MIMI Morristown, NJ
GIBBS, LLOYD Lubbock, TX
GIBSON, CAROLE Los Angeles, CA
GIBSON, GERALD K. Milan, IL
GIBSON, JOAN Cleveland, OH
GIBSON, KEVIN M. Herlong, CA
GIES, HAL Long Beach, CA
GIFFORD, ASTRID New York, NY
GIGLIO, KEITH V. Haywood, CA
GILBERT, COLIN Beverly Hills, CA
GILDEA, BARRY San Marcos, TX
GILDEA, JOHN East Falmouth, RI
GILDEA, RAY, III Steens, MS

GLASS, ED Los Angeles, CA
GLASSMAN, FREDRICK Whittier, CA
GLEN, DANNY Albuquerque, NM
GLENN, DAVID Beverly Hills, CA
GLOUDEMAN, JOSEPH F., DR. La
Canada Flintridge, CA
GLUCK, TRACY Stateline, NV
GOCHIS, EMILY Los Angeles, CA
GODFRED, GORDON Chehalis, WA
GOFORTH, WALT Yorba Linda, CA
GOLD, BONNIE Rockville, MD
GOLD, PHILIP Snellville, GA
GOLDEN, BRIGHAM M. South
Weymouth, MA
GOLDINGER, S. JAY Beverly Hills, CA
GOLDINGER, SYLVAN H.
Beverly Hills, CA
GOLDMAN, RONALD Encino, CA
GOLDSMITH, EVAN New Rochelle, NY
GOLDSTEIN, ANDREW Chesterland, OH
GOLDSTEIN, STEVE Detroit, MI
GOLDSTON, S. R. Phoenix, AZ
GOLDSTON, STEPHAN Phoenix, AZ
GOMEZ, JUAN Los Angeles, CA
GOMORY, ROBERT J. Fullerton, CA
GONSALVES, JORGE Rio de Janeiro,
Brazil
GONZALES, ANTHONY New York, NY
GONZALES, DOUGLAS A.
Long Beach, CA
GONZALES, GLORIA Costa Mesa, CA
GONZALES, JOHN M.
Redondo Beach, CA
GONZALEZ, ERIC JOHN Richmond
Hills, NY
GOODING, CHARLES A., M.D. Mill
Valley, CA
GOODMAN, DAWN Morrison, CO
GOODRICH, BRIEN Santa Monica, CA
GOOLSBY, TERESSA Lonoke, AR
GORDER, STEVEN Rudyard, MT
GORDON, ALBERT Tucson, AZ
GORDON, CLIFFORD San Diego, CA
GORDON, ROBIN New York, NY
GORDON, TERESA D. Glenview, IL
GOSHIMA, MAYUMI Kobe, Japan
GOSINK, LEONARD J. San Diego, CA
GOSNAY, DAVID Houston, TX
GOSS, DEAN Cerritos, CA
GOTLIEB, ADAM Denver, CO
GOTO, STEVEN J. Alhambra, CA
GOTOH, KUMI Okayama, Japan
GOTT, JOHN O. La Fayette, LA
GOTTWALD, JAMES
South Pasadena, CA
GOUGH, DIDI Laguna Beach, CA
GRAAFSTRA, THOM Everett, WA
GRACIA, MARTHA Monterey Park, CA
GRADY, DON Mobile, AL
GRAF, ROBERT F. Sepulveda, CA
GRAFF, SYLVESTER M. Pasadena, CA
GRAKAL, CHRISTOPHER H.
Brentwood, CA

Lexington, KY

GAUGHAN, ROBERT Boston, MA
GAUVIN, DENISE, Johnston, RI
GAYER, FRAN ALLEN
Zephyr Cove, NV
GEBHARD, DEBBIE Laguna Beach, CA
GEIGER, BARBARA Fort Wayne, IN
GEISE, BEVERLY A. Casper, WY
GEISE, BONNIE Auburn, WA
GEIST, GLENN Costa Mesa, CA
GELBER, MILDRED Knoxville, TN
GELFANO, JANNA Los Angeles, CA
GELOW, BUD Napa, CA
GENTRY, G.M. San Diego, CA
GENTRY, RENE H. San Diego, CA
GEORGE, DAVID Tulsa, OK
GERFERS, JIM Buena Park, CA

GILL, CANDY El Cajon, CA
GILL, JAMES Denver, CO
GILLETTE, EDWIN F. Los Angeles, CA
GILLISPIE, RANDELL Alta Loma, CA
GILLOOLY, JOHN A. Coral Springs, FL
GILPIN, EARL, II Frederick, PA
GILROY, MELINDA A. Palos Verdes
Estates, CA
GILTNER, DICK Hinsdale, IL
GIOCOMO, ROBERT J. Kirkland, WA
GIRARDI, GEORGE R., JR. Athol, MA
GIRAUDI, RONALD V. Encinitas, CA
GIROUX, TODD LOUIS Los Angeles, CA
GIVAN, AMY Barrington, RI
GLADDEN, RICHARD P. Anaheim, CA
GLASKY, ALVIN J. Santa Ana, CA

GRANAUDO, INES Stamford, CT
GRANDEL, DONALD D., MAJ.
   Geneva, NY
GRANT, CROSBY Newport Beach, CA
GRANT, WILLIAM R. New York, NY
GRASS, HENRY, DR. Banks, OR
GRAVENSTEIN, EBERHARD
   Ft. Worth, TX

Ephrata, WA

GRAVES, RALPH East Greenwich, RI
GRAY, EDWARD J. Stockton, CA
GRAY, MARY T. Los Angeles, CA
GRAY, NORMAN A., JR. Medfield, MA
GRAYSON, ARTHUR Torrance, CA
GRAYSON, SUZANNE Los Angeles, CA
GREAR, DOUG Derby, KS
GRECO, SUE Niles, IL
GREEN, BOBBY EARL Pontiac, MI
GREEN, FRANK, JR. San Gabriel, CA
GREEN, HIX H., III Atlanta, GA
GREEN, LARRY Valencia, CA
GREEN, LEWIS G. Darien, CT
GREENBAUM, ROBERT S.
   Palm Springs, CA
GREENBERG, MICHAEL J. Glendale, CA
GREENE, RICHARD D. Novato, CA
GREENWOOD, LISA J. Tempe, AZ
GREER, EDWARD F., CAPT.
   St. Louis, MO
GREGORY, MIKE Charleston, WV
GREIG, WILLIAM, SR. Royal Oak, MI
GRIES, ROBERT D. Shaker Heights, OH
GRIFFIN, GARY DEAN Los Angeles, CA
GRILL, JOHNNY Amarillo, TX
GRIMES, AL Strongsville, OH
GRIMES, JAMES West Paterson, NJ
GRIMES, KEVIN Atlanta, GA
GRINER, JOE San Diego, CA
GRISSOM, JOANN TERRY
   Indianapolis, IN

GRISSON, LEE San Diego, CA
GRIZZARD, CLAUDE H. Stone
   Mountain, GA
GROARK, PATRICK Beverly Hills, CA
GRONEK, NANCY Cleveland, OH
GROOTHUIS, DEREK Englewood, CO
GROSMAN, BILL Fremont, CA
GROSS, GEORGE, III
   South Weymouth, MA
GROSSMAN, DAVID Encino, CA
GROTH, HOLGER Waxahachie, TX
GRUELER, JANET La Puente, CA
GRUNDEN, NANCY San Ramon, CA
GRUNDHAUSER, RUSSELL
   Seattle, WA
GRUNDY, CAROLYN Clarksburg, MD
GUARNIERI, MICHAEL W. Palos Verdes
   Estates, CA
GUEITS, ROBERT Rego Park, NY
GUERINDON, PIERRE C. Peoria, IL
GUEVARA, MARIA ALEXANDRA
   Southgate, CA
GUIDON, CARELLA Ione, CA
GUINZBURG, MICHAEL T. New
   York, NY
GUMMA, NAOMI Tokyo, Japan
GUTHRIE, L. C. Redondo Beach, CA
GUTIERREZ, ANTHONY J. San
   Diego, CA
GUTIERREZ, RICHARD R., JR. Los
   Angeles, CA
GWYNNE, RUSSELL M., JR.
   Riverside, CA

H

HAAS, AMY Stilwell, KS
HAAS, HAROLD Kentfield, CA
HAASE, KAREN La Mirada, CA
HABERECHT, ROLF R. Dallas, TX
HABERMAN, RICHARD E. Jerome, ID
HAGY, NOREEN South Lake Tahoe, CA
HAHN, ERNES, II Rancho Santa Fe, CA
HAHN, JEAN Rancho Santa Fe, CA
HAHN, JENNIFER Rancho Santa Fe, CA
HAHN, LINDA Rancho Santa Fe, CA
HAHN, RONALD Rancho Santa Fe, CA
HALE, JASON Akron, OH
HALE, RAY G. Salt Lake City, UT
HALE, TOMMY Redwood City, CA
HALKIAS, THEODORE San Marino, CA
HALL, BROOKE PHISTER
   Costa Mesa, CA
HALL, CHARLES Beverly Hills, CA
HALL, GARY H. Citrus Hall, CA
HALL, JAMES L. Florence, OR
HALL, PORTER J. Sandy, UT
HALL, ROBERT Chicago, IL
HALL, SUSAN Westlake Village, CA
HALLIDAY-THOMAS, DEBRA
   Temecula, CA
HALLIGAN, BILL Munhall, PA
HALLING, JIM Atlanta, GA
HALPORN, ETHAN Northridge, CA

HAMAN, CLAUS Los Angeles, CA
HAMANAKA, MASAYUKI Tokyo, Japan
HAMBLIN, MARTHA Mebane, NC
HAMILTON, BILL Santa Barbara, CA
HAMILTON, CHARLES T.
   Tunkhannock, PA
HAMILTON, DICK Tahoe, NV
HAMILTON, JAMES D. Pomona, CA
HAMLIN, FREDERICK WRIGHT New
   York, NY
HAMMOND, DAVID Huron, OH
HAMMOND, SEAN C. D. Savannah, GA
HAMPDON, KEVEN Boulder, CO
HAMPTON, FREDERICK B. Upper
   Saddle River, NJ
HAMRELL, MIRIAM E. Los Angeles, CA
HANBY, JOSEPH J. Birmingham, AL
HANDEL, JON Marina Del Rey, CA
HANDEL, RICHARD Los Angeles, CA
HANDEL-COHEN, NANCI
   Los Angeles, CA
HANDLEY, STEVE Azusa, CA
HANES, VICKI Los Angeles, CA
HANEY, HARRY V. Imperial Beach, CA
HANEY, MICKEY G. Redondo Beach, CA
HANG, CHANG Lompoc, CA
HANIFORD, BOB Los Angeles, CA
HANNAH, KATHY Salt Lake City, UT
HANNON, PETER Wappingers Falls, NY
HANSEN, ANDY Danville, CA
HANSEN, DANNY Carmichael, CA
HANSEN, TONYA L. Uiola, KS
HANSON, BRETT Van Nuys, CA
HANSON, ROBIN Royersford, PA
HARDWICK, KEN Oklahoma City, CA
HARMON, BRADLEY ALDEN Lake
   Winnebago, MO
HARMS, JACK R. Plymouth, MI
HAROS, PAUL Fresno, CA
HARPER, FAITH Redondo Beach, CA
HARPER, HANK
   Rancho Palos Verdes, CA
HARPER, HARRY
   Palos Verdes Estates, CA
HARPER, LINDA LEE Palos Verdes
   Estates, CA
HARRELL, DANIEL Greenville, SC
HARRINGTON, MICHELE Huntington
   Beach, CA
HARRIS, JEFF Anaheim, CA
HARRIS, MICHAEL W. Rosemead, CA
HARRIS, PAM Anaheim, CA
HARRIS, WALLACE Richmond, VA
HARRISON, CHET Corona Del Mar, CA
HARRISON, KENNETH Northville, MI
HARRISON, MARK D. Pontiac, MI
HARRISON, PATRICK J. Naperville, IL
HART, MARY Los Angeles, CA
HARTBARGER, STEVE Lithonia, GA
HARTCH, TODD Greenwich, CT
HARTE, GENE L. Van Nuys, CA
HARTLEY, BOYD Glendale, CA
HARTLEY, DON Pacific Palisades, CA

HARTMAN, JOHN H. Orange, CA
HARTMAN, WILLIAM Secane, PA
HARTMANN, BUTCH St. Louis, MO
HARTMENN, BETTY L. Chester, VA
HARVEY, CHARLENE San Francisco, CA
HARWOOD, LOWELL Jersey City, NJ
HASEBE, KEIJI Kouhoku-ku Yokohama,
   Japan
HASKINS, JUDY Belvedere, CA
HASS, CARL E. San Marino, CA
HATHAWAY, CHARLES Pacific
   Palisades, CA
HATHAWAY, DOUGLAS W. Costa
   Mesa, CA
HAUSCH, BILL Manhattan Beach, CA
HAVLICK, JAMES D. La Canada, CA
HAWKES, DIANA West Hempstead, NY
HAWKINS, BECKY San Luis Obispo, CA
HAWKINS, CHERYL
   South Lake Tahoe, CA
HAWKINS, LORENE Pittsburgh, PA
HAWKINS, TOMMY Malibu, CA
HAWKS, PAMELA Pennington, NJ
HAWLEY, CRAIG Fullerton, CA
HAYDEN, TOM Santa Monica, CA
HAYEK, JOLA Hollywood, CA
HAYES, PATRICIA Davis, CA
HAYNES, JEFF Prescott, AR
HAYWARD, SUSAN Seattle, WA
HAZEL, CHARLES Mountain View, CA
HEALY, MICHAEL J. Houston, TX
HEARNES, DICK Kirkwood, MO
HEATON, JIM Topeka, KS
HECKEL, JACK Del Mar, CA
HEDGECOCK, ROGER, MAYOR San
   Diego, CA
HEFFERMAN, PAUL Cleveland, OH
HEFFERN, GORDON E.
   Shaker Heights, OH
HEFFLEY, GARY Richmond, CA
HEFTY, PAUL M. Bartlesville, OK
HEIDECKER, DUANE Indianapolis, IN
HEINDL, ANN MARIE Akron, OH
HEINZ, MICHAEL Winnetka, IL
HEIZER, ERIC Rochester, MI
HELD, DEBRA LYNN
   Glendale Heights, IL
HELDFOND, BENJAMIN
   San Francisco, CA
HELDFOND, NICHOLAS
   San Francisco, CA
HELLMAN, WARREN San Francisco, CA
HELOW, RONALD J. Belvedere, CA
HELTON, PAMELA Stateline, NV
HEMPHILL, GINA Chicago, IL
HENDERSON, MARK W. Larkspur, CA
HENDERSON, MELBA Portland, OR
HENDERSON, MIKE New York, NY
HENDRICHS, TIM Alcoa, TN
HENDRICKS, DAVE San Diego, CA
HENDRICKSON, MARK M. Aurora, CO
HENDRICKSON, RACHAEL Chicago, IL
HENDRIX, KEN Moss Lake, WA

HENLEY, MARKIDA Sunnyvale, CA
HENLEY, PARTICIA Rocky Hill, CT
HENSLEY, JACK O. Indianapolis, IN
HERMAN, HEATHER Lebanon, NJ
HERMANN, RICHARD J. Little Rock, AR
HERNANDEZ, CARLOS Fremont, CA
HERNANDEZ, CATALINA
   Los Angeles, CA
HERNANDEZ, DAVID E. Cerritos, CA

Tulsa, OK

HERNANDEZ, GEORGE Sparks, NV
HERNANDEZ, JUAN J. Van Nuys, CA
HERNANDEZ, PETE Santa Paula, CA
HERRERA, MAGDALENA GARCIA Los
   Angeles, CA
HERRICK, JOE La Habra Heights, CA
HERSHBERGER, JIM Wichita, KS
HESS, PETER A. Winnetka, IL
HEVERLY, KATHY Richardson, TX
HEWSER, COLLEN Richmond, VA
HEYM, WILLIAM J. Valley Stream, NY
HEZLEP, ROSEMARY
   Newport Beach, CA
HIBBS, DREW South Lake Tahoe, CA
HICKERSON, TODD Visalia, CA
HICKEY, JILL Vallejo, CA
HICKEY, JOSEPH M., JR. Bratenahl, OH
HICKEY, LORI Los Angeles, CA
HICKS, LISA Ventura, CA
HIGGINS, LARRY Wyckoff, NJ
HIGHT, MICHELLE Beverly Hills, CA
HIGLEY, JON M. Renton, WA
HIGUCHI, RICARDO Los Angeles, CA
HILAND, MIKE Ottawa, IL
HILDEBRAND, JULIE Tacoma, WA
HILL, BARBARA GIUS Long Beach, CA
HILL, BUFORD Tustin, CA
HILL, GERI Huntington Beach, CA
HILL, LYDA Dallas, TX
HILL, THOMAS Jonesboro, AR
HILLMAN, MAYOR R. New York, NY
HILLMAN, ROBERT D., JR. Pacific
   Palisades, CA
HINCKLEY, BRUCE C. Glendale, CA

HINDERT, MIKE Kalamazoo, MI
HINES, PAUL G. La Jolla, CA
HINNERSCHITZ, CLARENCE
   Brooklyn, NY
HINNINGSON, JOHN Worcester, MA
HIRSCH, FRANK Baltimore, MD
HIRSH, BRIAN Beverly Hills, CA
HIRSH, KEVIN Beverly Hills, CA
HITCHCOCK, WILLIAM B. South
   Pasadena, CA
HOCKLEITNER, DIETER Ft. Worth, TX
HODGE, BRADY South Lake Tahoe, CA
HOEKSTRA, KIMBERLY San Diego, CA
HOEKSTRA, MARK San Diego, CA
HOEKSTRA, TODD San Diego, CA
HOFF, RONALD J. Los Osos, CA
HOFFMAN, BUD Chappaqua, NY
HOFFMAN, JOHN E., JR. Menlo
   Park, CA
HOFFMAN, MICHAEL R. Palm
   Harbor, FL
HOGG, WADE B. Fullerton, CA
HOGLAND, CLAIRE San Francisco, CA
HOLCOMB, LINDA Decatur, GA
HOLLAND, DANIEL Beverly Hills, CA
HOLLAND, KEVIN Corona, CA
HOLLAWAY, VICKIE LYNN Seattle, WA
HOLLIDAY, BOB Dallas, TX
HOLLINGSWORTH, JESSE
   Waynesville, NC
HOLMAN, JODY Denver, CO
HOLMES, JOHN Knoxville, TN
HOLST, LINDY Fair Oaks, CA
HOLSTON, LAURA Princeton, NJ
HOLTER, BOB Manhattan Beach, CA
HOOPER, MARTHA W. Los Angeles, CA
HOOPER, THOMAS R. Orange, CA
HOOVER, GEORGE
   Rancho Santa Fe, CA
HOOVER, HERBERT, III San Marino, CA
HORI, TOSHIHIDE Otus, Japan
HORIGUCHI, CHIYE Gardena, CA
HORNER, DENNIS Council Bluffs, IA
HOSLER, ROBERT M., JR. Cleveland
   Heights, OH
HOSOI, TOMOKO Okazaki, Japan
HOSTETTER, HARVEY D. Portland, OR
HOTCHKIS, CAREY Pasadena, CA
HOTCHKIS, JOHN F., JR. Pasadena, CA
HOTCHKIS, MARK B. Pasadena, CA
HOTCHKIS, SARAH Los Angeles, CA
HOUGH, HEIDI Chicago, IL
HOULE, DEAN West Hartford, CT
HOULE, MARC Webster, MA
HOUSE, WARREN Zephyr Cove, NV
HOUSER, DONALD F. Sacramento, CA
HOWARD, DAVID M.
   Newport Beach, CA
HOWARD, J. R., JR. Greenville, SC
HOWELL, CATHERINE A.
   Honesdale, PA
HOWELL, WENDI JO Lancaster, OH
HOWES, THOMAS P. Westport, CT

HOWITT, ROBERT M. Denville, NJ
HOXMEIER, ROGER Ventura, CA
HOY, SUSAN DANE New York, NY
HOYT, LAWRENCE Sonoma, CA
HUBAND, LOUIS J. Walnut, CA
HUBERMAN, BERNARDO R.
  Palo Alto, CA
HUBERTY, WILLIAM G. River Falls, WI
HUCKINS, GREG Douglass, KS
HUDSON, ROBERT J., JR. Seekonk, MA
HUEBNER, DEBORAH Carpinteria, CA
HUEBNER, DONNA Carpinteria, CA
HUFFMAN, J. R. Shoshone, CA
HUFFMAN, LEE Monroe, MI
HUFFMAN, SCOTT Boulder, CO
HUGHES, JOE Ottawa, IL
HUIZAK, SAM Santa Monica, CA
HULKOWER, M. WALTER
  Beverly Hills, CA
HUMPHREY, JOE Arroyo Grande, CA
HUND, SHELLEY Portland, OR
HUNT, CARRIE SUE Bowie, MD
HUNT, DEBORAH Artesia, CA
HUNTER, KEN South Lake Tahoe, CA
HUNTLEY, SHAWN Portland, OR
HURET, ROBERT San Francisco, CA
HURLEY, RICHARD R., JR.
  Baltimore, MD
HUSSEY, JOHN C. North Kingstown, RI
HUSTON, TERRI Lincoln, NE
HUTCHINSON, BOB Phoenix, AZ
HUTCHISON, ANDY
  Rancho Santa Fe, CA
HUTCHISON, SUE Rancho Santa Fe, CA
HUTH, STAN Newport Beach, CA
HUTTENBACK, ROBERT A., DR. Santa
  Barbara, CA
HUTTER, KARL GEORGE
  Carson City, NV
HUTTON, SCOTT A. Pittsburgh, PA
HWI, KIM WON Los Angeles, CA
HYINK, SHERRILL Thousand Oaks, CA
HYNES, STEVEN J. Newport Beach, CA

I

IBUKA, NOBUKO Miyagi, Japan
IHARA, TOMOO Gunma, Japan
IKEGAME, MIHO Tokyo, Japan
INGLEE, PHIL R. Golden, CO
INGLEHART, BILL Houston, TX
INLOW, RICK Roselle, IL
INLOW, STEPHANIE Mexico, MO
INMAN, MICHAEL Redford, MI
INOUE, TOMOYOSHI Tokyo, Japan
IRRERA, DOMENICK, SGT. MAJ. Camp
  Pendleton, CA
ISAACS, DIANA Beverly Hills, CA
ISAACS, GREGORY B. Charleston, WV
ISAACS, RUSSEL Charleston, WV
ISCH, HEIDI San Clemente, CA
ISHIKAWA, TAKESHI Los Angeles, CA
ISOLA, VIRGIL M. Mount Pleasant, PA
ISOM, ANNETTE H. Santa Ana, CA

ITTLESON, H. ANTHONY
  New York, NY
ITTLESON, MARIANNE New York, NY

J

JAASTAD, K. SIGURD E. Des Moines, IA
JACK, ROSEMARY J. Signal Hill, CA
JACKMAN, TOM Marina Del Ray, CA
JACKSON, BILL Denver, CO
JACKSON, CHRISTIE Southfield, MI
JACKSON, DONALD Gardena, CA
JACKSON, DURRELL Downey, CA
JACKSON, JEFF Birmingham, AL
JACKSON, RANDY E. Placentia, CA
JACKSON, STEVEN Z. Toledo, OH
JACOB, YOLANDA R. Kenner, LA
JACOBI, RAYMEND Anaheim, CA
JACOBI, ROBERT A. Canoga Park, CA
JACOBS, DAN Riverside, CA
JACOBS, PEGGY Chicago, IL

Boonton, NJ

JACOBSON, JENNIFER SUE
  Sacramento, CA
JACOBSON, LEE Berkeley, CA
JACOBY, FRED Arnold, MD
JAEHNE, JILL San Jose, CA
JAFFE, BRUCE Santa Monica, CA
JAMES, ALLISON Omaha, NE
JAMES, BESS San Jacinto, CA
JAMES, BRENT Seattle, WA
JAMES, BRIAN Inglewood, CA
JAMES, CHARLES, SGT. Camp
  Pendleton, CA
JAMES, WENDI Schaumburg, IL
JAMISON, CHARLES W.
  Santa Barbara, CA
JANASZAK, JAMES J. Bay Shore, NY

JANICICH, LOU Vernon, CA
JANN, JOHN R. Niles, MI
JANOS, CLEON A.
  Lakeview Terrace, CA
JARRETT, SHARON Minden, NV
JENKENSON, WILLIAM K. Willow
  Grove, PA
JENKINS, NANCY L. Wichita, KS
JENKINSON, DENISE Willow Grove, PA
JENNER, BRUCE Malibu, CA
JENSEN, BRIAN Beaumont, TX
JENSEN, CHRIS Bellevue, WA
JENSEN, TIMOTHY Pacific Palisades, CA
JEWETT, TRACY North Attleboro, MA
JIMENEZ, MICHAEL Northwood, OH
JOBE, NASIYA Richmond, CA
JOHANSEN, OLIE Fresno, CA
JOHN, MAURICE E., DR. Louisville, KY
JOHNKE, JOHN New York, NY
JOHNSON, BEVERLY San Francisco, CA
JOHNSON, BOB Bakersfield, CA
JOHNSON, BURT Duarte, CA
JOHNSON, CHARLES W. Racine, WI
JOHNSON, DALE H. Renton, WA
JOHNSON, ERIC Costa Mesa, CA
JOHNSON, FORREST F. Doraville, GA
JOHNSON, GEORGE Ingleside, IL
JOHNSON, HEIDI L.
  Huntington Beach, CA
JOHNSON, LELAND Concord, CA
JOHNSON, LINDA Lansdale, PA
JOHNSON, MARIA Manchester, NH
JOHNSON, RAFER Dallas, TX
JOHNSON, ROBERT A. Santa Rosa, CA
JOHNSON, RODNEY New York, NY
JOHNSON, RONALD A. Detroit, MI
JOHNSON, SAMUEL T. Dana Point, CA
JOHNSON, SCOTTIE Atlanta, GA
JOHNSON, SONNY Muncie, IN
JOHNSON, VICTOR
  North Highlands, CA
JOHNSTON, KATIE Kansas City, MO
JOHNSTON, MARY THERESA
  Southfield, MI
JOHNSTON, SALLY L. Phoenix, AZ
JONES, ANDREA A. Los Angeles, CA
JONES, ARTIS Decatur, GA
JONES, BENJAMIN F. Somers, CT
JONES, BOB M. Wilmington, CA
JONES, BRUCE C. La Crescenta, CA
JONES, BRYAN Taft, CA
JONES, CONNELL J. Evansville, IN
JONES, GEORGE A. Glendora, CA
JONES, KARL Carrollton, TX
JONES, MARCUS Houston, TX
JONES, MARY Newport Beach, CA
JONES, RONALD
  Palos Verdes Estates, CA
JONES, SHERRIL South Lake Tahoe, CA
JOOS, LESLIE Huntington Beach, CA
JORDAN, HOMER Gainesville, GA
JORDAN, HUGH M. Rome, GA
JORDAN, WAYNE San Francisco, CA

JOSEPH, STEPHEN A. San Marino, CA
JOURDANE, MAURICE Salinas, CA
JOYCE, REGINA Edmonds, WA
JOYCE, TOM Staten Island, NY
JUBERT, DAVID M. Green Bay, WI
JUDD, COREY DEREK
   Thousand Oaks, CA
JUGUM, DEBBIE Sacramento, CA
JUNG, SOHN KIN Los Angeles, CA
JUSTIS, RICKY Dallas, TX

K

KAHAN, ROBERT L. Los Angeles, CA
KAHN, MORT Bridgewater, NJ
KAHN, ROZ San Francisco, CA
KALB, STEVE Las Vegas, NV
KALMBACK, SUSAN Pittsburgh, PA
KAMITA, KEITH Kaneohe, HI
KANADA, TOSHIMASA Ohbu, Japan
KANAZAWA SHOJI Tokyo, Japan
KANE, KRISTINA ELLEN
   Walla Walla, WA
KANEMAKI, TOSHIO Tokyo, Japan
KANSAKU, TERUYUKI Chibaken Chiba,
   Japan
KAPHING, GERALD E. Tucson, AZ
KAPLAN, JON Highland Heights, OH
KAPPESSER, ROGER Louisville, KY
KARATSIS, EDNA Fresno, CA
KARMA, ARTHUR
   Rancho Palos Verdes, CA
KASHAWA, HANK Denver, CO
KASIANCHUK, ANDY Honolulu, HI
KASS, GORDON Saratoga, CA
KASTEN, JIM Herculaneum, MO
KATANIK, JOSEPH Brooklyn, NY
KATES, HENRY E. Providence, RI
KATTO, DENNIS L. Long Beach, CA
KATZ, ALLEN M. Corona Del Mar, CA
KATZ, RICHARD, Panorama City, CA
KATZMAN, ANDREW Los Angeles, CA
KAU, CHERYL Redondo Beach, CA
KAUFFMAN, KEN Sacramento, CA
KAUFFMANN, KENNETH
   Canoga Park, CA
KAUFMAN, DONALD R. North
   Hollywood, CA
KAVANAGH, KATHLEEN Corona, CA
KAVATZAS, CHRIS Westminster, CA
KAY, JEROME HAROLD, M.D. Los
   Angeles, CA
KEANCEVIC, JAMES
   Mayfield Heights, OH
KEARNEY, RICHARD Sandown, NH
KEATING, KRISTA KAY Phoenix, AZ
KEEGAN, HOWARD W. Manchester, NH
KEEN, BILLY Knoxville, TN
KEEN, ROBERT Knoxville, TN
KELLER, DENNIS M. Fairmont City, IL
KELLER, OLEANA Tulsa, OK
KELLETT, KEVIN Atlanta, GA
KELLEY, ERIC Dallas, TX
KELLEY, HAROLD A. Maumee, OH

KELLEY, JOSEPH Akron, OH
KELLY, PATRICK Los Angeles, CA
KEMP, MARGARET Thousand Oaks, CA
KEMPEN, LAURIE Bakersfield, CA
KENEDA, SCOTT Oklahoma City, OK
KENNEDY, CAROLE Baltimore, MD
KENNEDY, CINDY L. Vista, CA
KENNEDY, MIKE Torrance, CA
KENT, PAUL M. Boulder, CO
KERSHAW, GUS Boulder, CO
KESSELMAN, FRANK Wilmington, DE
KESSLER, EDWARD Los Angeles, CA
KETCHUM, DARCY C. New York, NY
KETCHUM, SCOTT M.
   Newport Beach, CA
KEWLEY, JAMES Cleveland, OH
KEYSOR, DAVID MEYER Canyon
   Country, CA
KEYSOR, ROBERT E. Newhall, CA
KEZAS, GEORGE Solana Beach, CA
KHAN, MUKARAM Rochester, MI
KIDD, JAMES ALLEN San Francisco, CA
KIESER, C. WILLIAM Bala-Cynwyd, PA
KIESSLING, JAMES A. Sunnyvale, CA
KILGORE, DARYLL Reno, NV
KILKENNY, JAMES Oberlin, OH
KILLION, NELLIE R. Loma Linda, CA
KILMAN, GRACE Altadena, CA
KILPATRICK, RANDY San Diego, CA
KIM, SEE MYUN Torrance, CA
KIMBROUGH, JENNIE Little Rock, AR
KINCAID, PATRICK J. Bolingbrook, IL
KINERY, TYRONE, SGT. Twenty-nine
   Palms, CA
KING, ANGELA Pasadena, CA
KING, BRIAN Greer, SC
KING, DAVID A. Long Beach, CA

Dallas, TX

KING, WALLACE V., San Diego, CA
KING, WILLIAM J. Glendale, CA
KINGAARD, SEAN ERIK
   Costa Mesa, CA
KINION, NATHAN, F., JR.
   Carrollton, GA
KINSELLA, JOHN Winnetka, IL

KINSLER, RUTHE Delaware, OH
KIPECKY, LONNIE Houston, TX
KIRKGAARD, VALERIE Los Angeles, CA
KIRKHAM, GATES Willoughby, OH
KIRKHAM, GEORGE Cleveland, OH
KIRKWOOD, CHRISTINE Huntington
   Beach, CA
KIRKWOOD, WALTER B. Indiana, IN
KISSLINGER, MARY BETH El Cajon, CA
KITAGAWA, KEIKO Tochigi, Japan
KITAGAWA, KEITH Buena Park, CA
KIVIAT, ABEL R. Lakehurst, NJ
KIYOTA, SEIKA Tokyo, Japan
KIZER, TRAVIS Eugene, OR
KLAAHSEN, KATHY San Diego, CA
KLASER, KASEY Chula Vista, CA
KLAUBER, PHILIP M. San Diego, CA
KLEE, HOWARD, JR. Naperville, IL
KLEIN, ARTHUR I. New York, NY
KLEIN, DAVID Honolulu, HI
KLEIN, JAMES E. Clinton, OH
KLEIN, KRISTIN Akron, OH
KLEINERT, ROBERT Franklin Lakes, NJ
KLICMAN, DENNIS Akron, OH
KLINGE, JOEL M. Mesa, AZ
KLINGSTON, GEORGE
   Elizabethtown, PA
KLIONSKY, SY Binghamton, NY
KLOPE, AMY ELIZABETH Ventura, CA
KNAPP, DONALD M. Greenfield, MA
KNAUB, JIM Long Beach, CA
KNIGHTER, CHIWAUKII
   Los Angeles, CA
KNUDSEN, ELIZABETH PAGE
   New York, NY
KNUTE, KRISTA Irvine, CA
KO, YOUNG El Cerrito, CA
KOCH, JEFFREY Chester, NJ
KOERNER, STEPHEN Portland, OR
KOESTER, MATTHEW Shawnee
   Mission, KS
KOFF, HOWARD M. Encino, CA
KOGUTEK, MICHAEL D. Orange, CA
KOHL, DOUGLAS R. Shauburg, IL
KOHN, STEVE Menomonee Falls, WI
KOHTZ, BOB San Jose, CA
KOKICHI, UYEHARA El Cajon, CA
KOLL, JACK Newport Beach, CA
KOLM, KAROL M. Waco, TX
KOMLOS, MIKE Beaver Falls, PA
KONSTIN, CONSTANTINE
   Mill Valley, CA
KORNING, GERD Ft. Worth, TX
KOVALIK, JOE P. San Jose, CA
KOWALSKI, DAN Sheridan, WY
KRAMER, KEN Glen Ellyn, IL
KRANENBURG, MARION
   Milwaukee, WI
KRAUSE, RUSSELL Canton, OH
KRAUSE, STUART New York, NY
KRAUSHAR, STAN Toms River, NJ
KRUSE, CARL Poway, CA
KRYSS, JOSEPH São Paulo, Brazil

KUANDE, THOR ANDREW
Philadelphia, PA
KUCEJ, JENNIFER Trumbull, CT
KUHLMANN, JOHN H. Villa Park, IL
KUNZ, DONNA Salt Lake City, UT
KURAKANE, MIE Tokyo, Japan
KURN, WERNER Encinitas, CA
KURTANICH, JAMES Pittsburgh, PA
KURTANICH, JANET, Pittsburgh, PA

L

LA HAYE, FRANK Cupertino, CA
LABARRE, DAVID J. Woodridge, IL
LACHAPELLE, MARC Scotia, NY
LAROCCA, MICHAEL Lynn, MA
LAVAUTE, STEVE Los Altos Hills, CA
LADEAU, MARK Woodstock, VT
LADERACH, YVONNE Erie, MI
LADWIG, JAMES Evanston, IL
LAHIRI, AURINDRO Bakersfield, CA
LAKE, MICHAEL R. San Diego, CA
LAKE, NORA Irvine, CA
LAMARRE, LEILANI Escondido, CA
LAMBIASE, VINCENT A. Irvine, CA
LAMM, RICHARD, GOV. Denver, CO
LAMPIRIS, CHRIS Albuquerque, NM
LANCOR, BILL Hicksville, NY
LANDER, BRADLEY Van Nuys, CA
LANDGREBE, GEORGE Weston, MA
LANDRY, DEBRA A. Denver, CO
LANE, DANNY Laguna Beach, CA
LANGEBERG, SHARON
Los Angeles, CA
LANGENBERG, OLIVER M.
St. Louis, MO
LANGSLET, AUDREY Long Beach, CA
LANO, SUE Waterbury, CT
LANTZ, ROBERT L. Casper, WY
LAPPEN, CHET Pacific Palisades, CA
LARA, DELORES Wichita, KS
LARSEN, JIM A. El Toro, CA
LARSON, CHRISSIE Glendale, CA
LARSON, CYNTHIA BARNETT Rancho
Palos Verdes, CA
LATIMER, BRENDA Bedford, VA
LATOUR, JOHN Goleta, CA
LATTANY, MEL Athens, GA
LATTIMER, GEORGE W. La Jolla, CA
LATTIMER, HEATHER San Diego, CA
LAUDI, MONICA C. Sacramento, CA
LAUTRUP, TIMMY San Francisco, CA
LAVALLI, DIANE M.
Redondo Beach, CA
LAVELLE, EDWARD Wilmington, DE
LAVIN, JEANNIE M. San Francisco, CA
LAWLER, J. Yardley, PA
LAWSON, JOHN M., JR. La Canada
Flintridge, CA
LAY, JEREMY Braintree Essex, England
LAZARUS, JOHN New York, NY
LAZZARETTO, ANDREW C.
Burbank, CA
LEFRANCIS, NOEL Chester, NJ

LEACH, LES Thousand Oaks, CA
LEACH, LOIS, Thousand Oaks, CA
LEACH, THOMAS A., III
Collegeville, PA
LEADINGHAM, HARRY P., JR.
Wheeling, IL
LEAK, DAVID Oceanside, CA
LEAL, GUADALUPE San Francisco, CA
LEAR, MILTON JOHN Los Angeles, CA
LEASON, AMELIA Newport Beach, CA
LEASON, TIMOTHY Newport Beach, CA
LEDERER, TIMOTHY P. Philadelphia, PA
LEDERMAN, MARK T. New York, NY
LEE, JACK Pittsburgh, PA
LEE, LILLY MU Los Angeles, CA
LEE, MAN YOUNG
Woodside, Queens, NY
LEE, MARY ELIZABETH Van Nuys, CA

Eugene, OR

LEE, NANCY C. Monterey Park, CA
LEE, SAMMY, DR. Los Angeles, CA
LEE, SOO MOO South Lake Tahoe, CA
LEEMING, JANICE E. Providence, RI
LEEPART, GERALD Lennon, MI
LEHMAN, BETSY Beaver, PA
LEIGHTON, ROGER Costa Mesa, CA
LEINERT, JOHN Linwood, NJ
LEITIZKE, JIM Marina, CA
LEMOS, CAROLYN Stateline, NV
LEMUCCHI, TIMOTHY Bakersfield, CA
LENNARTZ, WILLIAM R.
Rolling Hills, CA
LENNON, MARY WILSON Solon, OH
LENNON, MIKE San Diego, CA
LENNON, TIMOTHY C. Russel
Township, OH
LEPORE, STEVEN L. Wilmington, DE
LEPPER, JACK Yorba Linda, CA
LEPPER, MARK A. El Cajon, CA
LESEMAN, WILLIAMS Van Nuys, CA
LESNAR, RAYMOND R. St. Paul, MN

LESSER, RUSS Manhattan Beach, CA
LESTER, JOHN R. Sunland, CA
LESTER, STEPHEN Los Angeles, CA
LEVENTHAL, ELAINE OTTER Los
Angeles, CA
LEVINE, JASON El Monte, CA
LEVINE, MEL, CONGRESSMAN
Washington, DC
LEVY, J. LAMPERT Los Angeles, CA
LEWANDOWSKI, PAULA Troy, MI
LEWIS, KENNETH A. Newbury Park, CA
LEWIS, KEVIN Beverly Hills, CA
LEWIS, PAUL Santa Clara, CA
LEWIS, SUSANNA Halifax, Nova Scotia,
Canada
LEWIS, TIMOTHY Los Angeles, CA
LEY, CINDY Atchison, KS
LIBENSON, RICHARD El Cajon, CA
LIBUSER, ANDY Santa Monica, CA
LIEB, JACK San Diego, CA
LIEN, LARRY Los Angeles, CA
LILES, LESLIE Los Angeles, CA
LILLY, DAVID M. Los Osos, CA
LIMING, ROBERT Pasadena, CA
LIN, TANA Schaumburg, IL
LINAS, WILLIAM B. Trabuco, CA
LINDE, CHRIS Torrance, CA
LINDEN, HAL Beverly Hills, CA
LINDEN, THOMAS MICHAEL Laguna
Beach, CA
LINDHEIM, SUSAN Beverly Hills, CA
LINENHAN, ERIN Auburn, WA
LING, ROBERT A. Irvine, CA
LINQUIST, CINDY R. Denver, CO
LINTHICUM, LAURA Cupertino, CA
LINTON, TOM Santa Monica, CA
LIONE, MICHAEL D. West Orange, NJ
LIPSON, MARK L. Calabasas Park, CA
LISA, KATHLEEN Parsippany, NJ
LISAGOR, TERRI Camarillo, CA
LITCHFIELD, LINDA L. Los Angeles, CA
LITTLE, ARTHUR D. Providence, RI
LIVINGSTON, RONALD
Laguna Beach, CA
LLOYD, HAROLD L. Burbank, CA
LLOYD, JONATHAN D.
Santa Monica, CA
LLOYD, JULIE Orange, CA
LOCKE, JENNIFER E. San Diego, CA
LOFFARELLI, THOMAS C.
Studio City, CA
LOGAN, DAN Kansas City, KS
LOGGINS, LISA Gainesville, GA
LOGUE, ERIC Los Angeles, CA
LOGUE, RACHEL Los Angeles, CA
LOHMAN, DAVE Tenafly, NJ
LOMBARDI, MICHAEL J. Shaker
Heights, OH
LONDON, JULIE Sylmar, CA
LONG, CHUCK San Diego, CA
LONG, LONNIE R. Yuba City, CA
LONG, MICHAEL PATRICK
Stockton, CA

LOPEZ, ARMANDO J. San Francisco, CA
LOPEZ, DANIEL National City, CA
LOPEZ, DAVID E. Santa Ana, CA
LOPEZ, ELIAS Los Angeles, CA
LOPEZ, JACOB El Monte, CA
LOPEZ, LOUIS New York, NY
LOPEZ, MIKE Benson, AZ
LORELLO, MICHAEL Warren, OH
LOREN, DAVIDSON Alderwood
  Manor, WA
LORGE, LESTER L. Cerrito, CA
LORSCH, ANNIE Los Angeles, CA
LOUDON, KATE Capitola, CA
LOVECCHIO, DARREN J. Stockton, CA
LOVEY, CHRISTY Anaheim Hills, CA
LOW, JOHN Montebello, CA
LOWE, KEITH Morristown, NJ
LOWELL, GARY R. Fallbrook, CA
LOWKE, ERROL Compton, CA
LOWRY, KATHIE San Francisco, CA
LUCAS, DONALD San Jose, CA
LUCAS, MARK D. Napa, CA
LUCERO, MARK STEVEN Garden
  Grove, CA
LUDEMANN, RONALD Bowling
  Green, OH
LUGARDO, ROBERTO Los Angeles, CA
LUJAN, JOHN Alameda, CA
LUM, CHARLIE Los Angeles, CA
LUN, EARL Santa Rosa, CA
LUND, ARTHUR K. San Jose, CA
LUND, RONALD S. Aspen, CO
LUPBERGER, EDWIN New Orleans, LA
LUSH, LAURETTE J. Burbank, CA
LUSSIER, RACHEL Battle Creek, MI
LUTKE, KARL Huntington Beach, CA
LUTRIN, DAVID Marmora, NJ
LUX, RICK Mitchell, KY
LYKINS, LANA Breckenridge, TX
LYMAN, RICHARD Sacramento, CA
LYNCH, CAROLYN Vancouver, WA
LYNCH, MICHAEL Astoria, OR
LYNCH, PATRICK E. Ventnor, NJ
LYNN, SHIRLEY Los Gatos, CA
LYONS, CHRIS Pomona, CA
LYONS, PAUL G. White Plains, NY
LYONS, TOM Boulder, CO
LYSINGER, REX L. Birmingham, AL

M

MACDONALD, JOHN Dover, NJ
MACDONALD, JOHN A. Stone
  Mountain, GA
MACFARLANE, CRAIG Unionville, CT
MACHO, MICHELLE La Canada, CA
MACKI, GLEN Carlsbad, CA
MACKINNION, JOHN Holliston, MA
MACOMBER, GEORGE Boston, MA
MACURDY, JOHN Stamford, CT
MACZYNSKI, TONY Wilmington, DE
MADDOX, MARGUERITE Detroit, MI
MADIGAN, MIKE San Diego, CA

MADRID, ART La Mesa, CA
MAEHARA, RUSTY Sparks, NV
MAGEE, MELINA ISABELLA
  Piedmont, CA
MAGGIO, NICHOLAS Baltimore, MD
MAGNIN, JERRY Beverly Hills, CA
MAHAN, CHARLES E. Los Angeles, CA

San Francisco, CA

MAHONEY, TIMOTHY J., JR.
  Chatham, NJ
MAIO, FRANK L. Landover, MD
MAJETICH, MARK Zephyr Cove, NV
MALCOLM, ROBERT J., JR.
  Pittsburgh, PA
MALDONADO, AL Monterey Park, CA
MALEKOF, MICHAEL E. Oakland, CA
MALEKOS, GEORGE Eagle River, AR
MALONE, ANDREW E.
  San Clemente, CA
MALONE, TERRANCE Milwaukee, WI
MAMBEL, LUIS Sun Valley, CA
MAMOLA, RANDY Woodside, CA
MANCHESTER, DOUGLAS F.
  La Jolla, CA
MANELL, MICHAEL Orange, CA
MANES, MICHAEL Louisville, KY
MANION, ROD J. Chula Vista, CA
MANN, PETER B. Laguna Beach, CA
MANNINO, JODI Manhattan Beach, CA
MANNINO, ROBERT S. Chatsworth, CA
MANOLAKIS, MARY San Mateo, CA
MANSOUR, JACK Los Angeles, CA
MARA, DONALD Metairie, LA
MARADA, TEDDY C. Washington, DC
MARANDA, RAYMOND P.
  Bakersfield, CA
MARCOTT, DARLA Phoenix, AZ

MARCOVSKY, SHARON LYNN
  Southfield, MI
MARGULIES, MICHAEL D. Marina Del
  Rey, CA
MARILLOTTA, SAM Cleveland, OH
MARINARO, LINDA New York, NY
MARION, MICHAEL S. Anaheim, CA

MARKLEY, JAMES S. Washington, PA
MARKMAN, DAVID A. Lawndale, CA
MARKMAN, JOSH Los Angeles, CA
MARKSTEIN, TRAVIS Auburn, CA
MARLIN, BRAD Panorama City, CA
MARSH, HENRY Bountiful, UT
MARSH, SHARON Spring Valley, CA
MARSHAL, DAN Gardena, CA
MARSHALL, FRANK Santa Monica, CA
MARTENSON, GENE H.
  Swarthmore, PA
MARTIN, DIANE Fremont, CA
MARTIN, EARL E. Pasadena, CA
MARTIN, WILLIAM M. Springfield, MA
MARTINDALE, LLOYD A., JR.
  Portland, OR
MARTINELLI, ANTHONY
  Staten Island, NY
MARTINEZ, DAN
  Rancho Palos Verdes, CA
MARTINEZ, ISIDRO Mountain View, CA
MARTINEZ, JUANITA L.
  Long Beach, CA
MARTINEZ, LORETTA Irwindale, CA
MARTINEZ, RONNIE Los Angeles, CA
MARTINI, JIM Miami, FL
MARTONHEGYI, STEFANIE ANN
  Columbus, OH
MARTUCCI, JAMES V., DR. Warren, OH

MARVELL, HUBERT E. Muncie, IN
MARX, GILDA Beverly Hills, CA
MARX, ROBERT Danville, CA
MASHBURN, JESS Oklahoma City, OK
MASON, JAY Gallup, NH
MASON, MARC New York, NY
MASSAD, MICHAEL, JR. Dallas, TX
MASTERS, MATTHEW A.
   Redwood City, CA
MATAS, ANTHONY Rosemead, CA
MATEAS, ELMER, H.
   Fountain Valley, CA
MATELJAN, GEORGE Montebello, CA
MATHEWS, MAURICE M.
   Los Angeles, CA
MATHIAS, BOB Colorado Springs, CO
MATLIN, REID ERIC Los Angeles, CA
MATSON, MIKE Lake Bluff, IL
MATSUBARA, RANDY Burbank, CA
MATSURA, HIROKAZU Osaka, Japan
MATT, PAUL J. Newport Beach, CA
MATTENSON, MYLES Los Angeles, CA
MATTONE, ALAN Staten Island, NY
MATTONE, MICHELE Staten Island, NY
MAUSETH, CANDICE J. Redmond, WA
MAUZY, SCOTT Raleigh, NC
MAY, MICHAEL G. Kirkwood, CA
MAYBERRY, LES Carmichael, CA
MAYER, LORETTA San Diego, CA
MAYERSON, FREDERIC H.
   Cincinnati, OH
MAYFIELD, DAVID S. Anaheim, CA
MAYNARD, JIM Claremont, CA
MC CAFFREY, EDDIE New York, NY
MC CALL, PETER New York, NY
MC DERMOTT, CHARLES
   New York, NY
MC KEAN, KAREN Oxnard, CA
MC LAUGHLIN, ANN
   Manhattan Beach, CA
MC LAUGHLIN, DAVID Medford, OR
MC MILLAN, RAYMOND A. Long
   Beach, CA
MC NAIR, TERRY Washington, DC

Mahwah, NJ

MC PHERSON, RONALD C.
   Glendora, CA
MCBRAYER, JACK Dothan, AL
MCBRIDE, MIKE Tempe, AZ

MCCALL, LESTER DeSoto, TX
MCCALLISTER, DOUGLAS
   Des Plaines, IL
MCCALLON, DALE H. Irvine, CA
MCCANN, KATHE Sacramento, CA
MCCARL, F. JAMES Beaver Falls, PA
MCCARTHY, J. THOMAS
   Los Angeles, CA
MCCARTHY, MOLLY Ashtabula, OH
MCCLAVE, WILLIAM H., JR.
   Piedmont, CA
MCCLENDATHAN, GORDON J.
   Goleta, CA
MCCLOUD, ROBERT Beverly Hills, CA
MCCORMICK, LAURA C.
   Chatsworth, CA
MCCOY, BRIAN F. San Marcos, TX
MCCOY, DENNIS P. San Marcos, TX
MCCOY, EMMET F. San Marcos, TX
MCCOY, MICHAEL E. San Marcos, TX
MCCOY, THOMAS A. Pawcatuck, CT
MCCULLEY, SCOTT R.
   San Bernardino, CA
MCCULLOUGH, JAMES D., M.D.
   Birmingham, MI
MCDANIEL, KEN Ventura, CA
MCDEVITT, PAT Seattle, WA
MCDONALD, ALEX San Diego, CA
MCDOUGAL, STUART Y. Ann Arbor, MI
MCEWEN, STEVE Irvine, CA
MCGARREY, KEVIN Trenton, NJ
MCGILL, KELLY Ogden, UT
MCGUIRE, PAT San Francisco, CA
MCILROY, ROBERT Laguna Beach, CA
MCINTOSH, KAREN M. Pacifica, CA
MCINTYRE, ANDREW Burbank, CA
MCINTYRE, ANNE Monroe, MI
MCKAY, DANIELE Klamath Falls, OR
MCKEAN, BILL South Lake Tahoe, CA
MCKEE FREDERICK J. Laguna Hills, CA
MCKENNON, ROBERT J. Lomita, CA
MCKEOWN, JAMES L. Fresno, CA
MCKINNEY, KEVIN Los Angeles, CA
MCKINNIS, DIANNE Topeka, KS
MCLAUGHLIN, MATTHEW P.
   Santa Ana, CA
MCLEAN, DENISE Philadelphia, PA
MCMAHON, DOUGLAS A. Atlanta, GA
MCMAHON, TIMOTHY J.
   Glastonbury, CT
MCMANUS, SEAMUS Boston, MA
MCMILLAN, ELLIOT Los Angeles, CA
MCNAMARA, JAMES Santa Ana, CA
MCNAMARA, KELLY Los Angeles, CA
MCNAMARA, STEVE Mission Hills, CA
MCNARRY, GENE St. Louis, MO
MCNEAL, JERRY Minnetonka, MN
MCNEELY, EDWARD L. La Jolla, CA
MCWHORTER, TED Garden Grove, CA
MEACH, JOHN Bowling Green, OH
MEAD, JAMES C. Denver, CO
MEADOWS, ANTHONY
   Los Angeles, CA

MEALINGS, MICHAEL J. Wellington,
   New Zealand
MEANS, ANTHONY Washington, DC
MECCA, MICHAEL Los Angeles, CA
MEDINA, MARIO Las Cruces, NM
MEDINA, VICTOR New York, NY
MEDOVITCH, THERESA
   Cucamonga, CA
MEGONIGAL, ZADA B.
   Laguna Beach, CA
MEHAGIAN, A.S. Phoenix, AZ

Aurora, WV

MELE, TONI Simi, CA
MELENDEZ, GEORGE D. Tucson, AZ
MELGOZA, JESUS Los Angeles, CA
MELLOS, TONY Pacific Palisades, CA
MELLOW, DANIEL Stafford, VA
MENDOZA, SALVADOR Santa Ana, CA
MENELY, MATT Portland, OR
MENENDEZ, STANLEY J.
   Bridgeport, WV
MENNIG, JAN C. Culver City, CA
MERRICH, JEAN MARIE
   Laguna Niguel, CA
MERRY, SALLY Hartford, CT
MESSER, KRISTIE Plano, TX
MESTA, CENK Cambridge, MA
METALLINOS, CONSTANTINE
   Glendale, CA
METCALF, BOBBY Sun Valley, CA
METCALFE, LAUVE Philadelphia, PA
METZGER, MONTE Corona Del Mar, CA
MEYER, BILL Simi Valley, CA
MEYERS, ERNIE La Mesa, CA
MEYERS, IRA S. Highland Park, IL
MEYERS, SHARLEEN G. Vincentown, NJ
MICHEL, KRIS Huntington Beach, CA

MICHIE, DAVID D. Newbury Park, CA
MICKLON, WARREN Salem, NH
MIDDLEBROOK, PAUL Los Angeles, CA
MIEHE, ARNIE Darlington, WI
MIHALIC, JOSEPH Warren, MI
MILBRATH, SCOTT Klamath Falls, OR
MILDREN, RICHARD A.
   Oklahoma City, OK
MILES, JEROLD L. Beverly Hills, CA
MILISTITS, CATHERINE Bronx, NY
MILLER, ALAN Staten Island, NY
MILLER, CHRIS New Orleans, LA

Klamath Falls, OR

MILLER, DAN B. Dallas, TX
MILLER, DAVID A. Niles, IL
MILLER, DOUGLAS Asheville, NC
MILLER, EDWARD F., JR. San Diego, CA
MILLER, JEFFREY D. Norcross, GA
MILLER, LARRY L. San Lorenzo, CA
MILLER, LAURA Los Alamitos, CA
MILLER, LAWRENCE Philadelphia, PA
MILLER, LENNOX V., D.D.S.
   Altadena CA
MILLER, LILLIAN V. Loma Linda, CA
MILLER, RALPH A. Balboa Island, CA
MILLER, SANDRA L. Chicago, IL
MILLER, SUSAN Shaker Heights, OH
MILLER, SUZANNE T. Sacramento, CA
MILLS, BILLY Fair Oaks, CA
MILLS, DARRNE Chevy Chase, MD
MILLWARD, MARK Redwood City, CA
MINIX, J.R. Springfield, OR
MINOR, PRESTON Hemet, CA
MINTER, LEIGHANNE Summit, NJ
MINTURN, AL Torrance, CA
MISSETT, JUDY SHEPARO Carlsbad, CA
MITCHELL, JAMES Cumberland, IN

MITCHELL, MIKE Los Angeles, CA
MITCHELL, STEVE Sandy, UT
MITCHELL, TINA R. Grand Blanc, MI
MITCHELL, TONY California City, CA
MITCHELL, WARREN G.
   Mount Clemens, MI
MITTELMAN, JOSEPH B. Encino, CA
MIXON, EDWARD W. Arlington, VA
MIXON, JAUDON Gainesville, GA
MIZUMACHI, MARIKO Jonan-Ku
   Fukuoka, Japan
MOELLER, JAMES Upland, CA
MOEN, CHERI El Cajon, CA
MOENICH, MATTHEW Strongsville, OH
MOFFA, SHERRY Burbank, CA
MOFFETT, PATRICK Long Beach, CA
MOLINA, OSCAR Ft. Worth, TX
MOLITOR, WENDY Lakeside, CA
MOMII, KATHY Santa Monica, CA
MOMINEE, BERNIE Erie, MI
MONFETTE, BRUCE J.
   Los Angeles, CA
MONROE, ELEANOR Diamond Bar, CA
MONROE, WILLIAM A. Bay Village, OH
MONTES, SUSAN Kensington, MD
MOOMAW, DONN, REV.
   Los Angeles, CA
MOON, RONALD North Adams, MA
MOORE, BEN A., JR. Annapolis, MD
MOORE, BOB Lake Tahoe, NV
MOORE, JASON Lakeside, CA
MOORE, LARRY Birmingham, AL
MOORE, MACK Wichita, KS
MOORE, MARJORIE A. San Jose, CA
MOORE, MELVIN Huntsville, AL
MOORE, MICHAEL Carson, CA
MOORE, RICHARD A.
   Garden Grove, CA
MORA, TERESITA LASES
   Montebello, CA
MORALES, DAVID J. Buena Park, CA
MORELAND, ROBIN Tucson, AZ
MORENO, ALEXSANDER Whittier, CA
MORENO, JOANNE Sunnyvale, CA
MORGAN, A. C., IV Darien, CT
MORGAN, JESS S. Los Angeles, CA
MORILLO, TIM Lindsay, CA
MORISHIMA, KATSUMI Tokyo, Japan
MORLAND, BARBARA L. Hollins, VA
MORPHY, TIMOTHY A. Pasadena, CA
MORRIS, EILEEN Chicago, IL
MORRIS, MERVYN C. Menlo Park, CA
MORRIS, MICHELLE Los Gatos, CA
MORRIS, PAUL South Lake Tahoe, CA
MORRIS, RICHARD G.
   Sherman Oaks, CA
MORRIS, SCOTT Thousand Oaks, CA
MORSE, BEVERLY Beverly Hills, CA
MORSE, TIMOTHY Hackensack, NJ
MORTON, JOHN Los Angeles, CA
MOSCOTTE, JULIO Los Angeles, CA
MOSELLE, MERRITT Los Angeles, CA
MOSMAN, ELAINE T. Los Angeles, CA

MOTT, MICHAEL P. Rochester, WA
MOULTON, JOHN Riverwoods, IL
MOUNT, RICHARD L. Saratoga, CA
MOYER, JAMES M. Bay Village, OH
MULDER, LARRY Zeeland, MI
MULLALLY, PETE Santa Ana, CA
MULLANE, DONALD A. Hacienda
   Heights, CA
MULVIHILL, JOAN K. Manoloking, NJ
MUNDY, THOMAS C. Gainesville, GA
MUNNELL, FRED Orange Village, OH
MUNOZ, DAVID AUGUSTINE Los
   Angeles, CA
MUNOZ, JULIO Brooklyn, NY
MUNSTER, SANDRA Beverly Hills, CA
MURAKAMI, HIROSHI Hachioji-Tokyo,
   Japan
MURCHLAND, MARCY Aliquippa, PA
MURDOCK, DAVID Westwood, CA
MURDOCK HAROLD, III
   Rolling Hills, CA
MURDOCK, JUSTIN Westwood, CA
MURPHY, EDDIE Atlanta, GA
MURPHY, ELAINE E.
   Hacienda Heights, CA
MURPHY, JIM Provo, UT
MURPHY, JIM Wilmington, DE
MUSSEN, JEFF Santa Paula, CA
MUSSMAN, GALEN Overland Park, KS
MUTH, MARION Manhattan Beach, CA
MUZZUCO, DENTON A. San Jose, CA
MYERS, GEORGIA Pomona, CA
MYERS, PETE Oceanside, CA
MYLENEK, BOB Canoga Park, CA
MYLIUS, FRED Castro Alley, CA

N

NABORS, JOHN Pasadena, CA
NAFTZGER, R. E. Beverly Hills, CA
NAKAGAWA, KANAKO Kumamoto,
   Japan
NAKAMORI, TAKESHI Mie, Japan
NAKAO, ESUKO Nagasaki City, Japan
NAKASHIMA, CHIKAKO Pre Fukuoka,
   Japan
NAKAZATO, TOSHIHIRO Kiryu-City
   Gunma, Japan
NAKAZAWA, NORIKO Tochigi, Japan
NAKOMURA, MASAKO Nagasaki, Japan
NARUSHIMA, MAKI Tokyo, Japan
NATHANIEL, KEITH Los Angeles, CA
NAYLOR, ASSEMBLYMAN San
   Francisco, CA
NEAL, DAVID Dallas, TX
NEAL, TYLER Pacific Palisades, CA
NEFF, GREGORY, Newport Beach, CA
NEHER, CLARK D. De Kalb, IL
NEHRA, CHANDRA P. Hackensack, NJ
NEILSON, HILDRED Union Lake, MI
NELDER, WENDY San Francisco, CA
NELLESON, EARL Anaheim, CA
NELSON, BRANDON Seattle, WA
NELSON, FRED A. Los Angeles, CA

NELSON, JAMES N., M.D.
    Long Beach, CA
NELSON, NORMAN Tulsa, OK
NELSON, RALPH Montecito, CA
NELSON, ROBERT Troy, NY
NELSON, ROBERT LaGrange, IL
NEMECEK, MIKE San Francisco, CA
NERI, STEPHEN North Providence, RI
NESEN, KARLA NELSO Westlake,
    Village, CA
NEWMAN, DAN St. Louis, MO
NEWMAN, KEVIN T. Santa Monica, CA
NEWSOME, CHARLEY Kearns, UT
NEWTON, CORY Manhattan Beach, CA
NEWTON, RICK Salt Lake City, CA
NEWTON, SHARI Newington, CT
NEWTON, WILLIAM C. Los Angeles, CA
NGUYEN, HIEU TRONG Seaside, CA
NICCOLI, DENNIS A., JR. Brockton, MA
NICHOLLS, BARBARA L. Eugene, OR
NICHOLSON-WOODWARD, LENOR
    Pasadena, CA
NICKEL, TY Placerville, CA
NICKLAS, DOBY Springfield, VA
NIDY, REBECCA Ontario, CA
NIGHTINGALE, STEVEN Reno, NV
NILES, RICKY Oklahoma City, OK
NIMEE, JENNIFER Spring Valley, IL
NIX, NANCY MAE Gainesville, GA
NOBLE, ALAN Redlands, CA
NOBLE, JOHN South Lake Tahoe, CA
NOCERA, FRANK Clinton, CT
NOESNER, FREDERICK W. Glenside, PA
NOLAN, ARTHUR F. Glendale, CO
NOLAND, JOHN Woodland Hills, CA
NOLAND, LEAH Woodland Hills, CA
NORDSTROM, DAYL JANETTE
    Costa Mesa, CA
NORDSTROM, JOHN Seattle, WA
NOREHAD, DAVID C. Winnetka, IL
NORELIUS, DALE Sunnyvale, CA
NORLANDER, GREG Ventura, CA
NORRIS, SIG Crowley, LA
NORTHROP, EDWARD H. Arden
    Heights, NY
NORTHROP, WILL Arden Heights, NY
NORWOOD, BILL Denver, CO
NOUQUE, DANIEL San Francisco, CA
NOVASEL, SUE Tahoe Paradise, CA
NUBER, GAIL Ridgewood, NJ
NUNN, BETTY Hayward, CA
NUNNALLY, MATT Avon, NJ

━━━━━ O ━━━━━

O'BRIEN, CHARLENE Jacksonville, NC
O'BRIEN, DAVID C. Annapolis, MD
O'BRIEN, FRANK C. Independence, OH
O'CONNOR, TIM South Pasadena, CA
O'DELL, LES Excelsior Springs, CA
O'DONNELL, JOEY Indianapolis, IN
O'DONOGHUE, CHRIS Towson, MD
O'KEEFE, THERESE Boston, MA
O'KELLY, MICHAEL St. Louis, MO

O'LEARY, BARRY J. Randolph, MA
O'LEARY, MARY Pasadena, CA
O'NEAL, PAUL Irwindale, CA
O'NEIL, RANDALL R. Battle Creek, MI

Jefferson City, MO

OATEY, WILLIAM R. Bay Village, OH
OBERMAN, ARI Pacific Palisades, CA
OBINATA, SATOSHI Tokyo, Japan
OBLER, BRANDI San Diego, CA
ODAMAKI, CATOMI Shizuoka, Japan
ODERMATT, RICHARD San Diego, CA
OGILVIE, DONALD G. New York, NY
OGLE, DEBRA L. Charlotte, NC
OHASHI, TORAO Tokoname, Japan
OHER, GERRY Irving, TX
OHLER, ERVIN CHRISTOPHER San
    Bernardino, CA
OKUMURA, YOSHIKAZA Akashi, Japan
OKURA, SUSAN Dana Point, CA
OLAZEWSKI, PAUL ROBERT, JR.
    Carnegie, PA
OLDENBURGER, TOM, JR. Lombard, IL
OLESON, ALAN M. Santa Ana, CA
OLIP, JOHN Chatsworth, CA
OLIVER, BARRY Leucadia, CA
OLIVERA, ROBERTO Los Angeles, CA
OLMSTEAD, AMY Great Falls, VA
OLMSTEAD, JOHN M. Great Falls, VA
OLMSTEAD, KATHERINE E.
    Great Falls, VA
OLSON, PETER Rancho Palos Verdes, CA
OLSON, TODD Rancho Palos Verdes, CA
ONEAL, PATTY San Jose, CA
ONO, SHIORI Tokyo, Japan
ORDWAY, DOUG Molgate, OH
ORENSTEIN, DAVID M., M.D.
    Memphis, TN
ORGIAS, SHIRLEY Greensboro, NC

ORLOVE, JACK I., JR. Milpitas, CA
ORR, CHERYL Redwood City, CA
ORTEGA, JERRY Los Angeles, CA
OSBORN, LOIS Painesville, OH

OSBORN, THOMAS G.
    Woodland Hills, CA
OSBORNE, ROBERT D. Bremerton, WA
OSHIRO, GLENN H. Honolulu, HI
OSTER, VICTOR Los Angeles, CA
OSTINI, FRANK Santa Maria, CA
OTERO, DONALD G. Birmingham, MI
OTSUKA, YASUKO Venice, CA
OTTO, JAMIE LOUISE Frisco, CO
OTTONE, LOUIS, JR. Salinas, CA
OUKI, HIROO Yamagata, Japan

━━━━━ P ━━━━━

PACHECO, NICHOLE Riverside, CA
PACKARD, CHARLES Irvine, CA
PADDOCK, EDWARD Livonia, MI
PADILLA, CHEN West Covina, CA
PADILLA, JOE New York, NY
PADRICK, BILL Ft. Pierce, FL
PADRO, JOE Los Angeles, CA
PAINE, FLETCHER Stockton, CA
PALMER, STEVEN Columbus, GA
PALMQUIST, EVELYN
    Newport Beach, CA
PALMTAG, TOM San Diego, CA
PANASCI, ANTHONY
    Canyon Country, CA
PANEK, JAMES G. Florissant, MO
PANELLI, BRETT Oxnard, CA
PAOLETTA, LEN Eastlake, OH
PAOLETTI, JOHN West Los Angeles, CA
PAOLINI, KIM M. El Verano, CA

PAPAIORDANOU, ZELIA São Paulo
    Brazil
PAPE, DEAN Eugene, OR
PAPPAS, P. VASILING Berkeley, CA
PAPPAS, TONI Manchester, NH
PARDOW, JOSEPH Flushing, NY
PARILLA, NICHOLAS Oakland, CA
PARIS, JESSICA Fallbrook, CA
PARKER, ALBERT Orange, CA
PARKER, FELICIA Garland, TX
PARKER, JAMES West Warwick, RI
PARKER, PATTY Stone Mountain, GA
PARKER, TIM Pasadena, CA
PARKER, WAYNE J. Sacramento, CA
PARKER, WILL HAYTON Seattle, WA
PARKS, RICHARD B., JR. Fullerton, CA
PARKS, WILLIAM JEFFREY Austin, TX
PARRISH, HERBERT E. Tucson, AZ
PARSONS, LINDA Los Angeles, CA
PASCHAL, ANDREA Y. Garland, TX
PASHUCK, RAYMOND Carrollton, TX
PASSO, WILLIAM O. Santa Ana, CA
PATMAN, DAVE Macon, GA
PATSAOURAS, TANYA Tarzana, CA
PATTEN, EVELYN THERESA
    Berkeley, CA
PATTIZ, CATHY Beverly Hills, CA
PATTIZ, DAVIDSON Tarzana, CA
PATTON, AARON Long Beach, CA
PATTON, KELVIN Dallas, TX
PAUKEY, BILL, SEN. Littleton, CO
PAULIN, LINDSEY A. Broomall, PA
PAULIN, MICHAEL V. Honolulu, HI
PAULUS, GEORGE Salem, OR
PAYNE, GARY R. La Mesa, CA
PAYNE, JANICE S. Los Angeles, CA
PAYNE, JOHN T. Malibu Beach, CA
PAYNE, ROBERT A., SR. Raymond, ME
PAYTON, WALTER Chicago, IL
PEARSON, CHARLOTTE
    Washington, DC
PEARSON, PAUL M. Annapolis, MD
PEBWORTH, EUGENE Croton-On-
    Hudson, NY
PEBWORTH, RUSSEL Croton-On-
    Hudson, NY
PEDDIE, ROD Houston, TX
PEDERSEN, BARBARA Arlington
    Heights, IL
PEDERSEN, JOHN S. Santa Ana, CA
PEEK, MIKE Shoshone, CA
PELTZ, RUSSELL B. Redondo Beach, CA
PENA, FREDERICO, MAYOR
    Denver, CO
PENA, ROSALINA Fresno, CA
PENALOZA, HECTOR JULIO
    Sun Valley, CA
PENCE, JEFF Corona Del Mar, CA
PEREZ, HENRY JOSEPH, JR. Los
    Angeles, CA
PEREZ, JACKIE Bell, CA
PEREZ, JESUS Los Angeles, CA
PERILLO, LEONARD Hayward, CA

PERKINS, FRANK N., JR. Huntsville, AL
PERKINS, JIM, D.D.S. Glendale, CA
PERKINS, NEALE Monrovia, CA
PERKOSKY, MATTHEW Rancho
    Cordova, CA
PERRY, CAROL J. Portland, OR
PETERSEN, ED Arlington Heights, IL
PETERSEN, GEORGE S., IV
    Mill Valley, CA
PETERSEN, ROBERT E. Los Angeles, CA
PETERSON, ANNE Fairway, KS
PETERSON, ROGER Westchester, CA
PETERSON, TRACI LENORE LEE Garden
    Grove, CA

Cleveland, OH

PETROVSKI, JANET Monterey Park, CA
PETTKER, JACK Pacific Palisades, CA
PFEIFFER, JON Denver, CO
PHAILA, MICHAEL A., SR. Newport
    Beach, CA
PHELAN, DESMOND R. Westlake
    Village, CA
PHELAN, JIM Morristown, PA
PHELPS, CHARLES F. Santa Monica, CA
PHILLIPS, CARL Euclid, OH
PHILLIPS, FREDDIE Venice, CA
PHILLIPS, ROGER Berlin Heights, OH
PHIPPS, RICHARD E. Burbank, CA
PICKETT, DANIEL St. Charles, MO
PICNICH, JOHN L. Gig Harbor, WA
PIERCE, DONALD L. Tustin, CA
PIERSON, FRANK E., JR. La Mesa, CA
PIERSON, JEFFREY LLOYD Irvine, CA
PILARA, ANDREW, JR. Lafayette, CA
PILZ, GEORGE I. Norristown, PA
PINKOSKY, PAUL M. Tulsa, OK
PIPES, ERICK Lubbock, TX

PISCIOTTA, NAT Whittier, CA
PITCHFORD, RICHARD Carlsbad, CA
PITKIN, NORMAN R. Danville, CA
PITT, SANDRA Nashua, NH
PLA, VINCE Anaheim, CA
PLACET, HAL Wheaton, IL
PLATT, GEORGE Oklahoma City, OK
PLUBELL, ANN MARIE Washington, DC
PLUNKETT, JIM El Segundo, CA
POLAND, BILL R. Ross, CA
POLITE, MARILYN New York, NY
POLITOSKE, E. J., DR. Orange, CA
POLLARD, JAMES, JR. Glendale, CA
POOL, WILLARD R. Garden Grove, CA
PORTER, ANNETTE Poway, CA
POSTON, KAREN Bonita, CA
POTTER, WENDI Ketchum, ID
POULOPLULAS, KOSTOS Norwalk, CT
POULSEN, ERIC H. El Cerrito, CA
POUND, DICK Los Angeles, CA
POWELL, FRED Falls Church, VA
POWELL, RICHARD Exeter, CA
POWELL, ROE Los Angeles, CA
POWERS, BRIAN Holbrook, MA
PRADO, RAMIRO Santa Ana, CA
PRATHER, MARGE Glen Ellyn, IL
PRATT, ARTHUR L.F. Sisters, OR
PREBLE, LEE Torrance, CA
PREBLE, WALLACE Portland, OR
PRECOURT, ANTHONY Denver, CO
PREHEIM, CHRISTINE Klamath Falls, OR
PREIS, TIM Northridge, OH
PRESICCI, MICHAEL Downey, CA
PRESNELL, ROBERT W. Greenville, SC
PREVATTA, RICKY EARL Charlotte, NC
PRICE, CHAUNA Rancho Mirage, CA
PRICE, DALLAS Santa Monica, CA
PRICE, DEIRDRE Salt Lake City, UT
PRICE, JOHN Salt Lake City, UT
PRICE, NADINE M. Haines, AL
PRICE, TED N. Oxnard, CA
PRICE, TOM Eaton Town, NJ
PRIKUPETS, VLADIMIR
    San Francisco, CA
PRINCE, HAIG MARQUIS, II
    Northridge, CA
PRINDIVILLE, GARY, SR. Arnold, MO
PRIVETT, JOHN, DR. Pasadena, CA
PRIZMICH, MICHAEL
    South Pasadena, CA
PROCACCINO, KEVIN Arlington, TX
PRODAN, NICK, Gardena, CA
PROVOST, LYNDA L. Biddeford, ME
PROWELL, R. WALT, DR. Antioch, CA
PRUDHOMME, BARBARA E. Mobile, AL
PRUEHS, ROBERT E. Flint, MI
PUGH, ROY Sparks, NV
PUNJ, BRIJ M. Overland Park, KS
PYLE, ORAN M. San Leandro, CA

Q

QUA, STEPHEN Chagrin Falls, OH
QUAGON, PHILLIP Tacoma, WA

QUAID, GLENN R. Riverside, CA
QUICK, SHELLY Madison, MS
QUINONES, JOSE D. Torrance, CA
QUINONES, JOSE, JR., III Torrance, CA
QUINTANILLA, NILDA F. McAllen, TX
QUINTERO, REBECCA Wenatchee, WA

R

RABIN, ROBBIE Chicago, IL
RACHOFSKY, HOWARD E. Dallas, TX
RACZKOWSKI, DIETER Smyrna, DE
RAGAN, ROBERT L. Inola, OK
RALSTON, SHIRLEY Orange, CA
RAMBERG, ISAAC Los Angeles, CA
RAMIREZ, RAY Oxnard, CA
RAMOS, GEORGE Los Angeles, CA
RAMOS, RALPH, CHIEF WRT. OFC.
   Camp Pendleton, CA
RAMOS, ROBERTO São Paulo, Brazil
RAMOS, ROCKY Holgate, OH
RAMSEY, KEN Concord, CA
RAMSEY, NICOLE Indianapolis, IN
RAMSEY, SHERRY Lakewood, CO
RAMSFDELL, ROB Pacific Palisades, CA
RANCE, MURIEL Chicago, IL
RANCOURT, NORRIS Carmichael, CA
RANDALL, TODD Centerville, UT
RANDOLPH, JOHN M. Greenwich, CT
RANEY, TAMMY RIOS Corona, CA
RANGEN, STEPHEN T. Beverly Hills, CA
RANKIN, RORY J. Kaaawa, HI
RANSOM, RICHARD W. Rochester, NY
RAPAPORT, H. LEWIS White Plains, NY
RASER, STEPHANIE Santa Ana, CA
RASMUS, JAMES L. Dallas, TX
RASTALL, SHAWN Willowwick, OH
RATTO, GERRI Alameda, CA
RATZ, JEAN Toledo, OH
RAWLINGS, AL J. Canoga Park, CA
RAWSON, SUSAN Lakewood, CA
RAYBOULD, WARREN A. Pasadena, CA
RAYMOND, DEAN C. Stockton, CA
REAGAN, MICHAEL Sherman Oaks, CA
REBER, JOHN El Cajon, CA
RECACHINA, DION A. Beverly Hills, CA
RECH, GARY Penfield, NY
REED, JUDY Los Angeles, CA
REED, KEITH Oceanside, CA
REEL, ANN K. Shelbyville, IN
REES, CHARLOTTE Lynchburg, VA
REES, DAVE Lynchburg, VA
REGELLO, TIMOTHY San Diego, CA
REILD, DONALD F. El Cerrito, CA
REILLY, BETH CORRIE Manhattan
   Beach, CA
REILLY, CHRISTOPHER JOHN
   Manhattan Beach, CA
REILLY, MICHELLE Warminster, PA
REILLY, MICKEY Oakland, CA
REINHART, DAVE Kingwood, TX
REINISCH, MARY ADAMS
   Los Angeles, CA
REISS, AMY New York, NY

REITER, JAMES Toledo, OH
RELLA, FRED Waldwich, NJ
REMANICK, ELIZABETH Pasadena, CA
RENDON, RALPH A. Encinitas, CA
RENSHAW, DAVID San Jose, CA
RETTON, SHERRY Charleston, VA
REVILLA, ANTHONY
   City of Commerce, CA
REYNOLDS, BRUCE Morristown, NJ
REYNOLDS, DON West Covina, CA
REYNOLDS, JIM North Kingston, RI
REYNOLDS, NANCY Vacaville, CA
REYNOLDS, THOMAS B. La Canada, CA
REYNOLDS, TRISHA Bakersfield, CA
RHEINSCHILD, MARY RUTH Crescent
   City, CA
RHODE, JAMES M. Chicago, IL
RHODES, JIM Birmingham, AL
RHODES, RON C. Shoshone, ID
RIACH, MICHAEL JAMES
   Northridge, CA
RICAN, JERRY Lakewood, CA
RICE, BOB Long Beach, CA
RICHARDS, CHRIS Bryn Mawr, CA
RICHARDS, KENWYNN Fullerton, CA
RICHARDS, MIMI Ventura, CA
RICHARDSON, CHARLES D.
   Walnut, CA
RICHARDSON, ELMER J. Arlington
   Heights, IL
RICK, ERICA K. San Marcos, CA
RICK, HORST San Marcos, CA
RICK, ROLAND R. San Marcos, CA

RING, HAROLD Encino, CA
RING, RICHARD Sun Valley, ID
RINGER, JERRY San Diego, CA
RIPPEE, EARL F. Irvine, CA
RISEMAN, MARCI Los Angeles, CA
RITTER, DANIEL E. Roswell, GA
RITTER, KATHY Los Angeles, CA
RIVARD, SCOTT Seaford, VA
RIVERA, RHONDA Toledo, OH
ROBB, PATTI Lake Zurich, IL
ROBBINS, ALAN, SEN. Pacoima, CA
ROBBINS, DONALD E. Tustin, CA
ROBBINS, KATHERINE Phoenix, AZ
ROBERTS, CATHERINE
   Huntington Beach, CA
ROBERTS, DAVID Beverly Hills, CA
ROBERTS, JOHN M. San Diego, CA
ROBERTS, MARY LEE Twin Falls, ID
ROBERTS, RHODE L. La Honda, CA
ROBERTSON, FRANK D. Upland, CA
ROBINSON, CAROLINE Tarzana, CA
ROBINSON, DAVID K., JR. Coeur
   d'Alene, ID
ROBINSON, DEBBIE Asheville, NC
ROBINSON, JANICE Denver, CO
ROBINSON, LINDA Coeur d'Alene, ID
ROBINSON, PHILIP Pacific Palisades, CA
ROBINSON, WILLIE Memphis, TN
ROBLES, JOHN Los Angeles, CA
ROCCO, RALPH M., JR.
   Rocky River, OH
ROCHA, GILMAR FERREIRA
   Westchester County, NY

Leonidas, MI

RICKERT, JOHN Banning, CA
RIDDLE, ROSS Long Beach, CA
RIDINGS, LESTER Cedar Grove, NJ
RIEHL, WILLIAM J. Sacramento, CA
RIELLY, JOHN Darien, CT

ROCK, JANELLE Los Angeles, CA
RODDA, DAVE Long Beach, CA
RODGERS, NICK South Lake Tahoe, CA
RODRICK, PATRICK Bronx, NY
RODRIGUEZ, RANDY Cupertino, CA

RODRIGUEZ, YURI ANN San Diego, CA
RODRIQUEZ, ARMANDO Bronx, NY
RODRIQUEZ, J. ROBERTO Monterey Park, CA
ROE, JENNIFER La Jolla, CA
ROE, SUSAN Tiburon, CA
ROGER, ROBISON Alturas, CA
ROGERS, BILL Boston, MA
ROGERS, GRANT H. Los Gatos, CA
ROGERS, JENNIFER Covington, LA
ROGERS, JUNE S. Los Angeles, CA
ROGONE, ANTHONY Sacramento, CA
ROLLINS, MARY ELLEN Oceanside, CA
ROLLO, CHARLES J. Simi Valley, CA
ROM, JEFF Santa Cruz, CA
ROMAN, MARCELINO, JR. West Covina, CA
ROMAN, MIQUEL San Mateo, CA
ROMANO, JAMES M. Bartlett, IL
ROMANS, BRIAN Dallas, TX
ROMERO, JOSE Venice, CA
ROMESSER, GARY Indianapolis, IN
ROMO, CARLOS La Habra, CA
RONCONE, CHRISTOPHER Vista, CA
RONQUILLO, LETICIA Whittier, CA
ROOP, DWIGHT Akron, OH
ROOS, ROBERT A. Stroudsburg, PA
ROGOWSKI, BRUCE L Norwalk, CT
ROSARIO, DAVID Madera, CA
ROSAS, MAURICE MAURY Saugus, CA
ROSE, EDWARD W., III Dallas, TX

West Point, NY

ROSE, JAMES R., JR. Matteson, IL
ROSENBERGER, GARY Bedminster, NJ
ROSENDAHL, ROGER W. Marina Del Rey, CA
ROSENKJAR, SERENA Los Angeles, CA

ROSENTHAL, RICHARD San Ramone, CA
ROSER, JIM Beaver Falls, PA
ROSS, RICKY Dallas, TX
ROTHSCHILD, LINDA BROWN Newport Beach, CA
ROTHSTEIN, MICHELE LEE Long Beach, CA
ROTHWELL, PATRICIA Thousand Oaks, CA
ROTKIN, CHARLES J. Tarzana, CA
ROUSE, MARTIN Moorpark, CA
ROWE, BECKY Malta, IL
ROWE, DAVID Rolling Hills, CA
ROWE, STEVEN Monterey Park, CA
ROWELL, JAY L. Richardson, TX
ROWLEY, JANET Boston, MA
RUBENSTEIN, JOEL Los Angeles, CA
RUBIO, JOSE Napa, CA
RUDDER, MARY ELLEN Neshanic Station, NJ
RUDELL, WILLIAM B. Burbank, CA
RUDOLPH, WILMA St. Louis, MO
RUEGG, STEVEN L. Berkeley, CA
RUELAS, MARK Azusa, CA
RUGGIRO, JO ANNE Hicksville, NY
RUNNELS, JAMES Oklahoma City, OK
RUPLE, ROD Montecito, CA
RUPPMAN, WALTER C. Washington, IL
RUSAW, CLINTON P. Sacramento, CA
RUSSELL, DOUGLAS A. La Canada, CA
RUSSELL, PAT Oklahoma City, OK
RUSSELLO, AL San Leandro, CA
RUSSELLO, GARY J. San Leandro, CA
RUSSO, LEE Pomona, CA
RUST, JOSEPH San Jose, CA
RUTH, ANN Rancho Palos Verdes, CA
RUTH, KEVIN J. Warminster, PA
RUTHER, CARL A. P. Akron, OH
RUTHERFORD, JOSEPH Hatfield, PA
RUTLEDGE, ELIZEBETH ANNE Lakewood, CA
RYAN, MARY ROSE Northampton, MA
RYAN, TIMOTHY Chagrin Falls, OH
RYAN, TIMOTHY DAVID La Costa, CA
RYDER, CYNTHIA West Townsend, MA
RZEPPA, CHRISTOPHER St. Louis, MO

S

SABA, FRED, II Toledo, OH
SABA, STEPHANIE SUE Toledo, OH
SABIN, SHAWN New York, NY
SACKHEIM, RON Wheeling, IL
SADLE, RICHARD L. Berkeley, CA
SADLER, ANITA Los Angeles, CA
SADRUDDIN, HADIYAH Portland, OR
SAFRAN, THOMAS L. Los Angeles, CA
SAGE, KEVEN Stockton, CA
SAGE, PAUL M. Swartz Creek, MI
SAGE, ROBERT Waltham, MA

SAITO, NAOKO Toyota, Japan
SAITO, TOMOHIDE Yoshi-ku Osaka, Japan
SAIZ, ARTURO Albuquerque, NM
SAKAZAKI, YOSHITAKA Camarillo, CA
SAKURAKO, ISUTSUI New York, NY
SALECKER, JOHN New York, NY
SALISBURY, H. GRAHAM Salt Lake City, UT
SALISBURY, HOWARD Seattle, WA
SALISBURY, MARILLA San Diego, CA
SALTER, LINDA San Pedro, CA
SAMFORD, FRANK P. Birmingham, AL
SAMUELSON, PETER Los Angeles, CA
SANCHEZ, EDWARD Duarte, CA
SANCHEZ, EMILIO Temple City, CA
SANCHEZ, JOSEPH D. Riverside, CA
SANCHEZ, NANCY MORAN Corona Del Mar, CA
SANCHEZ, SABRINA Tujunga, CA
SANDAHL, JOHN Klamath Falls, OR
SANDEFER, JULIE Oklahoma City, OK
SANDEFUR, ROBERT L. Florissant, MO
SANDOVAL, EMIDGIO Rosemead, CA
SANDRIDGE, GENE A. Great Falls, VA
SANTORO, JOSEPH Linden, NJ
SANTOWSKI, FRANCES J. Elk Grove Village, IL
SANTOWSKI, STEPHEN J. Elk Grove Village, IL
SAPPER, STEPHANIE Beverly Hills, CA
SARGENT, DICK·Los Angeles, CA
SARMENTO, TOM Carmichael, CA
SARTAIN, ROD Grand Prairie, TX
SARVER, JACK L. Wadsworth, OH
SATARIANO, ANDREA C. Clifton, OH
SATTERFIELD, BUDDY Mesa, AZ
SAUNDERS, JOHN D. Atlanta, GA
SAUNDERS, MARK Santa Barbara, CA
SAVAGE, BRUCE B., DR. Seattle, WA
SAWTELL, GREGORY P. Twin Falls, ID
SAWYER, BUZZ Mt. Prospect, IL
SAWYER, MARY ANN Whittier, CA
SAWYER, VICKI KAYE Ventura, CA
SAXTON, WILLIAM Wayland, MA
SCHAFERKOTTER, DAVID San Diego, CA
SCHEITLIN, TED Dallas, TX
SCHELLENBERG, WILLIAM K. Sherman Oaks, CA
SCHENONE, DAVID Foster City, CA
SCHIAVONE, GENE Waterbury, CT
SCHINDLER, BRIAN L. Bellflower, CA
SCHISLER, JULIE Klamath Falls, OR
SCHLICK, DAVID Ivanhoe, CA
SCHMIDT, JOHN O. Torrance, CA
SCHMIDT, MERRILL E. Newport Beach, CA
SCHMITT, WOLF Wooster, OH
SCHNABEL, CHRISTY Malibu, CA
SCHNABEL, DARRIN Malibu, CA
SCHNABEL, EVAN Malibu, CA
SCHNEIDER, ANN Millbrea, CA

SCHNEIDER, CLAUDINE
  Washington, DC
SCHNEIDER, ERIC, SR. Washington, DC
SCHNORR, JACK Pelham, NH
SCHOELLKOPF, ALAN Dallas, TX
SCHOELLKOPF, LAURA Dallas, TX
SCHOELLKOPF, WILSON Dallas, TX
SCHOEMEHL, VINCENT St. Louis, MO
SCHOENROCK, TODD
  South Holland, IL
SCHOLL, MICHAEL Newport News, VA
SCHUH, JOSEPH C. Wyckoff, NJ
SCHULER, CHRISTINE Bellevue, WA
SCHULER, DORIN Bellevue, WA
SCHULLER, CAROL Anaheim, CA
SCHULMAN, GAIL N. Hollywood, CA
SCHULMAN, GARY N. Hollywood, CA
SCHULMAN, JOHN Beverly Hills, CA
SCHULMAN, LINDA N. Hollywood, CA
SCHUMACHER, JOHN C., DR.
  Carlsbad, CA
SCHUMACHER, STEVE Irvine, CA
SCHUMAN, CARL J. Litchfield, CT
SCHWAB, LOU Palm Springs, CA
SCHWAB, RICHARD
  Shaker Heights, OH
SCHWARTZ, JOEL Studio City, CA
SCHWERS, MANFRED San Francisco, CA
SCOFIELD, ANGIE Gastonia, NC
SCOTT, BART H. Los Angeles, CA
SCOTT, JIM Sacramento, CA
SCOTT, MARY Encinitas, CA
SCOTT, STACEY Burbank, CA
SCOVILL, JASON Chiloquin, OR
SCUDDER, DAVID Manhattan Beach, CA
SEAMON, STORMY Vista, CA
SEARIGHT, TERRY San Francisco, CA
SEARLE, DANNY Payson, UT
SEARS, PETER Grand Rapids, MI
SEATON, BILL San Diego, CA
SEATON, JAMES M. Elm Grove, IL
SEAVER, CHRISTOPHER
  Santa Monica, CA
SEAVER, MARTHA Cupertino, CA
SEAVER, PATRICK Long Beach, CA
SEAVER, RICHARD CARLTON
  Pasadena, CA
SEAVER, RICHARD C. Los Angeles, CA
SEAVER, VICTORIA Cupertino, CA
SECIOMBE, MARILYN San Diego, CA
SEEGOTT, PAUL L. Chagrin Falls, OH
SEGALAS, RICHARD A.
  San Francisco, CA
SEGURA, MARGO MARIE
  Richmond, CA
SEIDULE, J. M. Mobile, AL
SEIGEREID, DALE L. Indianapolis, IN
SEK, JON Milpitas, CA
SELFRIDGE, ROBERT Whittier, CA
SELIG, MARTIN Seattle, WA
SELLONS, KEITH Long Beach, CA
SEMBROSKI, ANELYA North
  Hollywood, CA

SEMEL, SCOTT B. Van Nuys, CA
SEMES, PAUL Butler, PA
SEMOS, VASILI Memphis, TN
SENNER, GORDON D. Fair Oaks, CA
SENNEY, WALTER F. Lakewood, OH
SENO, YUKI Shiga, Japan
SEPULVEDA, VICTOR Burbank, CA

Edwardsburg, MI

SHAERBAN, GEORGE A., JR.
  Brooklyn, OH
SHAFFER, HEATHER Camarillo, CA
SHAFI, MOHAMMAD, M.D. Edison, NJ
SHANAHAN, ERIN MARIE
  Sepulveda, CA
SHANE, BILL Huntington Beach, CA
SHAPIRO, RICHARD B.
  Beverly Hills, CA
SHAPIRO, ROBERT Beverly Hills, CA
SHAPIRO, ROBERT D. Milwaukee, WI
SHAPIRO, MAX Corte Madera, CA
SHARLUP, JEROME Mission Viejo, CA
SHARPE, CHRIS Grand Rapids, MI
SHAW, CHRISTOPHER R.
  Sacramento, CA
SHAWNEGO, SUSIE V. Santa Rosa, CA
SHEA, BRIAN W. Pacific Palisades, CA
SHEA, KEVIN P. San Francisco, CA
SHEAFFER, DOUGLAS
  Mountain View, CA
SHEEHAN, JAMES Southington, CT
SHEEHAN, MICHAEL New York, NY
SHEFFEY, LYNN Escondido, CA
SHELBOURNE, K. DONALD
  Indianapolis, IN
SHELTON, B. Rochester, MI
SHELTON, JOHN MICHAEL
  Arlington, VA

SHELTON, JOHN P. Los Angeles, CA
SHEN, ELIZABETH
  Palos Verdes Estates, CA
SHEPHERD, KAREN
  Santa Cruz, CA
SHEPPARD, AL Atlanta, GA
SHERGOLD, DAVE Santa Clara, CA
SHERIDAN, MATTHEW G. San Jose, CA
SHERMAN, GEORGE N. San Diego, CA
SHERMAN, NILES Burbank, CA
SHERRY, TIMOTHY Fremont, CA
SHIELD, KIM Anaheim, CA
SHIELDS, DONNA Pittsburgh, PA
SHIFFMAN, DAVE Wayne, NJ
SHILLING, DAVID M. Arlington, VA
SHINE, JACK Encino, CA
SHIPP, GARY Stamford, CT
SHIVES, KATHY Tustin, CA
SHOENBERG, DAVE
  West Hollywood, CA
SHOOK, JEFFREY Northwood, OH
SHOONG, ELOISE San Francisco, CA
SHOONG, MILTON San Francisco, CA
SHOONG, ROSEMARY
  San Francisco, CA
SHOTWELL-GUSTAFSON, ALICE
  Pontiac, MI
SHRADER, J. A. Amarillo, TX
SHUCK, STEVE Colorado Springs, CO
SHYVER, CRAIG Washington Boro, PA
SIDNEY, ALICE Beverly Hills, CA
SIDOTI, A. FRANK Montauk, NY
SIEBACH, PAUL Arlington, VA
SIEGAL, ARLO Woodmere, NY
SIEGAL, RICHARD D. New York, NY
SIKKING, JAMES Los Angeles, CA
SILAS, STEPHEN Mt. Kisco, NY
SILBER, JAMES G. Los Angeles, CA
SILBER, JULIE A. Los Angeles, CA
SILIGO, WAYNE Fremont, CA
SILVERMAN, MARV, DR. Tarzana, CA
SIME, NATALIE Lincoln, NV
SIMES, MARY M. Hebron, IL
SIMMONS, EUGENE G. Fremont, OH
SIMMONS, LEO San Francisco, CA
SIMMONS, LESLIE Fallbrook, CA
SIMON, BILL Los Angeles, CA
SIMON, DALE ANN Orange, CA
SIMON, DAVID Los Angeles, CA
SIMON, JEANNE Carlsbad, CA
SIMONYAN, GARY River Edge, NJ
SIMPSON, NANCY Perry, MI
SIMPSON, O. J. New York, NY
SIMPSON, WILLIAM R.
  Hermosa Beach, CA
SIMRIL, CLINTON Fremont, CA
SIMS, JESSICA Indianapolis, IN
SINASEK, BARBI Newport Beach, CA
SINGLETON, MARK A. Marietta, GA
SIRACUSA, JON SISTI
  Capistrano Beach, CA
SIRIANNI, PHILIP S. Los Angeles, CA
SIRKO, MICHELLE Chicago, IL

SITTON, TRENT L. Wilkinson, IN
SITZER, MIKE Burbank, CA
SKIDMORE, EUGENIA H. Dallas, TX
SLADE, JOHN H. New York, NY
SLADKEY, JOHN R. Leawood, KS
SLAGLE, JERRY Anaheim, CA
SLAUGHTER, RAY Venice, CA
SLAVIK, SUSAN Pasadena, CA
SLAVIN, JOSEPH P., III Palm Desert, CA
SLIVKA, TROY M. Flint, MI
SLUSHER, JOHN F. Rolling Hills, CA
SMALL, DAVID Saratoga, CA
SMART, HILARY H. Weston, MA
SMART, JOHN Bedminster, NJ
SMITH, BALLARD F. San Diego, CA
SMITH, CHARMIN A. Olivette, MO
SMITH, CHERYL Concord, CA
SMITH, CHERYL Seattle, WA
SMITH, CLINTON TODD Canyon
    Country, CA
SMITH, DAVID L. Silver Spring, MD
SMITH, DIANE L. Princeton, NJ
SMITH, DON HYRUM Hemet, CA
SMITH, DONALD C.
    Manhattan Beach, CA
SMITH, DOTTIE HOWE La Jolla, CA
SMITH, ED New Rochelle, NY
SMITH, EDWARD V., III Dallas, TX
SMITH, GARY A. Kansas City, MO
SMITH, GLEN La Habra, CA
SMITH, GREG Rancho California, CA
SMITH, HUBERT L. Tome, GA
SMITH, JENNIFER Century City, CA
SMITH, JODY LYNN Portland, OR
SMITH, JOHN SKIPPER Lubbock, TX
SMITH, KELLY JEANNE
    Newport Beach, CA
SMITH, MARK Westport, CT
SMITH, MARK A. Redlands, CA
SMITH, MARY DORIS Seattle, WA
SMITH, MICHAEL Oakland, CA
SMITH, OZZIE St. Louis, MO
SMITH, PAUL JOSEPH Culver City, CA
SMITH, PETER B. Sacramento, CA
SMITH, PHYLLIS San Diego, CA
SMITH, RAYMOND W. Swarthmore, PA
SMITH, TERRI CHAPMAN Palo Alto, CA
SMITH, TODD S. Boulder, CO
SMITH, TYLENE ANN San Jose, CA
SMITH, WILLIAM H. Deerfield, IL
SMITH, WILLIAM N., JR. Richmond, VA
SMITH, WILLIAM W. Birmingham, AL
SNODGRASS, ELIZABETH BRIM
    Portland, OR
SNOW, JOE L. Glenwood Springs, CO
SNYDER, CURTIS Pomona, CA
SNYDER, ROBERT E.
    Rancho Cordova, CA
SNYDER, SANDI West Covina, CA
SOBOROFF, STEVE Santa Monica, CA
SOHN, MARK Arlington Heights, IL
SOLOMON, LEONARD A. Ft.
    Lauderdale, FL

SOLOMON, MICHAEL JAY Fort Lee, NJ
SONHEIM, RICHARD Glendale, CA
SOODIK, TRISH Santa Monica, CA

Topeka, KS

SORENSEN, R. E. Omaha, NE
SOTOMAYOR, TRISTEN Norwalk, CA
SOUTH, CHRISTOPHER
    Woodland Hills, CA
SOUTHWORTH, KELLY Rancho Palos
    Verdes, CA
SOUZA, DAVID R. Alameda, CA
SOWERWINE, HANNAH C.
    Menlo Park, CA
SPAAR, THOMAS Hereford, PA
SPADONE, PAUL G. Palos Verdes
    Estates, CA
SPANGLER, JAMES E., JR. Pasadena, CA
SPARKS, KEVIN Indianapolis, IN
SPEARS, MELVIN S. Encino, CA
SPECA, BOBBY Broomall, PA
SPERTY, SUE Los Angeles, CA
SPIGHT, ELENA Orange, CA
SPINELLI, JOSEPH A. Long Beach, CA
SPIRES, BRAD Stateline, NV
SPOONER, JULIAN MICHAEL
    Richmond, VA
SPRAGUE, DAVID H. Williamstown, MA
SPRAGUE, ELIZABETH P. Bronxville, NY
STAGER, PHILIP C. Johnstown, PA
STAGG, JEFFREY A. Indianapolis, IN
STALEY, BARRY B., D.D.S. Aptos, CA
STANFORD, SCOTT St. Louis, MO
STANICH, CHRISTINE Warren, OH
STANSBURY, CLAUDE Beverly Hills, CA
STANTON, WILLIAM Sandy Springs, GA
STAPP, JERRY Oceanside, CA
STARK, MICHAEL La Habra Heights, CA

STARK, NORM Green River, WY
STARNER, JOHN Phoenix, AZ
STARZAK, ROBERT, M.D. Marina Del
    Rey, CA
STATTIN, ERIC L., JR. La Canada, CA
STAUFFER, FLOYD RANDALL, DR.
    Downey, CA
STEADMAN, JOHN Baltimore, MD
STECHMANN, VICKY Far Rockaway, NY
STEELE, RUSS Garden Grove, CA
STEENBLOCK, ERIK Laguna Beach, CA
STEGER, ROBERT A. J. La Habra, CA
STEIN, GARY Tustin, CA
STEIN, STANTON Santa Monica, CA
STEINEKE, CHRISTOPHER
    Olivenhain, CA
STEINHARDT, BARRY Tarzana, CA
STEPHAN, NICHOLAS D. Upper
    Montclair, NJ
STEPHENS, MARYLIN
    Manhattan Beach, CA
STEPOVICH, ALEX D. San Jose, CA
STERN, MICHAEL J. Canoga Park, CA
STEVENSON, TRENA Inglewood, CA
STEWARD, MICHAEL Corte Madera, CA
STEWART, AL Sacramento, CA
STEWART, KERRY D. Salt Lake City, UT
STEWART, WILLIAM JOHN Santa
    Barbara, CA
STICK, STEPHEN J. Toledo, OH
STILES, DOUGLAS M. Klamath Falls, OR
STOCKMAN, DAVID E. La Canada, CA
STOCKWELL, RICHARD Beloit, WI
STOIKE, R. D., M.D. Chula Vista, CA
STOKES, HERBERT L. Omaha, NE
STONE, GARY Rancho Palos Verdes, CA
STONE, JANET Barrington, RI
STONE, LEWIS Burbank, CA
STONE, VIC San Gabriel, CA
STORMS, JENNY Boulder, CO
STOYANOFF, JIM Tucson, AZ
STRADER, TIMOTHY L.
    Corona Del Mar, CA
STRAND, LAUREL PATRICIA
    Montclair CA
STRANG, SHEILA Burbank, CA
STRASHENSKY, DEBBIE Manor, PA
STRAUS, BARBARA G. Beverly Hills, CA
STRAUS, LINDA J. Beverly Hills, CA
STRAUSS, KARL H. Asheville, NC
STRAUSS, LEONARD Beverly Hills, CA
STRAUSS, NANCY Los Angeles, CA
STREATER, STEVE Cherokee, NC
STRINE, SUZANNE Rockville, MD
STROMBERG, ANN HELTON, PH.D.
    Claremont, CA
STROMBERG, CARL Los Angeles, CA
STROMME, TINA Kankakee, IL
STRONG, KEVIN Westport, CT
STRUDWICK, PETER Buena Park, CA
STRUMSKY, JOHN J., JR.
    Millersville, MD
STRUVE, KRISTA LYNN Claremont, CA

STUART, CLAUDE K. Orange, CA
STUBBART, WINSTON Honolulu, HI
STUCKY, BRIAN D. Goessel, KS
STUMP, ROGER L. Aurora, CO
SUAREZ, RAQUEL Berkeley, CA
SULLIVAN, CHRIS Anderson, SC
SULLIVAN, LONNIE Englewood, CO
SULLIVAN, STANTON T.
   San Francisco, CA
SUMMERS, HARRY L. La Jolla, CA
SUMMERS, LINDA San Diego, CA
SUMMERS, SUANNE La Jolla, CA
SUMMERS, SUSAN HAMILTON
   La Jolla, CA
SUNDBERG, RICHARD Agoura Hills, CA
SUPPES, BART Portland, OR
SUYEHIRO, TOKIHIKO Livermore, CA
SUZUKI, YIUKO Tokyo, Japan
SWAIN, ROBERT J. Pasadena, CA
SWANSON, HAROLD D. La Crosse, WI
SWARY, KEITH New Bavaria, OH
SWEENEY, KERI M. Thousand Oaks, CA
SWEET, DARLENE Drums, PA
SWEET, DEREK Burbank, CA
SWEIRDERK, LOUIS Millville, NJ
SWIRSKY, KAREN LESLIE
   La Canada, CA
SWOTEK, ED Sacramento, CA
SZABO, DIANE Spotswood, NJ
SZCZUBELAK, SUZANNE Newark, DE

T

TABORI, LASZLO Culver City, CA
TACHIYAMA, GLENN J. Seattle, WA
TACLAKAZU, SATO Tokyo, Japan
TAHARA, TOSHIHIKO Los Angeles, CA
TAKACH, GASPER GEZA
   Seal Beach, CA
TAKAHASHI, OSAMU Tokyo, Japan
TAKATA, SHINGO Tokyo, Japan
TAKEDA, HISAO New York, NY
TAKEI, GEORGE Los Angeles, CA
TAKESHITA, HIROKO Hyogo, Japan
TALIAFERRO, MARYANN
   West Covina, CA
TAMAYO, ERMA Bell Gardens, CA
TAMBERLING, KERRY M. Lexington, SC
TAMBOLLEO, PATT
   Huntington Beach, CA
TANASE, MARK Bellevue, WA
TANNER, MAURICE R. Phoenix, AZ
TANZINI, STEPHANIE
   W. Bloomfield, MI
TAPIA, ALFREDO H. Montebello, CA
TARBELL, RICHARD Santa Ana, CA
TATUM, KAREN Klamath Falls, OR
TAUPMANN, JEFFREY S. Edmond, OK
TAVAGLIONE, CHRISTOPHER J.
   Riverside, CA
TAYLOR, BRANDON Artesia, CA
TAYLOR, DWYAN Cleveland, TN
TAYLOR, JAMES A., JR. Mequon, WI
TAYLOR, JAMES H. Asheville, NC

TAYLOR, JEFF Jay, OK
TAYLOR, JEFFREY Pawtucket, RI
TAYLOR, JOYCE University City, MO
TAYLOR, NATHANIEL Washington, DC
TAYLOR, WILLIAM Lincoln, NE
TEACHWORTH, WILLIAM R. Santa
   Monica, CA
TELLER, WILLIAM Beverly Hills, CA
TEMPLE, BOB New London, OH
TERRELL, SANDY Carmichael, CA
TERRY, CHARLES, JR. Los Angeles, CA
TERRY, KEITH Bloomfield Hills, MI
THARP, DONALD W. Pleasanton, CA
THARPE, STEVE St. Louis, MO
THASEN, SHERRY Simi Valley, CA
THEDFORD, CHAROLEESE D. Lakeview
   Terrace, CA
THEIUBALTU, MAUDE Paso Robles, CA
THEODOSOPOULOS, LAMBROS
   Manchester, NH
THEODOSOPOULOS, WILLIAM
   Manchester, NH
THERIOT, PETER Tulsa, OK
THISSELL, JERRY Eureka, CA
THOHBS, BRETT Highland Heights, OH
THOMAS, GORDON M.
   Salt Lake City, UT
THOMAS, IAN Rancho Palos Verdes, CA
THOMAS, JAMES Coon Rapids, MN
THOMAS JAMES N. Agoura, CA
THOMAS, JOHN New York, NY
THOMAS, SUZANNE Irvine, CA
THOMAS, WILLIAM
   Arlington Heights, IL
THOMPSON, CARLA Anaheim, CA
THOMPSON, DAVID Dallas, TX
THOMPSON, DOUG Dallas, TX
THOMPSON, FRED T.
   North Adams, MA
THOMPSON, JENNIFER L. Huntington
   Beach, CA
THOMPSON, LARRY A.
   Los Angeles, CA
THOMPSON, RACHEL Ten Mile, TN
THOMPSON, RICK Burbank, CA
THOMPSON, STANLEY I., DR.
   Reno, NV
THOMPSON, STEPHEN R. Lafayette, CA
THOMSON, RICHARD South Lake
   Tahoe, CA
THORNE, ALICE Chehalis, WA
THORPE, BILL JR. Cleburne, TX
THUENTE, JULIA Long Beach, CA
TIEDE, RICH Murray, UT
TINI, THOMAS Bayville, NY
TINNEN, RAY Dallas, TX
TIRRELL, DER-LING Kentfield, CA
TITSWORTH, LAWRENCE W. Port
   Hueneme, CA
TIURLEY, WINDLE Dallas, TX
TOCKETT, SHIRLEY Arkadelphia, AR
TODD, KEN Paso Robles, CA
TODD, RICHARD K. Pomona, CA

TODD, RON, JR. Pomona, CA
TOGNOLI, LORRAINE K. Alameda, CA
TOKUNAGA, JOHN Yuba City, CA
TOLLAKSON, C. DAVID Studio City, CA
TOMKO, ROBERT Chagrin Falls, OH
TOOLEY, WILLIAM Los Angeles, CA
TOOMEY, THERESA Los Angeles, CA
TOPOLSKI, VERNON Timonium, MD
TORGERSON, CLYDE L. El Centro, CA
TORGERSON, TIM Austin, MN
TORINO, FRANCIS P. Torrance, CA
TORRES, DAVID C., III Portland, OR
TORREZ, ALMA Los Angeles, CA
TORUNA, DAL Gardena, CA
TOUCHSTONE, GIFFORD Dallas, TX
TOUCHSTONE, RANDY Dallas, TX
TOVER, EDWARD LAWRENCE, JR.
   Palmdale, CA
TOWERS, TIMOTHY Levittown, NY
TOWNSEND, SUSAN Upland, CA
TOY, FRANK Monterey Park, CA
TRABERT, DONALD San Francisco, CA
TRAMELL, BRIAN K.
   Fountain Valley, CA
TRAYERS, CHARLES Tucson, AZ
TREMALT, RICHARD Los Angeles, CA
TREMBLAY, CORINNE J.
   Manchester, NH
TRENT, SUZANNE Coronado, CA
TRIBULL, CHRISTOPH Beverly Hills, CA
TROXEL, DOUG Brea, CA
TUBBS, DENNIS Dallas, TX
TUNCAY, FIRAT Alta Loma, CA
TUNE, CHARLES Portland, OR

New Creek, WV

TUREAUD, CHRISTIAN B.
   Palm Beach, FL
TURLEY-EMETT, MARY ANNE
   Balboa, CA
TURNER, ERIC Goleta, CA
TURNER, HENRY E. Laguna Beach, CA
TURNER, MARSHA
   Manhattan Beach, CA

TURNER, RITA Huntington Beach, CA
TURNEY, CYNTHIA A. Newark, DE
TWEEDY, JAMES Bolton, MA
TWIST, GWENDOLEN HALL Newport Beach, CA
TWIST, JORDAN ROBERT Newport Beach, CA
TYMAN, LISA A. Redondo Beach, CA

U

UEBERROTH, JOEY Los Angeles, CA
UEBERROTH, VICKI Los Angeles, CA
UEDA, JIRO Osaka, Japan
UEMURA, MASASHI Kagawa, Japan
UENO, ETSUZIRO Isumtotsu-Shi, Japan
UHRIG, VICKY LYNN Topeka, KS
UJCICH, CHRIS Willoughby Hills, OH
UMPHENOUR, RUSSELL V. Atlanta, GA
UNTERHOLZNER, STEPHAN Fair Oaks, CA
UPCHURCH, STACY Easley, SC
UPHAM, ROBERT Mineral Wells, TX
UPTON, JOHN South Lake Tahoe, CA
URICH, AURORA JAMES Whittier, CA
URNESS, RICH Des Moines, WA
URSTADT, CHARLES J. Bronxville, NY

V

VALDEZ, DANIEL A. Pico Rivera, CA
VALDEZ, RICH Orange, CA
VAN AELST, MARCEL P. San Francisco, CA
VAN ARTSDALEN, VICKIE Eugene, OR
VAN BREDA, BOB Los Angeles, CA
VAN DER HOEVEN, MARTIN Tempe, AZ
VAN DINE, SEAN Palos Verdes Estates, CA
VAN KIRK, RICHARD L. Arcadia, CA
VAN LOAN, EUGENE M., III Bedford, NH
VAN OSDOL, PERRY Hutchinson, KS
VAN PATTEN, BRUCE E. Brea, CA
VAN VOY, TOM Westlake Village, CA
VAN WINGERDEN, ESTHER Carpinteria, CA
VANACKER, JOHN P. Oregon City, OR
VANCE, NICOLE E. Elkins Park, PA
VANDENEKART, MARTIN A. Snohomish, WA
VANLANDINGHAM, MARK E. Irvine, CA
VANLANDINGHAM, SHERYL Irvine, CA
VANOVER, RON Indianapolis, IN
VANYO, LOUIS Cleveland, OH
VARNER, MELISSA Houston, TX
VARSOGEA, JENNY Monroe, MI
VASQUEZ, JAMES Brea, CA
VASQUEZ, TERRY Arcadia, CA
VAUGHAN, CHARLES Lake Geneva, WI
VAUGHN, CRAIG Oklahoma City, OK

VELMAN, STACY ANTHAN Des Moines, IA
VENDETTI, JEFFREY Canton, MA
VENDETTI, ROBERT A. Caldwell, NJ
VENEZIAN, JOSEPH, JR. Piscataway, NJ
VERDUZCO, ERNESTINA San Francisco, CA
VERES, JOHN Independence, OH
VERSCHELDEN, ELIZABETH Manhattan, KS
VICKERY, RUSSELL A. Anderson, SC
VIDALI, LYNN M. Morgan Hills, CA
VIEIRA, THERESA San Jose, CA
VIGIL, NORMAN R. San Diego, CA
VILLARI, JUDY Cranston, RI
VILLASENOR, DAVID Pico Rivera, CA
VINAS, ELIZABETH San Francisco, CA
VOGEL, KATHY Bristol, CT
VOLPE, DIANE Boston, MA
VOLTZ, BILLY Homestead, PA
VOLZ, GARRETT Englewood, CO
VONFELT, DOROTHY J. Colby, KS
VOSS, NED Berkeley Heights, NJ

W

WACHS, JOEL Los Angeles, CA
WACHSMAN, JAMES H. Oxnard, CA
WADDINGHAN, MARK Menlo Park, CA
WAGNER, DANA Englewood, OH
WAGNER, DAVID C. Louisville, KY
WAGNER, JACK G. Mesa, AZ
WAGNER, MICHAEL D. San Antonio, TX
WAITE, GARY Irvine, CA
WALECKA, SCOTT Cupertino, CA
WALKER, CYRIL A. Anaheim, CA
WALKER, LARRY A. Stratford, CT
WALKER, PAT Bedminster, NJ
WALKER, PHIL A. Brea, CA
WALKER, WAYNE San Francisco, CA
WALL, DONALD C. Irving, TX
WALLACE, ROB Napa, CA
WALNIK, PAUL South Holland, IL
WALSH, MICHAEL F. Pittsburgh, PA
WALSH, PAT M. Bartlesville, OK
WALSH, TOM San Francisco, CA
WALTERS, BILL Scotts Valley, CA
WALTERS, PETER D. Ridgway, PA
WALTON, DONALD W. Westmont, NJ
WALTON, REESE Hawthorne, CA
WARD, BERNARD Oakland, CA
WARD, LINC La Mesa, CA
WARREN, GREG Gastonia, NC
WARREN, MELINDA Louisville, KY
WARREN, NANCY San Juan Capistrano, CA
WARREN, WARD P. San Gabriel, CA
WATANABE, SUSAN Carson, CA
WATERS, GEORGE National City, CA
WATKENS, JOE Memphis, TN
WATSON, KENT Salt Lake City, UT
WATSON, PAULA Warren, OH
WATSON, RONALD L. Spokane, WA

WATTS, CYNTHIA G. Cerritos, CA
WATTS, MARCIE Mission Viejo, CA
WATTS, OSCAR Monroe, NC
WEATHERLY, MELISSA San Jose, CA
WEAVER, ANTHONY L. San Diego, CA
WEAVER, DENNIS Calabasas, CA
WEBB, DON Oklahoma City, OK
WEBB, KEITH Conneaut, OH
WEBB, LEE Cleveland, OH
WEBER, JILL ANNE Celina, OH
WEBSTER, CHARLES L. Westlake, OH
WEBSTER, ROBERT Woodstock, IL
WECKMAN, CAROL San Diego, CA
WEDMAN, BRADY Boulder, CO
WEEDOCK, ED Houston, TX
WEEKS, CHRISTIAN TESSANDORI Bakersfield, CA
WEGMANN, TED South San Francisco, CA
WEIGAND, LOU Circleville, OH
WEIGEL, TIM Evanston, IL
WEINBERG, SCOTT Reseda, CA
WEINER, DAVE Malibu, CA
WEINGARTENER, KARL Thousand Oaks, CA
WEINSTEIN, MICHAEL Cambridge, MA
WEINTZ, FRED J., JR. Riverside, CT
WEISER, DOREEN Lynbrook, NY
WEISER, LARMAN BLAINE Klamath Falls, OR
WEISMAN, JAMES Albuquerque, NM
WEISS, PAUL Cupertino, CA

Detroit, MI

WEITERMANN, MICHAEL Germantown, WI
WELBORNE, JOHN H. Los Angeles, CA
WELLMAN, MARK Cupertino, CA

WELLMAN, NED Pittsburgh, PA
WELLS, KENNETH H. Aurora, CO
WELLS, TOM Carthage, MO
WELLS, VIRGIL R. Los Angeles, CA
WELLS, WILLIAM T. Houston, TX
WELLS-MCELLIGOTT, DOROTHY
   Glendora, CA
WESELOH, BEN Oceanside, CA
WESSELN, HENRY B. Anaheim, CA
WESSON, ROBERT W. Southbury, CT
WEST, MITCH Oklahoma City, OK
WEST, SOL Los Angeles, CA
WEST, WILLIAM N. Willoughby, OH
WESTBROOK, SANDRA HUUSFELDT
   Cerritos, CA
WESTMORELAND, ANNE MARIE Santa
   Monica, CA
WHALEN, TOM San Francisco, CA
WHEELER, GARY Oxnard, CA
WHITE, GARY Dallas, TX
WHITE, JOSEPH E. Riverdale, GA
WHITE, KAREN V. Palo Alto, CA
WHITE, LISA Manhattan Beach, CA
WHITE, WILLYE Chicago, IL
WHITEHAIR, ARNOLD Chinle Navajo
   Nation, CA
WHITMIRE, RONALD, M.D.
   Gainesville, GA
WHITNEY, CORNELIUS V. Basking
   Ridge, NJ
WHITNEY, DAVID Northridge, CA
WHITNEY, RICHARD E. Santa Ana, CA
WHITTINGHAM, JULIE Steamboat
   Springs, CO
WIBERG, ED Swartz Creek, MI
WICHGERS, NATALIE Muskego, WI
WICK, RANDO Marysville, WA
WIEDER, HARRIETT M. Huntington
   Beach, CA
WIELIN, FRANCES E. Rolling Hills
   Estates, CA
WIGOD, JANE A. Long Beach, CA
WILEY, JOHN Northridge, CA
WILKES, DENNIS Louisville, KY
WILKES, JAMAL Santa Monica, CA
WILKINS, MAURY Baltimore, MD
WILKINSON, CHRYS
   Manhattan Beach, CA
WILKINSON, DEBRA Clawson, MI
WILLARD, KEVIN Cleveland, TN
WILLEY, SUSAN Sacramento, CA
WILLIAMS, ALAN F. San Gabriel, CA
WILLIAMS, JAMES, JR. Thayer, KS
WILLIAMS, JAMIE Carson, CA
WILLIAMS, JIM El Cajon, CA
WILLIAMS, LENNY G. Boise, ID
WILLIAMS, LEON San Diego, CA
WILLIAMS, RICHARD W. Westlake
   Village, CA
WILLIAMS, SHELAEN MONEE Flint, MI
WILLIAMS, THOMAS Burlington, NJ
WILLIAMS, TOMMY Birmingham, AL
WILLON, MYCHAEL COLE Laurel, MD

WILSON, DAVID San Diego, CA
WILSON, DAVID South Laguna, CA
WILSON, DEAN R. San Dimas, CA
WILSON, LARRY Dallas, TX
WILSON, LARRY Tustin, CA
WILSON, LIONEL Oakland, CA
WILSON, MIKE Dallas, TX
WILSON, TED, MAYOR
   Salt Lake City, UT
WILSON, PETER, SEN.
   San Francisco, CA
WINGTON, LORI LEE
   Huntington Beach, CA
WINSOR, DAVID, M.D. Los Angeles, CA
WINTERS, HILYARD, JR. Denver, CO
WISE, MARC Woodland Hills, CA
WISE, MEIER Woodland Hills, CA
WISNE, JUDY Farmington Hills, MI
WISSNER, CHARLES New Brighton, PA
WISSUCHEK, D. J. Canton, OH
WITT, SANDRA New Berlin, WI
WITZ, LEO W. Glencoe, IL
WOHLBACH, THOMAS K. Taylors, SC
WOHLLEBEN, GARY L. Hollywood, CA
WOLARY, CECILIA J. San Jose, CA
WOLF, DEAN Marina Del Rey, CA
WOLF, JOHN A. Dallas, TX
WOLF, SCOTT Lexington, MA
WOLFE, ERIC Davis, CA
WOLFSON, GEORGINA El Monte, CA
WOLLARD, RON Burbank, CA
WONG, FRANKLIN C. Berkeley, CA
WOOD, BRUCE A. Huntington, CA
WOOD, CLYDE O., JR. Los Angeles, CA
WOOD, JEFFREY D. Santa Ana, CA
WOOD, SALLY Piedmont, CA
WOODARD, STEWART C.
   Laguna Beach, CA
WOODROW, JOHN C. Milford, NH
WOODRUFF, BEN W. Columbia, SC
WOODS, BILL Lafayette, CA
WOOLFORD, ROBIN S., JR.
   Annapolis, MD
WORLEY, WILLIAM College Station, TX
WORTHINGTON, EMILY
   Los Angeles, CA
WORTHINGTON, WENDI
   Los Angeles, CA
WRATE, JENNIFER Westminster, CA
WRATE, JOHN Westminster, CA
WRIGHT, DEXTER S. Reno, NV
WRIGHT, DOUG, MAYOR Topeka, KS
WRIGHT, ROBERT Studio City, CA
WRIGHT, TIM Jackson, CA
WRIGHTSON, TERRENCE LLOYD
   Escondido, CA
WROTEN, ROPBERTOLD Chicago, IL
WULF, BRAD Salem, OR
WULFF, STERLING Lakeside, CA
WYANT, DANA WADE San Diego, CA
WYLIE, SARAH JANE
   Newport Beach, CA
WYMA, JOCELYN FINN Tujunga, CA

WYRICK, A. L. Fresno. CA

Y

YABU, SHIGERU Camarillo, CA
YACKEY, GEORGE Fullerton, CA
YAMADA, SABURO Kameoka City
   Kyoto, Japan
YAMAMOTO, MISAKO Kobe, Japan
YAN, CINDY Monterey Park, CA
YAN, KENNETH Escondido, CA
YANDELL, ROCKY Big Springs, TX
YARBROUGH, RICHARD C. Denver, CO
YEE, HERBERT H. Los Angeles, CA
YEOMANS, BILL HENRY Chino, CA
YERKS, BOB Vienna, VA
YESBERG, TERRY M., MAYOR Crystal
   City, MO
YOKAYAMA, NAOKO Achinomiya,
   Japan
YONEYAMA, MIEKO Tokyo, Japan
YOSHI, MARLO MASSAYUKI
   Norwalk, CT
YOSHIHASHI, MASAMICHI Chiyoda-ku
   Tokyo, Japan
YOSHIMURA, SALLY MAYUMI
   Salinas, CA
YOUNG, DANIEL New Hyde Park, NY
YOUNG, GARTH Canyon Country, CA
YOUNG, RICHARD D. Encino, CA
YOUNG, TONY Sycamore, IL
YOW, CHARLES W. Lawrenceville, GA
YU, VIKKI Los Angeles, CA
YUE, ALLEN J. Torrance, CA
YUNGLING, DOUGLAS T. San Luis
   Obispo, CA

Z

ZAMBANO, GINA New York NY
ZAMBARDI, ARMAND Avenel, NJ
ZAMPERINI, LOUIS Hollywood, CA
ZANUCK, RICHARD D.
   Santa Monica, CA
ZAPPIA, JEFFREY Pittsburgh, PA
ZAVICHAS, PENNY Pueblo, CO
ZAVORAL, JULIE A. La Palma, CA
ZELAYA, FERNANDO Bronx, NY
ZELIK, EDWARD J. Baltimore, MD
ZELL, NICOLE SOFIA New York, NY
ZESIGER, ALBERT New York, NY
ZEZAS, SPERO Buffalo, WY
ZIMMERMAN, SCOTT Milton, PA
ZOLIK, MARY BETH Toledo, OH
ZOVAK, MARI-KAY Los Angeles, CA
ZSCHAU, CONGRESSMAN San
   Francisco, CA
ZUBOR, JOHN Lincoln Park, MI
ZUCKERMAN, JEROME, DR.
   New York, NY
ZUKOWSKY, DAN Hamden, CT
ZURAWSKI, RONALD Covina, CA
ZUSINAS, BELINDA Finleyville, PA
ZYMAN, SERGIO Atlanta, GA

INDEX

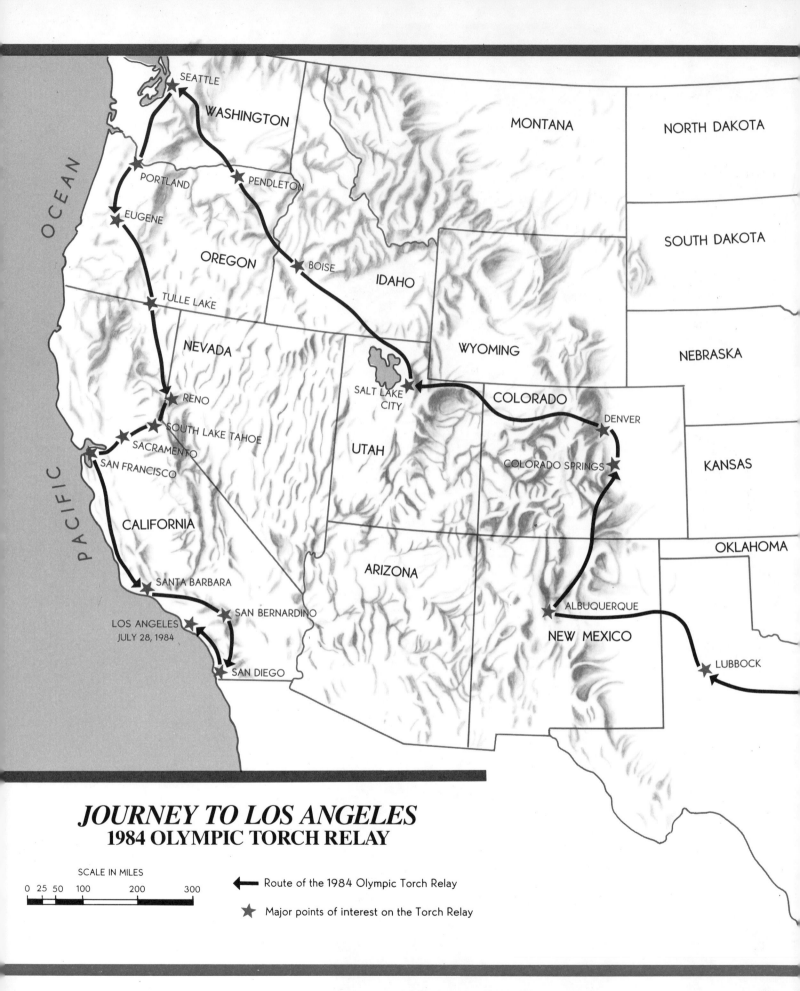

JOURNEY TO LOS ANGELES
1984 OLYMPIC TORCH RELAY

SCALE IN MILES

0 25 50   100   200   300

⬅ Route of the 1984 Olympic Torch Relay

★ Major points of interest on the Torch Relay

Map labels:
OCEAN
PACIFIC
SEATTLE
WASHINGTON
MONTANA
NORTH DAKOTA
PORTLAND
PENDLETON
EUGENE
OREGON
BOISE
IDAHO
WYOMING
SOUTH DAKOTA
NEBRASKA
TULLE LAKE
NEVADA
SALT LAKE CITY
UTAH
COLORADO
DENVER
RENO
SOUTH LAKE TAHOE
SACRAMENTO
SAN FRANCISCO
COLORADO SPRINGS
KANSAS
CALIFORNIA
ARIZONA
SANTA BARBARA
SAN BERNARDINO
LOS ANGELES
JULY 28, 1984
ALBUQUERQUE
NEW MEXICO
OKLAHOMA
SAN DIEGO
LUBBOCK